Corporate Finance,
Mergers & Acquisitions

3.2 & 3.5.4.1

3.6.4

Corporate Finance, Mergers & Acquisitions

General Editor

Paul Rylance BA, Solicitor

Associate Dean, Faculty of Law, UWE
Director, Bristol Institute of Legal Practice

Contributors

Pauline Bearblock, BSc, Solicitor
Associate Partner in Compliance at Oriel
Securities Limited

Visiting Lecturer, Bristol Institute of Legal
Practice, UWE

Diana Johnson, BA, Solicitor
Senior Lecturer, Bristol Institute of
Legal Practice, UWE

Joanne Weston, BA, Solicitor

Corporate Professional Support, Burges Salmon
Visiting Lecturer, Bristol Institute of Legal
Practice, UWE

Ben Reeves, BA, LLM, Solicitor,

Principal Lecturer, Bristol Institute of Legal
Practice, UWE

Assistant Editors

Steven Dinning, BA, Solicitor

Deputy Director, Bristol Institute of Legal Practice,
UWE

Wendy Swinscoe, MA, Solicitor

Senior Lecturer, Bristol Institute of Legal Practice,
UWE

Research

James Goldblatt, BA, Solicitor

Director, Hermes Corporate Information Limited

OXFORD
UNIVERSITY PRESS

OXFORD

UNIVERSITY PRESS

Great Clarendon Street, Oxford OX2 6DP

Oxford University Press is a department of the University of Oxford.
It furthers the University's objective of excellence in research, scholarship,
and education by publishing worldwide in

Oxford New York

Auckland Cape Town Dar es Salaam Hong Kong Karachi
Kuala Lumpur Madrid Melbourne Mexico City Nairobi
New Delhi Shanghai Taipei Toronto

With offices in

Argentina Austria Brazil Chile Czech Republic France Greece
Guatemala Hungary Italy Japan South Korea Poland Portugal
Singapore Switzerland Thailand Turkey Ukraine Vietnam

Oxford is a registered trademark of Oxford University Press
in the UK and in other certain countries

Published in the United States
by Oxford University Press Inc., New York

First Published by Blackstone Press 1994

British Library Cataloguing in Publication Data
Data available

ISBN 0-19-927803-2

1 3 5 7 9 10 8 6 4 2

Typeset by Newgen Imaging Systems (P) Ltd., Chennai, India
Printed in Great Britain
on acid-free paper by
Antony Rowe Ltd, Chippenham, Wiltshire

OUTLINE CONTENTS

DETAILED CONTENTS

PREFACE

Whilst retaining the overall structure of the 2004 edition, Chapters 1, 2, 3, 4 and 8 have been substantially amended. In addition to general updating, these chapters now incorporate extensive references to primary sources and new material on:

- FSMA; Financial Promotions and the Code of Market Conduct;
- Companies Act regulation including: disapplication of pre-emption rights, UKLA's requirements and ABI guidelines; and the Companies (Acquisitions of Own Shares) Regulations 2003;
- statutory and regulatory controls including: Listing Rules obligations re director's dealing, the Model Code, the Combined Code and reporting requirements on director's remuneration;
- the key provisions of an underwriting agreement;
- tender offers;
- open offers;
- conditions for listing (including the role of the sponsor);
- the impact of European legislation;
- continuing obligations;
- proposals for change to the listing regime;
- schemes of arrangement in the context of takeovers; and
- merger control.

Whilst Chapters 5, 6, 7, 9 and 11 remain largely unchanged from previous editions, the contents of Chapter 10 are entirely new.

I am indebted to James Goldblatt of Hermes Corporate Information Limited for his invaluable research, to Pauline Bearblock, Jo Weston, Diane Johnson and Ben Reeves for their specialist contributions and to Wendy Swinscoe and Steven Dinning for their editorial assistance. I would also like to thank Lesley Bond for her help in co-ordinating the various contributions and compiling the final text. All worked tirelessly to tight deadlines in order to complete the new edition in a little over two months. In doing so I believe that we have supplemented Scott Slorach's (and Richard King's) highly regarded text so as to reflect recent changes in corporate finance regulation and practice and to respond to the particular needs of LPC students and their prospective employers.

Paul Rylance
Bristol
November 2004

TABLE OF CASES

TABLE OF PRIMARY LEGISLATION UK AND EUROPEAN

TABLE OF SECONDARY LEGISLATION FINANCE RULES, REGULATIONS AND CODES UK AND EUROPEAN

ABBREVIATIONS

ABI	Association of British Insurers
AGM	annual general meeting
AIM	Alternative Investment Market
ASB	Accounting Standards Board
CC	Competition Commission
CCD	concentration with a Community dimension
CGT	capital gains tax
City Code	City Code on Takeovers and Mergers
CMC	Code of Market Conduct
Combined Code	Combined Code on Corporate Governance
DPB	designated professional body
DTI	Department of Trade and Industry
FIMBRA	Financial Intermediaries, Managers and Brokers Regulatory Association
FRRP	Financial Reporting Review Panel
FRS	Financial Reporting Standard
FSA	Financial Services Authority (formerly SIB)
FS Act	Financial Services Act 1986
FSMA	Financial Services and Markets Act 2000
IMRO	Investment Management Regulatory Organisation
LAUTRO	Life Assurance and Unit Trust Regulatory Organisation
LIBOR	London Inter-Bank Offered Rate
LIFFE	London International Financial Futures Exchange
LR	Listing Rules
LSE	London Stock Exchange
MBO	management buy-out
MC	Model Code on Director's Dealings in Securities
NAPF	National Association of Pension Funds
OFT	Office of Fair Trading
PAL	provisional allotment letter
PIA	Personal Investment Authority
RAO	Financial Services and Markets Act 2000 (Regulated Activities) Order 2001
RIE	recognised investment exchange
RIS	Regulatory Information Service
RLA	renounceable letter of allotment (or acceptance)
RPB	recognised professional body
SARs	Rules Governing Substantial Acquisitions of Shares
SD	stamp duty
SDRT	stamp duty reserve tax
SEADS	Stock Exchange Admission and Disclosure Standards
SEAQ	Stock Exchange Automated Quotations
SFA	Securities and Futures Authority
SIB	Securities and Investments Board (now FSA (see above))
SRO	self-regulating organisation
SSAP	Statement of Standard Accounting Practice
UKLA	UK Listing Authority
USM	Unlisted Securities Market

The regulatory superstructure

This book is not primarily about regulation. It is about the core corporate finance transactions which lawyers are called to advise on. One particularly modern feature of these transactions is the regulation to which they are subject. The focus here is always on the underlying 'deal', though the regulation can never be all that far behind.

This order of priorities reflects the way in which regulation is often perceived, as something which does not tend to facilitate business activity: all the transactions we will look at could be done before regulation arrived. Regulation usually appears to control or systematise an area of corporate finance activity which has flourished in the absence of regulatory constraint—and perhaps because of that!

This is not to say that regulation is necessarily a bad thing. It does after all seek to create order where before there was none or little. It does aim to protect those who might otherwise be the victim of malpractice and to prevent abuses which are deleterious to the reputation of the market. All of these are obviously good things. But it is important to bear in mind that regulation is almost always superimposed over existing market practice. It may change it in the process—indeed, it is often intended to do precisely that—but you will not be able to understand how things are done in the corporate finance world simply by reading the regulations. They do not tell you how to do a deal. They will tell you what are the boundaries of acceptable conduct in the course of doing that deal. Therefore, this book will examine the transaction first, and regulation second.

This has at least two important consequences for us. The first is that much of the law relevant to the transactions discussed in this book is already familiar to you. The word 'transactions' implies give and take, and, indeed, we will see that most of the activities we look at here are constructed on the foundations of the law of contract. For instance, the sale and purchase of a business or shares is governed principally by the contract for the sale. An issue of shares is governed by the contract entered into between company and investor and underpinned by the underwriting contract between company and underwriter. An offer by one company to acquire the shares in another company, if accepted by the shareholders, will create an enforceable contract. Hence much of what we will focus on is the special nature of those contracts and the effect their various provisions are intended to achieve. But for you, the important consequence is that you are not entering waters entirely uncharted.

Second, the transactions have developed to achieve the business ends of the parties. If regulation emerges to intervene in that contractual relationship in some way, the parties can respond either by complying with the regulatory constraints, or by finding some way to achieve the same end but in a way that is not caught by the regulation. This is not because of a law-breaking mentality or even bloody-mindedness, but a recognition that regulation creates cost. This is the cost of delay, of completing the required paperwork, of the necessary professional advice, possibly of changing established business and working practices. If there is still a compelling business reason to enter into the transaction, there will also be very strong business sense in trying to do it at the cheapest price—which means avoiding the regulatory net.

There are in turn different ways of doing this. One is to exploit the holes in the net and escape through them. Another is to adapt the transaction so it still attains the desired outcome but assumes characteristics sufficiently distinct for it to avoid the clutches of the regulators and swim round the net altogether. There is therefore always a demand on the lawyer to be inventive.

Having said all this, the impact of regulation in this area is highly significant and we need to achieve some better idea of how it operates and when. Let us get a better idea first of what regulation actually is.

1.1 What is regulation?

'Regulation' in this book refers to any body of rules which has developed or is created to authorise or control business conduct or activity. The term does not embrace existing common law principles or precedents as these cannot properly be said to have been codified in any form, though their application and effect is sufficiently well established for us to be able to identify a body of law. Regulation, though, is pre-eminently codification. This is not to say that it comes into existence from nowhere and is then a static, once-and-for-all phenomenon. It may be the crystallisation of best practice which has been in existence for some time. Once it is introduced, it will evolve with changing conditions and new market practices.

Therefore, regulation for these purposes refers to statute first and foremost. Though far from complete, the Companies Acts represent an attempt to codify the formation and functions of companies and those persons connected with them. The Financial Services and Markets Act 2000 ('FSMA') provides a statutory framework for the regulation of banking, investment and insurance business. Of course these statutes and the others discussed in this book have effect as Parliamentary legislation. Their status as 'law' is therefore unquestioned.

There are other forms of codification which we will be looking at which are not statutory. There are the rules administered by the Takeover Panel in relation to takeovers of public companies. The rules, known as the City Code on Takeovers and Mergers, ('City Code'), are not law but something like rules for a professional sport. If you want to play the game, you have to play by the rules; if you break the rules, then the chances are you will not be allowed to play again. This is an oversimplification, but it introduces an important point.

When you break the law set out in a statute, you know that sanctions will follow if the breach is detected and enforced. When you break rules like those of the City Code, there may be sanctions provided for as part of the rules, but these lie essentially at the discretion of the regulator, the body which made the rules in the first place. And one thing is certain: those sanctions will not be criminal, as no such power is vested in these regulators. This is not to say the sanctions will not be serious—they are simply of a different order.

Beyond these non-statutory regulations (of which the City Code is only an example) there are other attempts at codification which amount to no more than principles of best practice. These could not properly be described as rules. This book refers to them as 'guidelines'. The critical distinction between them and rules is the absence of formal sanctions.

An example of such guidelines is the Investment Committee guidelines, which stipulate (amongst other things) what investing institutions regard as acceptable limits on the issue of shares by companies listed on the Official List. There is no formal sanction for failing to observe the guidelines, but any company which does so can be sure eventually to incur the wrath of its institutional shareholders who may accordingly use their influential power to show their displeasure (for example, by voting against company resolutions).

This kind of regulation is very easy to dismiss as inconsequential as it has no teeth. In fact, though its teeth are less visible, they can still give a company a nasty bite, and such guidelines are treated with care by companies anxious to show they are responsible.

1.2 What is regulation for?

This section looks briefly at the purpose of regulation so that when we come later to examine the application of regulations in practice, what we are looking at does not seem a senseless piece of rule-creation but rather something with a point.

As we have seen, regulation comes in different flavours and with different objectives. These are some of the most significant:

(a) *Protecting the public*

This is the background to just about every piece of regulation: the prime example in this context is the FSMA, though it is equally true of the City Code. The public in both these cases is the investing public. Preventing the perpetration of abuses is likewise the primary motivation behind the Companies Act 1985.

(b) *Licensing*

This is obviously linked to (a), as one way to protect the public is to impose certain thresholds in terms of standards on those who want to enter a market or deliver a product. The FSMA governs those who wish to provide financial services to the public. Another example is the Listing Rules ('LR') administered by the UK Listing Authority ('UKLA'), which govern what a company needs to do to get its securities listed on the Official List.

(c) *Financing requirements*

We will not be looking at these in the course of this book, but certain businesses clearly need to be properly financed to provide a proper service to clients: banking is a good example and banks regulated in the UK need a certain amount of capital to obtain and retain their authorisation (a requirement known as 'capital adequacy').

(d) *Compulsory insurance*

Again linked to (a), the assumption behind this is that some businesses in an industry will fail or make errors and be forced to compensate those who have suffered loss as a result of their failings. For the better protection of the investor, and shoring up the reputation of the industry in question, a fund needs to exist to which all market operators contribute (including those who never fail) so there is always money available for compensation. We will not look at this further in this book, but an example is provided by the solicitors' profession in the form of the Solicitors' Indemnity Fund.

(e) *Disclosure of information*

This applies to much of the regulation we will see. The idea is to improve the position of those investing in or affected by the business entity by obliging it to make adequate disclosure of relevant information. The investors and others are then free to make decisions based on 'transparency', i.e., the availability of clear data. Much of the Companies Act 1985 deals with disclosure requirements. The UKLA Listing Rules, the Stock Exchange Admission and Disclosure Standards and the City Code also place great emphasis on the accurate and prompt disclosure of information.

(f) *Fairness*

Some regulation aims to ensure the so-called 'level playing field', so that everyone competes by the same rules. Some of the regulations imposed under the Companies Act 1985 are a response to EC requirements which in turn are driven by the desire to harmonise regulatory obligations across the European Community so that companies in one jurisdiction are subject to no more or less regulation than their internal market competitors in other jurisdictions.

(g) *Competitiveness*

Ensuring competitiveness is again in the public's best interests. Antitrust regulation such as the Competition Act 1998 and the Enterprise Act 2003 are designed to give protection to UK consumers against the dangers of monopolies being formed which may lead to higher prices and less choice.

(h) *Systemic failure*

Another common reason for the existence of regulation is to guard against the collapse of a part of the financial system. Safeguarding the viability of an industry is in the best interests of the industry and vital if public confidence in it is to be maintained. The development of the City Code was a response to a growing number of scandals in the unregulated takeover market in the 1960s which threatened a state of chaos. The City Code was the solution to the survival of the market: there is always a risk if a market is excessively volatile or prone to abuse that investors will simply stay away.

1.3 Form of regulation

Regulation can be classified under two main headings: 'self-regulation' and 'statutory regulation'. The former is normally used to describe a system where rules are made by market professionals to regulate those who wish to operate in that particular market. The suggested strength of self-regulation is the responsiveness of the regulators to the needs of the market. Since they should have the best understanding of the market, they can develop flexible rules that best meet its needs. Statutory regulation is a term applied to directly imposed government regulation.

Currently, corporate finance transactions are governed by a mixture of forms of regulation. Self-regulation can be seen in the form of the rules for admission of securities to trading, which are made and enforced by the London Stock Exchange ('LSE'), and the City Code, made and enforced by the Takeover Panel. In the area of financial services, there has been a move away from self-regulation, with the advent of the Financial Services Authority ('FSA') as the single regulator of banking, investment and insurance business. Previously, these industries were self-regulated by a variety of industry bodies, whose roles are now the ambit of the FSA. The FSA has powers derived from the FSMA and, together with the Treasury, makes rules for the conduct of a wide range of finance-related business.

Whilst the dichotomy between forms of regulation can raise interesting questions of policy, the main practical issue for corporate finance professionals is an awareness of the overlap between regulators.

Companies may find that corporate finance activities or transactions they want to pursue may give rise to the intervention or involvement of more than one regulator at a time. There is no central regulatory unit to which a company can go to get all its regulatory problems handled at once. They have to be confronted on a market-by-market basis.

The consequence, to take an example, is that a public company takeover offer involving the issue of securities to be listed on the Official List as consideration for the offer will be regulated by the FSA, UKLA, the LSE and the Takeover Panel simultaneously: the FSA and UKLA, because of the promotion of and listing of securities, the LSE for admission of securities to trading, and the Takeover Panel because of the takeover offer. The checklist in **1.7.4** gives an idea of the questions which arise when a company is faced with such a multiregulatory transaction. The nature of regulation in the City means that the activities and transactions we are looking at in this book may intersect with any number of possible regulatory issues at any one time, depending on the nature of the deal, the parties involved and so on. A good grasp of the regulatory superstructure and its key institutions is therefore an essential foundation.

1.4 What is regulated, and by whom?

The checklist at the end of this chapter summarises the ways in which regulation superimposes itself on corporate finance transactions, and indicates which regulators are involved at different points. It is a useful way of seeing in the round the interaction of the various rules to which public company financing is subject. It is not, though, comprehensive: it covers only the most important aspects in passing, as a kind of overview, as other sections of the book (which are referred to where relevant) include a fuller treatment in context.

We concentrate in this book on three aspects of corporate finance regulation:

(a) the regulation of the financial services market as it affects corporate finance work;

(b) the key elements in the regulation of the securities market; and

(c) the regulation of public companies.

The rest of this chapter will look at the first two. Corporate regulation follows in **Chapter 2**.

1.5 Regulation of financial services

The term 'financial services' covers three principal types of business activity:

(a) investment;

(b) banking; and

(c) insurance.

1.5.1 The regulatory structure

1.5.1.1 Introduction

The regulation of financial services in the UK has recently been the subject of major reform.

A new regulatory regime was created by the FSMA, which came into force on 1 December 2001. The FSMA creates a statutory framework within which the FSA operates as sole regulator of the banking, financial services and insurance industries. Within this framework, the FSA and the Treasury have rule-making powers to regulate specific activities. The result is a large number of statutory instruments which give practical effect to the new regime. The regulations are backed up by detailed guidance. The FSA provides a Handbook of rules and guidance comprising numerous sourcebooks and manuals covering business standards, regulatory processes and means of redress. The Handbook is available in hard-copy form, on CD-ROM and online, at **www.fsa.gov.uk**.

Prior to FSMA, financial services were regulated by the Financial Services Act 1986 ('FS Act') under which operated a number of self-regulating organisations ('SROs') and recognised professional bodies ('RPBs'). To carry on investment business, a person had to be authorised and was required to comply with the rules of the FSA and those of its respective SRO or RPB. The move to a single regulator was prompted by a number of factors, which included: the blurring of the distinction between financial institutions such as banks, insurance companies, building societies and securities houses; a desire to reduce self-regulation, following scandals such as the mis-selling of personal pensions; and increasing powers to fight financial crime. The FSA now has four stated statutory objectives:

(a) maintaining market confidence;

(b) promoting public understanding of the financial system;

(c) protecting consumers; and

(d) reducing financial crime.

It is intended that these objectives are met through the effect of FSMA and related regulation.

1.5.1.2   The Financial Services and Markets Act 2000

The basic way in which FSMA regulates financial activity in the UK is through a general prohibition in s. 19 on any person carrying out regulated activities (defined in s. 22) unless that person is authorised by the FSA or is otherwise exempt. A regulated activity is defined in the Financial Services and Markets Act 2000 (Regulated Activities) Order 2001 (SI 2001/544) ('RAO'), which contains in Part II a list of a number of specific activities relating to a variety of defined investments ('Specified Investments', as listed in RAO Part III). The former include arranging deals in, advising on investments and discretionary managing of investments. The definition of investments includes shares, debt instruments and government securities. If a person carries out a regulated activity without authorisation, there are both criminal sanctions (FSMA s. 23) and civil sanctions (FSMA s. 26). To obtain authorisation, a person must apply for and be given a permission by the FSA under Part IV of FSMA to carry on one or more regulated activities. (Where a person was authorised under the previous regime, transitional arrangements allow for automatic permission to be given under the new regime.)

There are a number of excluded activities under RAO, for which authorisation is not required. Regulation 4(3) states that "each provision specifying a kind of activity is subject to the exclusions applicable to that provision". Each provision lies within its own chapter of Part II of RAO (subject to associated exclusions), and there are certain additional general exclusions in Chapter XVII of Part II of RAO. In addition, Part XX of FSMA provides for certain exempt regulated activities to be provided by members of professions, provided these activities are incidental to their mainstream business and are carried out under approved rules drawn up by the particular profession's designated professional body ('DPB'). As a result, solicitors are able to carry out certain financial and investment related activities under the Solicitors' Financial Services (Scope) Rules 2001. The Law Society is the relevant DPB for solicitors.

The significance of FSMA to corporate finance activities is that, as set out in Part III of RAO, shares, debentures and other interests in securities are investments under RAO and so most corporate finance work will fall within the definition of a regulated activity. Anyone involved in such work will therefore have to consider whether authorisation is required from the FSA or if the work in question is an excluded or exempt activity. In short, almost any activity during the transactions described in this book potentially has a FSMA dimension.

1.5.1.3   Regulation of specific activities

In addition to creating a general prohibition on carrying out regulated activities without FSA authorisation, there are a number of specific activities regulated by FSMA which should be noted at this stage:

(a) *Financial promotion*

Section 21 of the FSMA creates restrictions on financial promotion. A person is prohibited, in the course of their business, from communicating an invitation or inducement to engage in investment activity, unless that person is an authorised person or the content of the communication has been approved by an authorised person. The detail of the restrictions and relevant exemptions are set out in the Financial Services and Markets Act 2000 (Financial Promotion) Order 2001 (SI 2001/1335). These regulations draw a distinction in regs 7(1) and 7(2) between 'real time' communications (personal visits, telephone conversations and any other interactive communication process) and other 'non-real time' communications, such that, in some cases, one version is exempt whilst the other is not. Certain exempt communications in relation to all controlled activities are prescribed in Part IV of the Order, while Part V sets out exempt communications in relation to deposits and insurance, and Part VI sets out exempt communications in relation to more than 40 other controlled activities. Detailed discussion of these regulations is contained in **4.2.6.3**, and further guidance on the scope and application of the financial promotions regulations can be found in the FSA Handbook (see **1.5.1.1**), in the Authorisation manual (see Appendix 1 of the Authorisation manual, and, in particular, paragraphs 1.1.2 and 1.1.3 of that Appendix.).

The financial promotion regulations take the place of previous regulations under the FS Act which dealt with investment advertisements and unsolicited calls regarding investments.

(b) *Market abuse*

Part VIII of FSMA creates a civil regime which operates parallel to the insider dealing provisions of the Criminal Justice Act 1993. FSMA provides a general definition of market abuse in s. 118 which is backed by a Code of Market Conduct ("CMC") issued by the FSA pursuant to s. 119 accompanied by Guidance Notes issued pursuant to s. 157. This is available in the FSA Handbook (see **1.5.1.1**) and has annexed to it a useful set of 'frequently asked questions' on the Code of Market Conduct. The objective of these provisions is to make markets more open, transparent and fair. Market abuse is behaviour which is likely to be regarded by a regular user of the market as being a failure on the part of the person or persons concerned to observe the standard of behaviour reasonably expected of a person in his or their position in relation to the market. The behaviour in question must be in relation to qualifying investments on a market to which the provisions apply (s. 118 (1)(a)). There are three specific types of behaviour which may amount to market abuse:

(i) behaviour based on information not generally available to market users but which, if available to a regular user, would or would be likely to be regarded by him as being relevant in deciding the terms on which transactions in investments of the kind in question should be effected (s. 118 (2)(a));

(ii) behaviour likely to give a regular user of the market a false or misleading impression as to the supply of, or demand for, or as to the price or value of, the investments in question (s. 118 (2)(b)); or

(iii) behaviour which a regular user would or would be likely to regard as likely to distort the market in the particular investments (s. 118(2)(c)).

The FSA is required by FSMA to issue a code for the purpose of determining whether particular behaviour amounts to market abuse. In the event that market abuse occurs, the FSA has powers to impose penalties (s. 123), censure offenders, seek injunctions from the court (s. 381), seek restitution from the court (s. 383), or itself order restitution (s. 384). A more detailed discussion of the Code of Market of Conduct is contained at **1.8**.

(c) *Listing*

FSMA s. 72 provides that the FSA is the competent authority in the UK for the admission of shares to the Official List, which role it performs under the title of the UKLA. Part VI of FSMA contains provisions which deal with the powers and functions of the UKLA, applications for listing, and the content and registration of listing particulars and prospectuses.

(d) *Misleading statements and practices*

Section 397 of FSMA makes it an offence for a person, either purposely or recklessly, to make misleading, false or deceptive statements, promises or forecasts, or dishonestly to conceal facts, for the purpose of inducing someone to acquire investments. The section also extends the offence to any conduct which creates a false or misleading impression as to the market in or price of any relevant investments.

Specified activities and investments within the scope of s. 397 are set out in regs 3 and 4 of the Financial Services and Markets Act 2000 (Misleading Statements and Practices) Order 2001 (SI 2001/3645).

Specific provisions of FSMA and related regulations relevant to corporate finance transactions are dealt with in more detail later in the book.

1.5.2   Banking regulation

1.5.2.1   Authorisation and supervision of banks

On 1 June 1998, responsibility for the authorisation and supervision of UK banks was transferred from the Bank of England to the FSA. This change was implemented by s. 21 of the Bank of England Act 1998 as part of the government's aim to have a single regulator of all financial and banking services.

All those who wish to carry on banking business are required to be authorised to do so. Banking business is defined as accepting deposits in the UK whilst carrying on a deposit-taking business anywhere in the world. A deposit, broadly speaking, is money paid on terms that it will be repaid. To become authorised, a business must show that it will conduct its banking business prudently and that it has a certain amount of minimum net assets. Once authorised, the FSA supervises the operation of the bank. In particular, it oversees capital adequacy (sufficiency of capital reserves against potential losses), liquidity (sufficiency of cash) and large exposures (substantial losses to individual borrowers). These are monitored principally through reporting requirements.

1.5.2.2   The Bank of England

The Bank of England is owned by HM Treasury and governed by the Bank of England Act 1946. It is the UK central bank, in which capacity it manages the UK national debt, the issue of currency and the foreign exchange reserves. It also advises the government on economic and monetary policy. Since 1997, it has had the power to set interest rates.

1.5.3 Insurance regulation

This is another feature of the regulatory landscape, which is covered here to complete the picture. Once again, we will not be returning to this subject.

The Insurance Companies Act 1982 states that no person shall carry on any insurance business in the United Kingdom unless authorised to do so. Failure to obtain authorisation when required is an offence. The regulator under the Act is the Treasury, although it has contracted out many of its functions in this regard to the FSA.

1.6 Regulation of the securities market

There are two main markets in company securities. The first of these is the stock market, regulated and supervised by the UKLA and the LSE. In this section, we shall examine the general roles and functions of the UKLA and the LSE. In addition, we shall examine the CREST (see **1.6.2**) electronic framework for share trading. The second market is the takeover market. Unlike the stock market, the takeover market is not centred around a formal exchange. However, takeovers are still subject to regulation, in the form of the City Code, and governance by the Takeover Panel. The nature of the City Code and the role of the Takeover Panel are also examined below.

1.6.1 The UK Listing Authority

On 1 May 2000, by virtue of the Official Listing of Securities (Change of Competent Authority) Regulations 2000 (SI 2000/698), responsibility for the admission of shares to the Official List was transferred from the LSE to the FSA, which is now the 'competent authority' for listing under the FS Act. The FSA, in its guise as the UKLA, has re-issued the Listing Rules, the rules under which companies may apply for their securities to be listed and which impose a series of continuing obligations on those companies whose shares are admitted to the Official List. (These rules were formerly issued by the LSE and were contained in the 'Yellow Book', so named because of its colour. The Listing Rules are now contained in a purple volume, reflecting the corporate colour scheme of the FSA.)

As a result of the transfer of responsibility for admission to the FSA, companies wishing to have their securities listed and traded on the LSE must now apply to the UKLA for admission to listing and to the LSE for admission to trading (see **1.6.1.2**).

1.6.2 The stock exchange

The LSE, as a term, refers both to the market in which securities are exchanged and to the body which oversees the operation of that market.

1.6.2.1 The market

Looking first at the market, there are a number of separate markets comprised within the LSE:

(a) the UK equity market, in which shares are bought and sold in UK companies either listed on the LSE itself or admitted to the Alternative Investment Market ('AIM') (see **4.1.1**);

(b) the international equity market for trading in shares in overseas companies and companies listed on exchanges outside London (such shares can be bought and sold through the LSE); and

(c) the debt market in which debt securities issued by the government and other bodies (known as 'gilt-edged securities', or 'gilts' for short) are traded.

1.6.2.2   The regulatory body

The LSE is governed by a Board of Directors, which is assisted by a series of departments. As a body, it has a number of functions:

(a) It admits securities to trading (such securities having been admitted to the Official List by the UKLA) and imposes disclosure requirements to be observed by companies seeking admission whose shares are already traded. These are set out in the Admission and Disclosure Standards issued by the LSE. Sanctions for breach of these rules include private or public censure, suspension of trading and, ultimately, cancellation of the right to have securities traded (see paragraph 3.21 of Part 2 of Admission and Disclosure Standards).

(b) It monitors share price activity on the equity market to identify evidence of possible insider dealing (see **8.14**).

(c) It regulates those who wish to become members of the LSE and buy and sell shares through it. These trading members are distinct from the companies listed on the LSE whose shares are actually bought and sold.

(d) It sets the rules for share trading and the settlement of payment on trades (see **1.6.3**).

(e) It supervises the development and operation of the various computer systems and services needed to support the markets referred to above.

The LSE as a market revolves around broker dealers. Often referred to as 'brokers', they act for investors who want to buy and sell securities. Traditionally, brokers have not themselves bought and sold—they have done this through market makers. Market makers (who 'make markets' in the securities they are prepared to buy and sell) are broker dealers who specialise in the dealing function. They quote prices for UK equities through an electronic price display system called SEAQ (Stock Exchange Automated Quotations). The brokers select the appropriate market maker for the shares they want and the market maker trades the shares. This is known as quote-driven trading. Settlement and physical transfer of the shares follow later. The overseas equity market uses a similar system known as SEAQ International.

The LSE is replacing this system with what is called order-driven trading. This was introduced in October 1997. The system was initially introduced for trading in the shares of the FTSE 100 index companies but now includes the shares of the most liquid FTSE 250 companies. The SEAQ system is replaced with an automated order book. Investors place orders for the purchase and sale of shares at a stated price through LSE member firms for inclusion in the order book. Orders will remain on the book until a counterparty emerges at the desired price (in which case the trade will be executed automatically), the order is cancelled or the order expires. This system (known as SETS (Stock Exchange Electronic Trading Service) or the 'Order Book') is said to have more than halved the cost of trading for institutions in the UK equity market. It has also brought increased speed and transparency to the market. The majority of trades in the FTSE 100 companies are now being made through SETS.

The scale and importance of the LSE is illustrated by the fact that the turnover of UK and international equities traded on the Exchange was nearly £1700 billion in the six months to June 2003. In the same period, over £100 billion was raised in new issues. There were 2328 UK and 399 international companies listed on the LSE at the end of June 2003.

1.6.3 CREST

CREST is a computerised system for the settlement of stock transfer transactions on the LSE. Settlement is the way in which the stock is transferred from seller to buyer and payment is transferred from buyer to seller. CREST commenced operation in July 1996 and has now fully replaced the Talisman, paper-based, system formerly run by the LSE. It is now a condition of listing that all listed securities of a company incorporated in the United Kingdom should be eligible for electronic settlement. Amongst the benefits of CREST are quicker settlements and guaranteed payments to sellers.

1.6.3.1 Uncertificated Securities Regulations 2001

The operation of CREST is facilitated by the Uncertificated Securities Regulations 2001. These regulations:

(a) set out the legal framework for CREST;

(b) set out the conditions on which companies can allow their securities to participate in CREST;

(c) amend the requirement that shares need to be evidenced by a share certificate, thus allowing shares to be held electronically, in a dematerialised form; and

(d) provide for the transfer of securities without a written instrument such as a stock transfer form.

In addition, the regulations provide that legal title to securities is obtained at the point at which ownership of such securities is recorded on a CREST account register. This compares to certificated securities, where title is evidenced at the point of entry in a company's register of members.

1.6.3.2 How dematerialised shares can be held in CREST

There are three ways in which a shareholder can hold dematerialised shares in a company through CREST:

(a) as a member;

(b) as a personal member; and

(c) through a nominee.

Member

Members are electronically linked to CREST. The cost of this is likely to be prohibitive for small private shareholders. In practice, therefore, members tend to be brokers, market makers and institutions. Each member has an account which records the shares held within the system. A member is required to appoint a settlement bank through which payments on transfers will be made.

Personal members

Personal members of CREST hold their securities in secure electronic form within CREST and retain full legal title to their securities. This permits them to attend and vote at AGMs, and to receive corporate information directly from the issuing company. Those who opt for this method of holding shares in CREST are generally more likely to be more sophisticated investors, who hold a portfolio of shares and trade on a regular basis.

Nominee route

A shareholder using this route to hold shares within the system appoints a nominee who will be a member of CREST. The latter is electronically linked to CREST and has a nominee account, which can be used for a number of shareholders. Due to this, the nominee route is the cheapest way in which shares can be held under CREST. However, it is the name of the nominee CREST member, not that of the shareholder, which appears on the company's register. The shareholder is not, therefore, prima facie entitled to receive shareholder notices and dividends, since these are directed by the company to the nominee as the shareholder noted on the register. Separate arrangements have to be made between the nominee and the shareholder to deal with these matters.

It is not mandatory for a shareholder to hold shares in uncertificated, dematerialised form. The option remains to have a shareholding evidenced by a certificate. A company will maintain a register of members for certificated shareholdings and is also required to keep records of uncertificated securities. In practice, this will be a duplicate of the CREST register of uncertificated securities. Certificated shares are still traded through CREST, although this is slower and more expensive. This is because such shares first have to be dematerialised in order to be processed through the system and then rematerialised.

1.6.3.3 Transfers of shares under CREST

If a company decides to make its shares eligible for the system and shareholders decide to hold their shares in one of the uncertificated, dematerialised forms set out above, an electronic record of shareholdings will be held within an account on CREST. Transfers of shares can be made through this account. For example, a private investor holding shares through a nominee will instruct the latter to sell a number of shares. Once the nominee finds a market maker (also a CREST member) to purchase the shares, both the nominee and the market maker electronically send details of the transaction to CREST. The latter matches the messages and checks that the nominee holds sufficient shares within its account to make the sale. On settlement, CREST will instruct the market maker's settlement bank to make a payment to the nominee. CREST will update its own accounts and record the new shareholder's shareholding, at which point the latter obtains legal title to the shares. Stamp duty reserve tax ('SDRT') is payable on share transfers under CREST at a rate of $\frac{1}{2}$ per cent on the value of shares being transferred.

1.6.3.4 Other effects of CREST

The advent of CREST and uncertificated securities has implications for other areas of corporate finance covered in this guide. These include rights issues (see **3.6.4.4**), takeovers (see **8.5.7**) and notification of interests in shares (see **8.11**).

1.6.4 The Takeover Panel and the City Code on Takeovers and Mergers

The Takeover Panel is not a creature of statute or a government agency. It is not owned by anyone—in fact it is not even a legal entity in its own right. It came into existence in response principally to pressure from the Bank of England, but it is not answerable to the Bank. It occupies part of the LSE's premises, but that is where the formal relationship with the LSE ends. The Panel is simply a committee of best practice, designated from within the City by City institutions to oversee the takeover market. This committee draws its members from the various City institutions responsible for its inception and support.

A full-time secretariat has been established to oversee the takeovers market on a regular daily basis. This secretariat is known as the Panel Executive. The Executive is the first line of regulatory supervision and the committee, known now as the full Panel, is the second line—for instance, it is available to be summoned to hear appeals from decisions of the Executive (see **8.8.6**).

The nature of the City Code is itself sometimes a source of confusion. The City Code began life as a set of guidelines agreed by the same City institutions that set up the Panel, to constitute best practice in the conduct of takeovers. This was a response to questionable activities which took place in the almost unregulated takeover market in the early 1950s. Since these guidelines were not very successful at preventing further takeover-related scandals in the 1960s, these City institutions, at the behest of the Bank of England, revised the guidelines and simultaneously established the Takeover Panel as their 'authoritative interpreter'.

Since then, the City Code has expanded enormously and the Takeover Panel has changed in character, but there has been no fundamental shift in the basic nature of the City Code. It is not law. It has never been given any direct legal effect by statute in the way the LSE's Listing Rules have (see **4.2.5.1**). It remains essentially a set of principles as to best practice in these transactions, now regularly updated and refined by the Code Committee of the Takeover Panel. The City Code is therefore best described as a self-regulatory system. Importantly, though, the City Code and all its Rules (discussed in much more detail in **8.8**) are treated by takeover practitioners and companies operating in the market *as if they have the force of law*, and the Takeover Panel as if it carried the weight and firepower of any other regulatory authority. There are other financial services and securities markets operating in the City which there is simply not time to consider as they cover fields outside the scope of this book. We have looked at only those elements of the regulatory superstructure which relate most directly to the major aspects of corporate finance activity.

Before we move on, let us look at the work of the lawyer caught in the middle of such a system.

1.7 Regulation and the role of lawyers

1.7.1 Interpretation

Advising clients of the meaning and application of the rules in a given situation is the primary skill a lawyer will be expected to exercise. Many of these regulations, though, cannot be viewed or interpreted as a lawyer would view or interpret ordinary statute.

The first reason for this is that they are simply not law in the classical sense. Many are rules which operate like club rules; some are the distillation of best practice. They are not written to be treated like statutes.

The second reason is that, as we have seen, breach of the rules rarely gives rise to either criminal or civil liability. The sanctions are at the behest of the regulators. This is explained further below.

The third reason is that regulators may not draft to the standards of Parliamentary drafting.

These three factors mean lawyers have to take a different approach when interpreting regulation. The approach must be to discern the intention behind the regulation. The interpretative discipline is purposive, not literal. When you consider that generally the sanctions are exercised at the discretion of the regulator, there is really no point in attempting cleverly to circumvent a rule through a deftly constructed argument about its language. If the regulator considers that the spirit of the rule has been flouted, that will be conclusive. When you add to this the other factors mentioned above, there is really no alternative but to suspend classic legalistic analysis and concentrate on the underlying objective of the rule in deciding whether your client's conduct will be acceptable.

Where, however, you are dealing with a statute, normal principles of interpretation apply.

1.7.2 Understanding the market

Since the rules are written to make the relevant market operate prudently, efficiently and fairly, to understand and therefore interpret the rules properly, you need to understand the market. To determine whether your client's proposals or conduct can be accommodated within the rules, you need to understand the nature of what your client wants to do. Getting to grips with the commercial background to the transactions and the markets is consequently absolutely fundamental to the work of the lawyer, hence the focus of this book.

1.7.3 Compliance

An inevitable role the lawyer is called on to play, alongside that of the interpreter, is that of the compliance officer. Has the client done everything required of him by the rule book? Has everything gone into the relevant document that should be in the document? At times this is laborious and tedious, as it requires a checklist mentality. It is nevertheless a crucial task—you are paid to be painstaking.

1.7.4 Juggling the rules

We have seen an array of different rules from different regulators. Sometimes they intersect, overlap or run parallel to each other. You need to keep all these balls in the air at the same time and not lose sight of any of them. You cannot just be a master of the City Code when doing a public company takeover: you need to understand, amongst other things, the application of The Listing Rules and FSMA to the transaction. The checklist below will help you to know what is relevant. Advising on regulation is above all the art of the juggler.

Central to corporate finance work is the company which is raising or using its finance. Central to the functioning of a company is its management, owners and those who advise it professionally. We have now seen something of the regulatory superstructure: let us turn our attention to a specific area where regulation plays an important role, and which is relevant in all the transactions which are the subject of this book—the regulation of the governance of the company.

Table 1.1   Who will be the regulator?

Activity	Regulator and regulations	References
1 Are regulated activities to be carried out?	FSA (FSMA and related regulations)	FSMA is of major importance in corporate finance work and is covered in **1.5.1** above.
2 Is banking business to be carried out?	FSA (FSMA and related regulations)	Banking regulation as a subject in detail is outside the scope of this book. The basic structure of the banking regulatory system is covered above.

(Continued)

Table 1.1   Continued

Activity	Regulator and regulations	References
3 Is insurance business to be carried out?	Treasury, FSA (Insurance Companies Act 1982, FSMA)	Insurance regulation as a subject in detail is outside the scope of this book. The basic structure of insurance regulation is covered above.
4 Is a company to be formed?	Registrar of Companies (Companies Act 1985)	The regulation of public companies, insofar as it is different from that applying to companies more generally, is introduced below.
5 Are securities to be issued?	Registrar of Companies (ss. 80 to 89 Companies Act 1985)	This is covered in the *LPC Guide: Business Law*.
6a Is the company already listed on the LSE or admitted to the AIM?	UKLA LSE AIM (The Listing Rules) (LSE Admission and Disclosure Standards) (AIM Rules)	A listing or admission to the AIM for a company doing an issue of securities means there are continuing obligations to observe—see **4.2.10** and **4.3.5.2**.
6b	Investment Committees (IPC Guidelines)	A listed company doing a securities issue must also consider the Investment Committee guidelines (see **3.3.1.3**); the Committees are described below.
7 Is there to be an offer to the public?	Registrar of Companies LSE (Public Offers of Securities Regulations 1995) (as amended by the Public Offers of Securities (Amendment) Regulations 1999)	An offer to the public is discussed in **3.5**.
8 Are the securities to be admitted to the AIM?	LSE (Public Offers of Securities Regulations 1995) (as amended by the Public Offers of Securities (Amendment) Regulations 1999) (AIM Rules)	The AIM regulation is discussed in **4.3**; the LSE administers the AIM.
9 Are the securities to be listed on the LSE?	UKLA (Part VI FSMA) (The Listing Rules) LSE (Stock Exchange Admission and Disclosure Standards)	Obtaining a listing is discussed in **4.2**; the UKLA's and the LSE's overall function is described above.
10 Is the company listed and making a substantial acquisition or disposal?	UKLA (The Listing Rules) LSE (Stock Exchange Admission and Disclosure Standards)	Any listed company must observe the UKLA and LSE requirements.

(Continued)

Table 1.1   Continued

Activity	Regulator and regulations	References
11 Is there a substantial acquisition of shares?	Takeover Panel (Substantial Acquisitions Rules) (Part VI Companies Act 1985)	The Takeover Panel administers the Substantial Acquisitions Rules (SARs). These are described in **8.9**. The Takeover Panel is discussed above. Part VI of the Companies Act 1985 is discussed in **8.11**.
12 Is a public company being acquired?	Takeover Panel (City Code)	The Takeover Panel is responsible for the City Code. It is mentioned above and in much more detail in **8.8.5**.
13a Is there a referable merger under UK law?	Office of Fair Trading, Competition Commission (Competition Act 1998, Enterprise Act 2003)	The merger control regime in the UK is discussed in **8.16**.
13b Or a concentration with a Community dimension?	European Commission (EC Merger Regulation)	The EC merger control regime is explained in **8.16.2**.
13b Do any of the circumstances leading to the takeover constitute anti-competitive arrangements or abuse of a dominant position?	Competition Act 1998 (Chapter I and II prohibitions) or Arts 81 and 82 Treaty of Rome (if trade between Member States is affected)	The Chapter I prohibition is mentioned in **8.16.1.4**. The Chapter II prohibition is mentioned in **8.16.2.2**.

1.8   The Code of Market Conduct

1.8.1   Introduction

The control of market abuse under the FSMA is referred to in outline at **1.5.1.3(b)** and in the context of takeover activity at **8.15**. This section looks at the Code of Market Conduct in more detail. Very broadly, market abuse involves the misuse of relevant information not generally available to the market, or conduct likely to distort the market or give a false or misleading impression as to the market or price of securities.

1.8.1.1   Background

Prior to FSMA, regulators had only limited ability to penalise unregulated market participants for unacceptable market conduct, and market abuse was generally prosecuted primarily through use of the criminal law, where successful prosecutions were few and far between. In order to rectify this situation FSMA has created the market abuse regime under which the FSA is given civil powers to sanction both unregulated and regulated market participants whose conduct (on or off market) is deemed to be substandard. This new regime supplements the existing criminal law on insider dealing contained in the Criminal Justice Act 1993 (rather than replacing it) and has a broader remit which also deals with misleading and market manipulative practices as well as the misuse of information.

It should be noted that this civil legislation requires a lower standard of proof than the criminal legislation.

1.8.1.2 The Code of Market Conduct

The Code of Market Conduct (the 'CMC') which has been produced by the FSA in accordance with s. 119 FSMA gives guidance to market participants on the application of the market abuse regime to help determine whether or not their behaviour amounts to market abuse. It specifies certain types of behaviour which do not amount to market abuse—these are known a 'safe harbours'.

1.8.1.3 Penalties

Where the FSA finds that a person has been involved in market abuse or has taken any action encouraging another person to do so, the FSA has the power to either impose unlimited financial penalties or publicly censure that person.

1.8.2 What is market abuse?

1.8.2.1 Market abuse

Section 118 of FSMA describes market abuse as behaviour (which can be inaction as well as action) by one person alone or by two or more persons jointly or in concert. If a person's action or inaction encourages another person to engage in behaviour which amounts to market abuse, then they too may be held to have engaged in market abuse.

Conduct only amounts to market abuse if a hypothetical regular user of the market would regard the behaviour as falling below an acceptable standard.

1.8.2.2 Behaviour

Types of behaviour which fall within the scope of the market abuse regime are described in paragraph 1.3 of the CMC as including:

(i) dealing in qualifying investments;

(ii) dealing in commodities or investments which are the subject matter of, or whose price or value is determined by reference to a qualifying investment;

(iii) arranging deals in respect of qualifying investments;

(iv) Causing or procuring or advising others to deal in qualifying investments;

(v) making statements or representations or otherwise disseminating information which is likely to be regarded by the regular user as relevant to determining the terms on which transactions in qualifying investments should be effected;

(vi) providing corporate finance advice and conducting corporate finance activities in qualifying investments; and

(vii) managing investments which are qualifying investments belonging to another.

The behaviour must occur in relation to a qualifying investment traded on a market in the UK or which is accessible electronically in the UK (s. 118(5) FSMA). The behaviour must also satisfy one or more of the three statutory conditions in s. 118(2) being:

(a) *Misuse of information (para. 1.4 CMC):* behaviour based on information that is not generally available to the market, but which if made available would be likely to be regarded by a regular participant in that market (a "regular user") as relevant in

> deciding on the basis on which a transaction involving the investment in question should be effected; or
>
> (b) *Misleading practice (para. 1.5 CMC):* behaviour likely to give a regular user a false or misleading impression as to the supply, demand, price or value of the investment in question; or
>
> (c) *Manipulation/distortion (para. 1.6 CMC):* behaviour which would be regarded by a regular user of the relevant market as likely to distort the market for the investment in question.

'Behaviour' includes dealing in securities, dissemination of information and managing investments, and it covers actions as well as omissions (such as failure to make a required disclosure).

1.8.2.3   The regular user test (s. 118(10) FSMA, para. I.2 CMC)

Behaviour satisfying any of the above three market abuse conditions will only be subject to sanction if it fails to satisfy the 'regular user' test. A person's behaviour fails the regular user test if a regular user of the relevant market would be likely to regard the behaviour as a failure to observe the standard to be reasonably expected of someone in that person's position in relation to the relevant market.

1.8.2.4   Safe harbours under the Code of Market Conduct

In accordance with s. 122(1) FSMA, the CMC describes certain behaviour that, in the FSA's opinion, does not amount to market abuse. These paragraphs are marked throughout the code with a letter 'C' and are known as 'safe harbours'.

In addition, as required by s. 122(2) FSMA, the CMC also describes behaviour which the FSA believes does amount to market abuse. These paragraphs are marked with an 'E' throughout the CMC and may be relied upon for the purposes of FSMA.

1.8.3   Summary of Code of Market Conduct

1.8.3.1   Misuse of information

Conduct amounting to market abuse	MAR ref	Safe harbours	MAR ref
Dealing (including arranging deals) in a qualifying investment or relevant product where:		Dealing required to comply with a pre-existing regulatory/legal duty.	1.4.20
• The dealing is based on information;	1.4.4	Dealing not influenced by the possession of the relevant information.	1.4.21
• The information is not generally available;	1.4.5	Dealing based on 'trading information'.	1.4.26
• The information is likely to be regarded by a regulator user as "relevant information"; and	1.4.9	Dealing by a bidder in equity stakes in a takeover bid based on knowledge of his own bid.	1.4.28
• The information is (or potentially is) 'disclosable' (under a legal or regulatory duty) or 'announceable' (i.e. routinely the subject of public announcement).	1.4.12	Agreeing to underwrite securities	1.4.31

1.8.3.2   Misleading practices

Conduct amounting to market abuse	MAR ref	Safe harbours	MAR ref
Artificial transactions: Transactions in a qualifying investment or relevant product:	1.5.8(1)	Permitted transactions:	
• Where you know/ought to know that the principal effect is likely to be to artificially to inflate or depress the apparent supply of, demand for, price or value of a qualifying investment or relevant product so as to give a false or misleading impression to a regular user;	1.5.8(2) & (3)	• Transactions to take advantage of tax/cross-market arbitrages or lending or borrowing to meet underlying commercial demand;	1.5.24
• Unless the regular user would regard your principal rationale to be a legitimate commercial purpose and the manner of execution as proper	1.5.8(4) & (5)	• Where the regular user would regard your principal rationale to be a legitimate commercial purpose and the manner of execution as proper	1.5.8(4) & (5)
Disseminating information:		Required reporting or disclosure of transactions:	
Disseminating information that you know/ought to know is false or misleading in order to create a false or misleading impression	1.5.15	Reporting or disclosure in accordance with legal/regulatory requirements where expressly required or permitted by applicable regulations.	1.5.25
Dissembling information through an accepted channel of communication for a prescribed market that is likely to give a false/misleading impression where reasonable care is not taken to ensure that the information is neither false nor misleading.	1.5.18	Statutory exceptions: Behaviour conforming with specified rules in the Takeover Code or Rules on Substantial Acquisition of Shares as to the timing, dissemination or availability, content and standard of care applicable to a disclosure, announcement, communication or release of information if expressly required or permitted by those rules.	1.7.7
Course of conduct: Engaging in a course of conduct:		Behaviour conforming with r. 4.2 of the Takeover Code (restrictions on dealings by offeror and concert parties) if expressly required or permitted by that rule.	1.7.8
• Where you know/ought to know the principal effect is likely to convey a false or misleading impression to a regular user;	1.5.21 (1) & (2)		
• Unless the regular user would regard your principal rationale to be a legitimate commercial rationale and the manner of conduct as proper.	1.5.21 (3) & (4)	Chinese walls: Where an individual in an organisation disseminates information, the organisation will not be regarded that it knows/ought to know it was false/misleading where other information is held behind effe Chinese walls and the indi should not have know information was f	1.5.27

1.8.3.3   Market manipulation/distortion

Conduct amounting to market abuse	MAR ref	Safe harbours	Mar ref
Price positioning: Transactions with the purpose of positioning the price of a qualifying investment or relevant product at a distorted level.	1.6.9	Behaviour conforming with the London Metal Exchange rules set out in "Market Aberrations: The Way Forward" (Oct 1998) governing the behaviour expected of long position holders.	1.6.19
Abusive squeezes: Where you have significant influence over the supply of, or demand or delivery mechanism for, a qualifying investment or relevant product and you hold positions directly or indirectly in an investment under which the qualifying investment/relevant product is deliverable and you engage in behaviour with the purpose of positioning at a distorted level the price at which others have to deliver, take delivery or defer delivery to satisfy their obiligations.	1.6.13	Statutory exceptions: Behaviour conforming with specified rules in the Takeover Code or Rules on Substantial Acquisitions of Shares as to the timing, dissemination or availability, content and standard of care applicable to a disclosure, announcement, communication or release of information if expressly required or permitted by those rules.	1.7.5, 1.7.7
		Behaviour conforming with r. 4.2 of the Takeover Code (restrictions on dealings by offeror and concert parties) if expressly required or permitted by that rule.	1.7.5, 1.7.8

1.8.3.4   General safe harbours/statutory exceptions

Safe harbours	MAR ref
Behaviour conforming with the FSA's price stabilising rules or Chinese wall rules	1.7.3(1) & (2)
Behaviour conforming with specified rules in the UKLA's Listing Rules as to the timing, dissemination or availability, content and standard of care applicable to a disclosure, announcement, communication or release of information (or in relation to share buy backs).	1.7.3(3) & (4).

1.8.4   Market abuse—primary sources

In practice, where there is concern that activity (or inactivity) might amount to market abuse, you should refer to the primary resources governing this field. In addition to ss. 118–131, 144 and 397 FSMA, you will need to refer to:

- FSA Handbook MAR Chapter 1—Code of Market Conduct details the essential elements of market abuse regime and contains details of the safe harbours. Section 119 requires the FSA to draw up a code of market conduct to provide appropriate guidance to those who must decide whether certain behaviour amounts to market abuse.

- FSA Handbook MAR Chapter 2—Price Stabilising Rules and Traditional Provisions for the Price Stabilising Rules. Section 144 FSMA enables the FSA to make rules relating to stabilizing the price of new issues of securities. Stabilisation would in some circumstances constitute misleading statements and practices offences under s. 392(2) and (3) FSMA or insider dealing under the Criminal Justice Act 1993 and as a result would constitute market abuse under s. 118 FSMA. By complying with the price stabilisation rules, one is provided with a defence or "safe harbour" to such offences under the market abuse regime.

- Chapter 13, 14 and 15 of the Enforcement Module of the FSA Handbook, which have relevance to market abuse and authorised persons generally.

2

Corporate governance

Public companies have a wider range of opportunities open to them than private companies. They may offer their shares to the public. Their shares may be traded on the stock market. These offer the benefits of greater access to sources of finance. But they come at a price, in the form of more rigorous regulatory obligations. These tougher demands affect everyone connected with the company: the company itself, its directors, its shareholders and its advisers.

2.1 Companies Act regulation for public companies

The Companies Act 1985 ("CA") applies of course as much to public companies as to private companies. There are, though, a number of additional requirements imposed on public companies by the Act which do not apply to private companies, and a number of requirements imposed on all companies but more stringently on public companies. This section contains only a summary of some of the most important—many of these are covered in detail later on.

The abiding policy underlying all these provisions is to build in extra safeguards for investors, given the greater liabilities likely to be assumed by public companies.

2.1.1 Share capital requirements

Section 117 CA prohibits a public company (unless it has converted from being a private company) from trading without a certificate from the Registrar of Companies, which he will only issue if the company has the authorised minimum share capital of £50,000 (s. 118). At least one-quarter of the nominal value of the shares (£12,500) must be paid up (s. 101).

A public company may only disapply the pre-emption provisions of the CA if authorised to do so by its shareholders. Such authority must be limited in time to the directors' authority to allot shares and therefore may only be for a maximum duration of five years. The disapplication must be renewed by special resolution (s. 80) when the authority expires. However, the Investment Committees of the Association of British Insurers ("ABI") and the National Association of Pension Funds ('NAPF') (who represent the interests of institutional shareholders) regard disapplication of the statutory pre-emption provisions as a dilution of shareholders' rights. As such, although it is theoretically possible under statue to disapply pre-emption provisions for longer, the UKLA requires companies to disapply such rights annually by special resolution and the ABI currently advises its members to vote against resolutions seeking disapplication in respect of more than 5 per cent of the company's issued ordinary share capital.

2.1.2   Payment for shares

Public companies cannot accept payment for shares in the form of an undertaking from a person to perform work or services (s. 99)—the risks are that such an undertaking may never be performed and that its value is intangible and may be difficult to compare with the value of a share.

Non-cash payments for shares in public companies are not allowed if they are subject to an undertaking to be fulfilled more than five years after allotment (s. 102). This concerns payment by way of assets to be transferred to the company in the future, as these assets may decline in value.

Non-cash payments for shares in a public company must in any event be valued under s. 103. Exceptions exist where the company is issuing its shares in exchange for shares in another company (s. 103(3)) or is merging with another company by acquiring all its assets and liabilities (s. 103(5)). Section 108 CA sets out the required valuation procedure. Though often a mere formality this is time-consuming and expensive. Companies generally seek to avoid it wherever possible. In practice, for acquisitions or takeovers involving the issue of shares as consideration, the two exceptions mentioned usually provide the escape route needed.

2.1.3   Directors

Public companies must have at least two directors (s. 282), while private companies can have one. Other regulatory impositions to which directors of public companies are subject are covered in **2.2**.

2.1.4   Maintenance of capital

If a public company's net assets are half or less of its called-up share capital, the directors must call a meeting of shareholders to consider what to do (s. 142). For example, in a recession, when property companies may have to devalue their assets substantially. At the general meeting, directors will usually seek approval from shareholders for their strategy for survival.

2.1.5   Financial assistance for the acquisition of shares

Two additional restrictions apply to public companies. The first is that a public company cannot take advantage of the so-called 'whitewash' procedure under ss. 155 to 158. The second is that the exemptions under s. 153 (for example, permitting financial assistance for an employee share scheme) apply to a public company only if it does not thereby reduce its net assets, or it provides such assistance out of distributable profits. The financial assistance restrictions are discussed in more detail in **8.12**.

2.1.6   Purchases of own shares

Companies may buy back their own shares under certain conditions. A public company may not do so out of capital, unlike private companies (s. 171).

The Companies (Acquisition of Own Shares) (Treasury Shares) Regulations 2003 (which came into force on 1 December 2003) introduced a new regime whereby a quoted company which purchases its own shares is no longer required to cancel those shares.

Instead, subject to certain requirements and restrictions, they can be held 'in treasury' and then sold for cash (rather than the company issuing new shares), transferred under an employees' share scheme or cancelled. For the purposes of the regulations, 'quoted' means companies whose shares are admitted to the Official List, admitted to trading on AIM or listed in or traded on a regulated market in an EEA state.

2.1.7   Distributions

A public company may pay dividends only if the amount of its net assets is not thereby reduced to less than the value of its share capital and undistributable reserves (s. 264). This prevents public companies from paying out dividends against unrealised profits made from their assets, such as revised property values.

2.1.8   Accounts

A public company must put its annual accounts and directors' report to a general meeting, usually the AGM, and send them to the Registrar of Companies within seven months of the end of its accounting reference period (or six months if the company is listed on the LSE), not 10 months as in the case of a private company (s. 244). The relaxations from the accounting requirements for small and medium-sized companies in s. 246 do not apply to public companies.

2.1.9   Notification of interests in shares

Shareholders acquiring an interest in 3 per cent or more (or in some cases 10 per cent or more) of a public company's shares must notify the company within two days (s. 198). This requirement and the ensuing provisions are designed to help the company identify substantial and possibly hostile shareholders on its register. They are covered in much more detail in the context of takeovers (see **8.11**), when they are particularly important.

2.2   Statutory and regulatory controls on public company directors

Directors face an array of duties and controls at common law and under statute. These have already been examined in the *LPC Guide: Business Law*. This chapter looks at the additional regulatory restrictions to which directors of publicly traded companies are subject.

Broadly, these additional regulatory controls on directors affect two things: their dealings in securities and the composition and functioning of their own boards.

2.2.1   Directors' dealings: disclosure

You will already be familiar with what the CA requires of a director and his family when he or it owns, acquires or sells securities in his company or group company: s. 324 and associated provisions require notification of such transactions to the company, and s. 325 requires the maintenance of a register which may be inspected by the public. In addition, the directors' annual report must effectively relay to shareholders the information regarding directors' shareholding interests in the company and its group companies.

Where the company is listed, and under s. 324 the director notifies the company of a relevant interest, the company must transmit this to the LSE (s. 329), which publishes such data to the market through a Regulatory Information Service ('RIS'). In addition to the requirements under the CA, Chapter 16 of the Listing Rules imposes certain obligations relating to directors of listed companies including rules as to the disclosures a company must make about its directors and about dealings in securities of the company by directors and persons connected with them. In particular, LR para. 16.13 sets out in detail the information that a listed company must provide to a RIS relating to directors interests disclosed to the company in accordance with ss. 324 and 325 of the Act.

Furthermore, LR para. 12.43(k) asks that the annual report for a listed company distinguishes between each director's beneficial and non-beneficial interests in the company's securities, so that shareholders can get some idea of the voting control which directors actually have. These provisions ensure a degree of transparency in directors' dealings in their own or related companies. The concern remains that directors, given their access to so much privileged information about these companies, should be allowed to deal in their securities in the first place.

2.2.2 Directors' dealings: prohibitions

Again, we have already seen in the *LPC Guide: Business Law,* and we see later in **8.14,** how the Criminal Justice Act 1993 remedies this by making it an offence for directors to deal in their company's securities where they possess inside information about it, or for them to pass on such information improperly.

As far as listed companies are concerned, however, the UKLA is concerned that directors should be seen to be above suspicion in their share dealings. Preserving the integrity of the market is crucial. Acting on inside information erodes that integrity. Directors are most obviously party to inside information, and so the UKLA has a rigorous code to clamp down on the freedom of directors to deal in their own company's securities. The UKLA is not out to prevent directors holding shares in their companies—in fact, this is something it encourages, as it (a) gives directors a stake in the future of their companies as owners as well as managers, and (b) it is healthy for the company as it sends out positive signals to investors about its directors' view of its investment potential. However, there must be no suggestion that these shareholdings are acquired or sold with the benefit of privileged information.

2.2.2.1 The Model Code (on directors' dealings in securities)

The freedom of directors (and employees who are not directors but who are likely to possess unpublished price-sensitive information about the listed company which employs them) to deal in their company's securities is restricted in a number of ways—by statue, by common law and by the Listing Rules.

Following on from the disclosure of director's interests required in LR para. 16.13 LR para. 16.18 requires a listed company to ensure that its directors and certain employees and connected persons likely to possess unpublished price-sensitive information about the company comply with a code of dealing in terms no less exacting than those of the Model Code ('MC') before dealing in the company's securities. The Model Code is to be found in the Appendix to Chapter 16 of the Listing Rules. LR para 16.18 should therefore be seen as a continuing obligation of the company.

The Model Code applies to fully listed companies. AIM companies are not strictly required to adopt the code, as the AIM rules contain restrictions on dealings which are arguably wider than the Model Code itself. That said, an AIM company's nominated adviser is more than likely to require the company to comply with the Model Code as a matter of best practice.

Who is subject to be Model Code?

The Model Code applies to:

- directors of listed companies;
- employees of listed companies with access to unpublished price-sensitive information; and
- connected persons.

Purpose

The Model Code constrains the freedom of directors and those associated with them to deal in the company's shares (or other securities whose price is determined by reference to the company's shares). It gives guidance for the establishment of an agreed procedure for share dealings by directors and provides a minimum standard of good practice against which companies should measure their own dealing codes. It goes beyond the constrains imposed by the criminal legislation prohibiting insider dealing contained in Part V of the Criminal Justice Act 1993, which makes it a criminal offence for an individual who has information as an insider to deal (or disclose information which would encourage others to deal) on a regulated market in securities whose price would be significantly affected if the inside information were made public. LR para 16.19 allows companies to impose even more rigorous restrictions on dealings on directors and employees than those set out in the Model Code, if they see fit.

Prohibitions

The Model Code sets out the main occasions when a director of a listed company may not deal (i.e., essentially buy, sell or exercise an option) in his own company's securities, these being:

(a) *For short term gain*

A director may not deal himself and must take responsible steps to prevent any dealings by or on behalf of any person connected with him in any securities of the listed company on considerations of a short-term nature (MC para. 2). For example, this would prevent 'bed & breakfasting' or other short-term arrangements which may destabilise the market in those securities.

(b) *During a close period*

A director may not deal in the company's securities during a close period, which is defined as the two months immediately preceding the preliminary announcement of the company's annual results (or half-yearly results if applicable) or, if shorter, the period from the relevant financial period end up to and including the time of such announcement. If the company reports on a quarterly basis, the close period is the period of one month immediately preceding the announcement of the quarterly reports (or, if shorter, the period from the relevant financial period end to the time of such announcement) (MC para. 3). Note this is a total prohibition and applies whether or not the information contained in any such regular announcement is price-sensitive.

(c) *If in possession of unpublished price-sensitive information*

A director may not deal in his own company's securities at any time if he is in possession of unpublished price-sensitive information about the company (MC para.4)

Dealing

For the purposes of the Model Code, 'dealing' includes any acquisition, disposal or agreement to acquire or dispose of any of the company's shares (or other securities whose price is determined by reference to the company's shares)—including the exercise of options.

Clearance

Any dealing must in any event receive clearance from the company chairman or a director appointed to do this job (MC para. 6). In addition to the 'close periods', clearance will be refused when the dealing would take place after the need for an announcement to the market of unpublished price-sensitive information about the company has become reasonably probable (MC para. 7 (b)). A director may, however, sell securities to meet a 'pressing financial commitment' (MC para. 9). This would have to be exceptional to qualify. Where a director advises a company that he intends to deal in shares, the company must maintain a written record of such advice and any clearance given (MC para. 8). The company must also provide the director with written confirmation that such recording has taken place.

Connected persons

Where directors cannot themselves deal, they must seek to prohibit such dealings by their families and connected persons (see s. 346) of the Act and various other institutions connected with them, such as their investment managers (MC para. 11).

Exceptions

The Model Code also provides for a series of exceptions to its terms including taking up entitlements under a rights issue (MC para. 20 (a–d)) (see **3.6.4**), the acceptance of takeover offer (MC para. 20(e)) or an exercise of certain share options during a prohibited period under an employees' share option scheme (MC para. 20(g)).

The point of real importance is that the UKLA is looking for compliance with the spirit, and not simply the letter, of the MC.

It should be noted that in Consultation Paper 203 (CP203), the FSA proposed to streamline the Model Code once the Market Abuse Directive implementing measures have been finalised.

2.2.2.2   What if the Model Code is breached?

A breach of the MC will give rise to the same consequences as would apply to non-observance of any of the Listing Rules (on which see **4.2.11**). Note in particular that the failure by a director to discharge his responsibilities under the Model Code may lead to a fine or censure by the UKLA (LR para. 1.8) and possibly suspension (LR para. 1.15) or cancellation of listing (LR para. 1.19).

Of course, in certain circumstances, a breach of the Model Code could be a breach of the insider dealing legislation in the Criminal Justice Act 1993 or the market abuse provisions of FSMA, which carry much more serious connotations. This will not always be the case, though, given that the Model Code's provisions are more extensive than the legislation, and certainly a breach of the Model Code is not to be treated as a presumption of insider dealing. A technical breach of the Model Code does occasionally arise as a result of a dealing within one of the prohibited periods by an institution connected with the director, often because of a misinterpretation of the application of the Model Code (and the provisions are certainly quite complex)—but no insider dealing offence will have been committed.

By the same token it is dangerous to assume that compliance with the Model Code will automatically take particular conduct outside the insider dealing and market abuse regimes or act in any way as a defence to proceedings brought under them. Passing information on outside the course of the director's employment is not a breach of the Model Code but may fall foul of the Criminal Justice Act 1993 and FSMA.

2.2.3   Corporate governance: the Combined Code

2.2.3.1   Introduction and history of the Combined Code

The Combined Code ('the Code') is a set of main principles, supporting principles and provisions of good corporate governance. A listed company incorporated in the UK is required, by the Listing Rules, to make a corporate governance statement in relation to the Combined Code in its annual report and accounts (LR para. 12.43A (a)). The statement must report on how it applies the main and supporting principles, and either confirm that it complies with the Combined Code's provisions or, where it does not, provide an explanation for non-compliance (LR para. 12.43A (b)). The Combined Code is appended to but does not form part of the Listing Rules.

The current Combined Code has evolved from the work of various committees and reports on corporate governance. The Cadbury Committee produced a Code in 1992 which governed financial reporting and aspects of management. In July 1995, the Greenbury Code on good practice in determining directors' remuneration was issued. The Hampel Committee then published, in June 1998, a set of principles and a code which embraced the two earlier codes and the committee's own work. This became the Combined Code (Principles of Good Governance and Code of Best Practice). The current Combined Code ('the Combined Code on Corporate Governance') was published by the Financial Reporting Council in July 2003 and is based on Derek Higgs' review of the role and effectiveness of non-executive directors and Sir Robert Smith's report on audit committees. It supersedes and replaces the 1998 version, and applies to listed companies for reporting years beginning on or after 1 November 2003.

2.2.3.2   Content of the Code

The Combined Code comprises two sections, Section 1 applies to companies and Section 2 to institutional shareholders). Each Section contains a number of principles, supporting principles and code provisions, the provisions providing details of the way in which the principles and supporting principles should be observed.

Section 1 of the Combined Code, which deals with companies, is divided into four parts. The main principles are set out below:

(a) Directors
- Every company should be headed by an effective board, which is collectively responsible for the success of the company (Comb Code Section 1, A.1 'The Board' Main Principle).
- There should be a clear division of responsibilities at the head of the company between the running of the board and the executive responsible for the running of the company's business. No one individual should have unfettered powers of decision (Comb Code Section 1, A.2 'Chairman and Chief Executive' Main Principle).
- The board should include a balance of executive and non-executive directors (and, in particular, independent non-executive directors) such that no individual or small group of individuals can dominate the board's decision taking (Comb Code Section 1, A.3 'Board balance and independence' Main Principle).
- There should be a formal, rigorous and transparent procedure for the appointment of new directors to the board (Comb Code Section 1, A.4 'Appointments to the Board' Main Principle).
- The board should be supplied in a timely manner with information in a form and of a quality appropriate to enable it to discharge its duties. All directors should

receive induction on joining the board and should regularly update and refresh their skills and knowledge (Comb Code Section 1, A.5 'Information and professional development' Main Principle).

- The board should undertake a formal and rigorous annual evaluation of its own performance and that of its committees and individual directors (Comb Code Section 1, A.6 'Performance evaluation' Main Principle).

- All directors should be submitted for re-election at regular intervals, subject to continued satisfactory performance. The board should ensure planned and progressive refreshing of the board (Comb Code Section 1, A.7 'Re-election' Main Principle).

The principles highlight the board's role of providing entrepreneurial leadership of the company. All directors must take decisions objectively in the interests of the company. The board must not be so large as to be unwieldy, but should be of a sufficient size as to ensure a balance of skills and experience. There should be a strong presence on the board of both executive and non-executive directors, and power and/or information should not be concentrated in one or two individuals (A.3). The Code also emphasises the need for the non-executive directors to be independent. It states that the board shall identify in the annual report each non-executive director it considers to be independent and the board should determine whether the director is independent in character and in judgement and whether there are relationships or circumstances which are likely to affect, or could appear to affect, the director's judgement (A.3). These principles also pay particular attention to the responsibilities of the non-executive directors and suggest that they should constructively challenge and help develop proposals on strategy, scrutinise the performance of management in meeting agreed goals and objectives, and monitor the reporting of performance. The non-executive directors are also responsible for determining appropriate levels of remuneration of executive directors and have a prime role in appointing, and where necessary removing, executive directors and in succession planning (A.1). These are clearly key roles and a company must be diligent in choosing non-executive directors (particularly the independent non-executive directors) who are dedicated to fully and objectively carrying out such responsibilities.

The chairman and chief executive should be two separate people so that no one person has unfettered powers of decision. The Code also provides that a chief executive should not go on to be chairman of the same company unless the major shareholders have been consulted and the reasons for such an appointment have been explained to shareholders and subsequently set out in the next annual report (A.2). Further, the Code states that no individual should be appointed to a second chairmanship of a FTSE 100 company (A.4). The Code provides a helpful description of the role of the chairman; he is responsible for leadership of the board, ensuring its effectiveness in all aspects of its role and setting its agenda. The chairman is also responsible for ensuring that the directors receive accurate, timely and clear information. The chairman should ensure effective communication with shareholders. The chairman should also facilitate the effective contribution of non-executive directors in particular and ensure constructive relations between executives and non-executive directors (A.2). The chairman can chair the nomination committee but not when it is dealing with the appointment of his successor. The Code also states that the chairman should hold meetings with the non-executive directors without executive directors present.

In addition to the chairman, the Code also provides for a director to be appointed as the company's senior independent director and specific responsibilities are assigned to this role. For example, led by the senior independent director, the non-executive directors should meet without the chairman present at least annually to appraise the chairman's performance (A.1) and, again, led by the senior independent director, the non-executive directors should be responsible for the performance evaluation of the chairman, taking into account the views of executive directors (A.6). Also, the senior independent director should be available to shareholders if they have concerns which they cannot resolve through the normal channels of chairman, chief executive or finance director (A.3) and the senior independent director should attend sufficient meetings with a range of major shareholders to listen to their views (D.1). Arguably, the latter could be seen as duplication of the chairman's responsibility.

In order to preserve the standard of directors, the board is required to evaluate its performance and should state in the annual report how evaluation of the board itself, its committees and the individual directors has been conducted. (A.6).

Principle A.7 recommends re-election of directors at regular intervals and goes on to suggest that such intervals should not be longer than three years. Non-executive directors should be subject to rigorous review should they serve longer than two, three-year terms.

(b) *Remuneration*

- Levels of remuneration should be sufficient to attract, retain and motivate directors of the quality required to run the company successfully, but a company should avoid paying more than is necessary for this purpose. A significant proportion of executive directors' remuneration should be structured so as to link rewards to corporate and individual performance (Comb Code Section 1, B.1 'The Level and Make-up of Remuneration' Main Principle).
- There should be a formal and transparent procedure for developing policy on executive remuneration and for fixing the remuneration packages of individual directors. No director should be involved in deciding his or her own remuneration (Comb Code Section 1, B.2 'Procedure' Main Principle).

The 2003 version of the Combined Code does not contain material on disclosure of directors' remuneration. This is because the Directors' Remuneration Report Regulations 2002, SI 2002/1986, now require directors to prepare a remuneration report which is clear, transparent and understandable to shareholders (see **2.2.4.2** below).

Further directors' remuneration reporting requirements are contained in LR para. 12.43A and s.234B of the Act and are discussed at **2.2.4.1** below.

(c) *Accountability and audit*

- The board should present a balanced and understandable assessment of the company's position and prospects (Comb Code Section 1, C.1 'Financial Reporting' Main Principle).
- The board should maintain a sound system of internal control to safeguard shareholders' investment and the company's assets(Comb Code Section 1, C.2 'Internal Control' Main Principle). The Combined Code also includes guidance on how to comply with this principal entitled 'Guidance on Internal Control' which was produced by the Turnbull Committee.
- The board should establish formal and transparent arrangements for considering how they should apply the financial reporting and internal control principles and for maintaining an appropriate relationship with the company's auditors (Comb Code Section 1, C.3 'Audit Committee and Auditors' Main Principle). Guidance on Audit Committees which was produced by the Smith Group is also appended to the Combined Code.

(d) *Relations with shareholders*

- There should be a dialogue with shareholders based on the mutual understanding of objectives. The board as a whole has responsibility for ensuring that a satisfactory dialogue with shareholders takes place (Comb Code Section 1, D.1 'Dialogue with Institutional Shareholders' Main Principle).

- The board should use the AGM to communicate with investors and to encourage their participation (Comb Code Section 1, D.2 'Constructive Use of the AGM' Main Principle).

Schedules to the Combined Code set out provisions on the design of performance-related remuneration (Comb Code Schedule A), guidance on liability of non-executive directors (Comb Code Schedule B), and provisions on disclosure of corporate governance arrangements (Comb Code Schedule C).

Section 2 of the Code contains principles and provisions applicable to institutional shareholders with regard to their voting (Comb Code Section 2, E.3), dialogue with companies (Comb Code Section 2, E.1) and evaluation of a company's corporate governance arrangements (Comb Code Section 2, E.2).

2.2.3.3   Compliance with the Combined Code

Paragraph 12.43A of the Listing Rules requires all listed companies incorporated in the UK to include in their annual report and accounts:

(a) a narrative statement of how they have applied the principles set out in Section 1 of the Combined Code, providing an explanation which enables shareholders to evaluate how the principles have been applied; and

(b) a statement either confiming that they have complied with the Combined Code provisions or, where they have not, giving reasons for and the duration of any such non-compliance. This must be reviewed, at least in part (LR para. 12.43A (d)) by the company's auditors, who also have obligations to report in relation to Directors' Remuneration under Part 3 of Sch. 7A to the Companies Act 1985.

It should be noted that the Combined Code makes it clear that certain provisions are relaxed for smaller companies (for these purposes, a company which is outside the FTSE 350). Dispensations for smaller companies are that they should have at least two independent non-executive directors (rather than at least half the board) (A.3), that the remuneration committee should consist of two members (B.2) and the audit committee should consist of two members (C.3).

Companies are not required to report on whether and how they have complied with the provisions set out in Section 2 of the Combined Code relating to institutional shareholders. It was thought that the matters coveredin this section were inappropriate to be included within the Listing Rules disclosure requirements. However it is hoped that at least major institutions will disclose to their clients and the public the extent to which they are able to give effect to the provisionsof Section 2.

The overall intention is that the Combined Code and the Listing Rules reporting requirements should together result in high standards of corporate governance, transparent to shareholders and other outsiders. The main area where reporting requirements have been made more onerous is that of directors' remuneration. Where previously companies were only required to state that they had considered the Greenbury guidelines in formulating their remuneration policy, they are now required to state how they have applied all the principles. However, it should be remembered that the Combined Code does not form part of the Listing Rules: only the reporting requirements are mandatory. Surveys on the earlier codes showed that many companies were either ignoring guidelines or complying with them only to a limited extent. Companies have been loath to put their remuneration policies before shareholders: it remains to see whether the Combined Code will change this.

2.2.4 Reporting requirements on directors' remuneration

2.2.4.1 Listing Rules

Paragraph 12.43A(c) of the Listing Rules requires companies to report to shareholders on directors' remuneration, giving details of, *inter alia*, the following:

(a) the company's policy on executive directors' remuneration (LR para. 12.43A (c)(i));

(b) the amount of each element of each director's remuneration package (including salary, benefits in kind and bonuses) (LR para. 12.43A (c)(ii));

(c) share options for each director (LR para. 12.43A (c)(iii));

(d) long-term incentive schemes (LR para. 12.43A (c)(iv));

(e) any service contracts with notice periods in excess of one year (LR para. 12.43A (c)(vi)); and

(f) any defined benefit schemes or money purchase schemes (LR para. 12.43A (c)(ix) and (x)).

2.2.4.2 Companies Act 1985

The Directors' Remuneration Report Regulations 2002 have amended the CA such that s. 234B requires the directors of a listed company to prepare a directors' remuneration report for each financial year which contains the information specified in Sch. 7A. Such report is to be approved by the board and signed on behalf of the board by a director or secretary (s. 234C). It must also be offered for approval by the shareholders annually in general meeting (ss. 241, 241A).

The contents of such a report are set out in Sch. 7A CA and include the following elements:

(a) statement of the company's policy on directors' remuneration;

(b) performance graph showing the company's share price performance over the preceding five years;

(c) certain details of the directors' service contracts;

(d) amounts of each director's emoluments and compensation for the relevant financial year;

(e) directors' share options, long-term incentive schemes and pensions provisions.

Failure to deliver a properly executed directors' remuneration report may leave the company and its officers liable to a fine (ss.234C(4)(b), 241(2) CA).

2.2.5 Other restrictions

Directors are subject to a number of other regulatory constraints on their conduct which are addressed elsewhere in this book and so are mentioned here only for the sake of completeness:

(a) Any transaction between a listed company and one of its directors or his associates will be classified as a transaction with a related party under the Listing Rules (ch. 11). Typically, this will catch sales of assets to directors or their associates by listed companies. Exceptions which are considered in LR paras 11.7 and 11.8, include an issue of shares or options to a director by his company (LR para. 11.7 (c)(i)), or a company giving a director an indemnity (LR para. 11.7 (f)). Small transactions are also exempt (LR para. 11.7(i)). If the transaction is caught, a circular to shareholders and their consent in general meeting will normally be required under LR para. 11.4 (unless the UKLA is prepared to grant a waiver). This subject is covered in more detail in **5.6.4.1**.

(b) Any securities offering or takeover by a company will require the issue of some sort of public document regarding the transaction (prospectus, listing particulars or an offer document respectively). The UKLA and Takeover Panel respectively require the directors of the company to accept and declare publicly their responsibility for these documents on their face (LR para. 6.A.3, City Code r. 19.2 (a)). The precise effect this has on their legal liability is considered in **4.2.5.7**. The point to note for the time being is that the regulators place directors firmly in the firing-line in these major corporate finance transactions, irrespective of executive or non-executive status. This provides a useful stick (or carrot, depending on your point of view) with which occasionally to remind directors of the importance of their role in these transactions.

These points are in addition to any relevant statutory obligations directors may face.

2.3   The role of shareholders in corporate governance

There are two aspects to this:

(a) the regulation of shareholder activity in the affairs of a public company; and

(b) the influence which shareholders can exert over the affairs of a public company.

2.3.1   The regulation of shareholder activity in public companies

Although it seems less obvious, since good corporate governance is intended primarily for the benefit of shareholders, they too are subject to laws and regulations which aim to assist the effective and fair management of corporations. There are two particular areas to note:

(a) The provisions of the Companies Act 1985 which deal with the notification by shareholders of interests they hold in shares in public companies (ss. 198 to 220). These have nothing to do with the obligation of directors to disclose their own or their families' interests under s. 324 CA and related provisions. Sections 198 to 220 are examined in **8.11**. Their purpose is to help companies keep a close eye on developments on their share registers, so that any potentially controlling influence can be speedily identified. This is supported by the information requirement in LR para. 12.43(1), that any shareholding interest of 3 per cent or more in a listed company be disclosed in the annual report and accounts.

(b) The provisions in the Listing Rules described in **2.2.5** regarding transactions with related parties (between listed companies and their directors) apply equally to transactions between such companies and their substantial shareholders or their associates (LR para. 11.1 (b)(i),(iv)). Substantial shareholders are those currently holding, or who in the past year, held a 10 per cent interest or more in the company

(LR para. 11.1 (c)) . The idea of this is to offer smaller shareholders the right to object to deals involving their company which favour larger shareholders. Similar exemptions to those mentioned in **5.6.4.1** apply (as, for example, in LR para. 11.7 (j)), including that for small transactions.

2.3.2   Investment Committees

These are committees of the ABI and the NAPF. The ABI is the trade body for the insurance company market, the NAPF the equivalent for pension funds. They are very large organisations—the ABI comprises over 450 insurance companies. They were formed to represent the interests of their members, and these interests include their substantial holdings of shares in UK-listed companies. Though there has been a very significant growth in recent years in the number of private investors holding shares, the total number of shares held by private individuals has declined as institutional share ownership has increased. Roughly 80 per cent of all listed shares in the UK were held by institutional shareholders in 1993.

These stakes are held for investment purposes. The investment potential of shareholdings can be affected quite significantly by such things as fresh issues of shares, as these dilute the value of existing shares, and repurchases of shares, which require the company to spend money it might otherwise distribute by way of dividend. Hence the Investment Committees seek to capitalise on their powerful and often controlling position in listed companies by issuing guidelines expressing their members' views on questions such as new issues of shares (see **3.3.1.3**) and share repurchases. The Committees will also indicate their views on such aspects of corporate governance as the acceptability of proposed revisions to articles of association (which will of course require shareholder approval).

The nature of these guidelines is to alert companies to situations which the associations are likely to find unacceptable, so that a negotiation can be initiated with the association to arrive at a compromise. Sometimes the Committees insist on their guidelines being observed. The sanction they can exercise is their members voting against a resolution required to approve the proposed action. The guidelines are therefore of real concern to listed companies with significant numbers of institutional shareholders, though in practice they are usually observed by all listed companies.

2.4   The role of advisers in corporate governance

Advisers may seem an odd category of person to whom corporate governance principles should apply, for they are neither manager nor owner of the company. They do, though, play a significant and sometimes crucial role in its management and development and it is therefore in the company's best interests that this role is exercised responsibly.

You will already have seen in the *LPC Guide: Business Law* various legal provisions which affect the activities of a company's advisers.

2.4.1   Negligence

There is obviously the influence of the common law duty to take reasonable care in the advice proffered. This is considered particularly in the context of equity issues in **4.2.5.7**. Auditors have no greater duty than any other adviser, but their duty of care has recently been the subject of judicial analysis in cases referred to in that section.

2.4.2   Shadow directors

Statute imposes certain duties. Any adviser may be found to be a shadow director where the directors of the company are accustomed to act in accordance with the adviser's instructions or directions (s. 741 CA). This brings with it the liabilities associated with acting as a director. Accordingly, advisers would be well advised themselves to issue advice to their corporate clients in their professional capacity only and to take no managerial or supervisory role in the company's operations.

2.4.3   Auditors

Auditors are under a statutory duty pursuant to s. 237 CA to carry out investigations into, and report on the propriety of, the company's accounting records.

Section 235 requires auditors to report in particular on whether the company's balance sheet and profit and loss account at the end of each financial year give a true and fair view respectively of its state of affairs and profit and loss.

In the past, the accountancy profession established a series of accounting standards to assist the profession in determining what is true and fair. These are SSAPs, or Statements of Standard Accounting Practice. They are not law, but the major professional accounting bodies, such as the Institute of Chartered Accountants, will penalise any accountants who do not follow them. Essentially, therefore, they are statements as to best practice for auditors and their corporate clients, supported by the certainty of disciplinary action in the event of non-compliance.

Like all such statements, they are capable of differing interpretations, and this gave rise to considerable debate about the accuracy of some public companies' financial statements. In an attempt to improve public confidence in the quality of financial reporting, a new self-regulatory regime was introduced in 1990, under which the Accounting Standards Board (ASB) became responsible for the issue of new standards. These standards are called Financial Reporting Standards (FRSs). They are the contemporary equivalent of SSAPs. The old SSAPs have stayed in existence and are still referred to as SSAPs. FRSs have no greater legal effect than SSAPs. While some of the SSAPs have been superseded by FRSs, some remain in force.

Should a company depart from the SSAPs or FRSs, a Financial Reporting Review Panel (FRRP) may question and examine such a policy and publicise any such departures. The FRRP is part of the same self-regulatory regime to which the ASB belongs. Statutory procedures exist under ss. 245A–C CA to enable the Secretary of State for Trade and Industry or the FRRP to obtain a court order stating that a company's accounts do not comply with the Act and requiring the preparation of revised accounts. This supports the FRRP's enforcement role. Companies and their auditors will seek to avoid such public exposure of possible peculiarities in their accounting records, and this strengthens the regulators' arm in ensuring the 'true and fair view'.

2.4.4   Insider dealing and market abuse

Advisers are in a privileged position. They have access to confidential information about the company's strategy, products, financial status and so on. They could obviously benefit from that information if they chose. The Criminal Justice Act 1993 extends as much to them as to directors of companies. It prohibits advisers with access to information from dealing in securities of the company, and prevents them from passing the information on otherwise than in the proper performance of their job. Certain exceptions apply which will assist dealings by advisers in connection with certain transactions by the company in which they have been instructed to act, for example, acquisitions or disposals (see **8.14**, where this is explained fully).

In addition, advisers should be aware of the market abuse provisions of FSMA, especially in Part VIII (see **1.5.1.3(b)**). Any misuse of information or other behaviour falling within the Act could result in a fine or other sanction by the FSA.

2.4.5 Professional standards

The regulatory authorities expect advisers to act with probity and the highest standards of professionalism and care.

The Listing Rules indicate the importance the UKLA attaches to the role of a company's sponsor when it seeks admission to listing: this is examined in much more detail in **3.3.4**.

The City Code on Takeovers and Mergers (r. 3) stresses the importance of independent and competent professional advice for both sides in the course of a takeover bid.

Accountants and lawyers are regulated by their own professional bodies, which impose demanding standards of professional care on their members and take disciplinary action against them in the event of misconduct.

All these elements reinforce the common law remedies available to companies which receive negligent or incompetent advice or are the victims of malpractice.

3

Securities offerings

This chapter considers the various ways in which securities are offered to investors by companies raising finance from the stock market. These offerings may be by companies which do not yet have their shares traded on the market and which may therefore seek approval to have them admitted to the market at the same time as they offer them to the public. This first time they are admitted to the LSE is generally referred to as a 'primary offering'. Once their shares are admitted and trading, further issues of shares to raise additional capital are called 'secondary offerings', such as rights issues (**3.6.4**), placings (**3.2.3, 3.5.6**) and open offers (**3.6.5**).

This chapter looks at both types of offering.

The company will need to address at an early stage of any primary offering the question of which market it wants to join. In the UK, it is a choice between the LSE (a 'full listing' as it is sometimes described) and the Alternative Investment Market ('AIM'). The choice and considerations relevant to each are discussed in **Chapter 4**, as are the risks and legal liabilities attendant on these public share issues.

A preliminary subject to address is the nature of the securities the company is offering.

3.1 What are 'securities'?

'Securities' is not a term defined in the Companies Act 1985, though definitions exist in the Stock Transfer Act 1963 and the Criminal Justice Act 1993 which broadly include shares, stocks, debentures, bonds, warrants, options and the like. In general commercial usage, a security is some form of instrument representing an interest in a company. In ordinary company law terms, we are most likely to think of a share or a debenture when the term 'security' is used. The instrument here is the share or stock certificate representing the interest held by the investor in the company. The nature of that interest will vary, depending on the type of security in question.

The security the investor gets is literally the security of something in return for cash. The security is a necessary evil for the company. Ideally, the company would like to be given money for nothing! In reality, it has to give something back to the investor by way of rights or entitlements as a means of attracting capital in the first place.

We will look here at some of the questions relevant when choosing one type of security to issue rather than another.

The basic choice is between debt or equity, though we will see later how this boundary may be blurred.

3.1.1 Debt

The characteristics of a debt instrument are primarily a defined life and an agreed interest rate, referred to as the coupon. Debt is capital which is paid over on the understanding that it will be repaid (or redeemed) at a fixed point in time and in priority to shareholders on a winding up. That understanding is usually recorded in a contract between investor and issuer, and sometimes that contract may provide for an element of security in the form of a charge over assets. More usually, debt instruments will be unsecured.

A typical debt instrument in the UK market is loan stock. This is something like a single huge debenture carved into a number of separate debentures, each issued individually to different investors. A trustee is appointed to represent the collective interests of the assorted stockholders and ensure that the company complies with its obligations. A price may be quoted for the loan stock on the stock market so it can be traded.

A loan stock may be convertible into ordinary shares (see below) of the company. This is usually at the choice of the holder of the loan stock, who may choose to exercise this right when the ordinary shares are appreciating faster than the return on the loan stock.

Just as shares fluctuate in value on the stock market relative to both their nominal value and issue price, so traded debt instruments will at any point in time be worth more or less than their basic value at redemption, depending on the interest rate they carry in the current market and the underlying value of the company which issued them.

3.1.2 Equity

Equity does not have to be repaid to investors, save on a winding up (and even then shareholders usually come last in the priority of claims). The finance paid by an equity investor is available to the company for all time—unlike the finite life of debt capital. This has obvious attractions for the company.

The attraction of equity to an investor is the prospect of a return through a dividend, essentially a distribution from available profit, and capital appreciation of the equity interest (or share) as the company's performance improves. Ordinarily, there is no legal entitlement to receive a dividend. If the profit is not there to pay one out, the investor has no claim on the company. The dividend will be paid out after the company has met its interest payment obligation on outstanding debt.

Equity comes in a number of different forms.

3.1.2.1 Ordinary shares

As well as the right to receive a dividend when it is declared, and the right to receive on a winding up the proportion of capital represented by the size of the equity interest, an ordinary share also carries the right to vote at shareholders' meetings. Occasionally, a company may choose to have different classes of ordinary shares to represent different rights—this may be useful in a joint venture company (see **Chapter 6**) or where family members wish to retain enhanced voting rights. For companies seeking admission to the Official List, it is as well to be aware that the UKLA and the Investment Committees do not like a share capital structure in which some of the shares carry restricted voting rights (though the possibility of that is specifically contemplated in LR para. 6.B.5).

Ordinary shares may be issued as redeemable so that the shares may be bought back by the company. Sometimes the price and date of this redemption is fixed at the time of issue, though this is unusual (see **9.8**).

The great majority of shares traded on the LSE are ordinary shares. Usually the liquidity in the preference share market is quite low. This tends to depress their share price in comparison with the much more extensive market for ordinary shares. Ordinary shares may therefore have more appeal to the investor.

3.1.2.2 Preference shares

Holders of preference shares are entitled to receive a fixed dividend in priority to ordinary shareholders. This dividend is usually based on a percentage of the nominal value of the shares. It is also cumulative so that if the company has insufficient profits to pay out one year, the right accumulates until there is enough money to satisfy the deferred entitlements. In practice, this cumulative right is attractive to companies as they are not obliged to pay out a dividend every year (as compared with the need to make an annual interest payment on debt instruments). Of course, deferring the dividend payment is often unpopular with the shareholder.

Preference shares also generally precede ordinary shares in the priority of claims in a winding up of the company if this is expressly provided in the terms of issue.

Preference shares may also be redeemable, that is, they can be bought back at some date in the future at their nominal value (i.e., a fixed price). They will then generally carry a lower dividend as the guarantee of redemption is felt to be a significant investment inducement.

Preference shares may be convertible into ordinary shares at a definite future date and price. Usually the right to convert is exercisable at the discretion of the investor.

Participating preference shares have the right to receive an additional dividend on top of their fixed dividend. The additional dividend is usually a proportion of the dividend paid out to ordinary shareholders, so the preference shareholders are 'participating' in the profit performance of the company.

One of the characteristics of these more specialised instruments is that they confuse the boundary between debt and equity. An example is the redeemable preference share, which confers on the investor the right to be repaid a fixed amount in the future and an entitlement to a fixed dividend (not unlike interest). This is why it matters much less what an instrument is called and much more what rights it carries.

In view of this plethora of differing rights and interest, what factors will influence the decision as to which instrument to choose?

3.1.3 Debt or equity?

3.1.3.1 Interest rates

If interest rates are high, that will make the issue of debt more expensive for the company. When they are low, conversely it may be difficult to get investors excited about debt capital.

3.1.3.2 Cash flow

Interest payments need to be made regularly on debt instruments. If the company has limited supplies of cash, the interest obligation will prove difficult to service.

3.1.3.3 Market conditions

If the company's existing share price is depressed relative to the company's true value, raising finance through the issue of equity will be an expensive choice—it is better to issue equity when the company is able to get full value for each share. The overall state of the stock market may have an influence on this. Clearly there is little to be gained from attempting an equity issue in the wake of a significant fall in stock market values generally.

3.1.3.4 Cost

Different types of instruments may carry broadly comparable rights—we have already seen the similarities between the redeemable preference share and a debt instrument.

However, in this case, a redeemable preference share will be more expensive to service as the dividend cannot be set off against tax, unlike interest on a debt instrument. It is this tax benefit which often makes debt attractive to the issuer.

Set against this, of course, is the fact that an ordinary share theoretically carries no cost: the dividend is not an enforceable entitlement. The reality is slightly different. Attempts by companies to suspend or reduce dividend payments are often met with hostility from the Investment Committees (see in particular **2.3.2**).

The size of a dividend on a convertible or redeemable preference share is generally lower than for a normal preference share, and this may sway the issuer in their favour if the difference in cost is significant.

3.1.3.5 Flexibility

Equity offers flexibility in that dividends may be deferred in a bad year, both for ordinary and preference shares, whereas the interest on debt must always be paid because of the consequences for the company if it goes into default.

Convertible instruments, whether preference shares or loan stock, offer a 'hybrid' interest to investors which allows them some choice between the security of the fixed entitlements of debt or preference shares, and the greater risk but possibly greater rewards of equity.

3.1.3.6 Voting power

Preference shares are attractive to some companies in that they do not dilute the voting power of ordinary shareholders (most preference shareholders have an entitlement to vote only at their own meetings and not the company's general meetings). Debt instruments generally carry no voting rights at all (save that some loan stock instruments entitle the holders to vote at stockholders' meetings).

3.1.3.7 Accounting factors

A factor in selecting debt or equity is how it will be accounted for on the issuer's balance sheet. This is now governed by FRS 4. In essence, this requires securities to be accounted for not simply in accordance with their legal form but in a way that reflects the obligations of the issuer. It used to be relatively easy for a company to issue an instrument which carried debt obligations but, by virtue of a right of conversion into the company's shares, was treated as if it was share capital. FRS 4 requires that any security which 'contains an obligation to transfer economic benefits' (including a contingent obligation) be classified as a liability, rather than an equity interest. Thus, a convertible debt instrument would now have to be treated as a liability.

The point of this is that classification of a security as a liability rather than an asset (which would be the case with a share) will worsen the company's debt-equity ratio, which has an impact on its credit rating, and so affects its general standing in the financial markets. It may also raise questions in the minds of investors about the long-term viability and security of the business. FRS 4 therefore effectively requires a company choosing to issue debt to classify it as such on its balance sheet.

3.1.3.8 Conclusion

There is no right answer to which is the best sort of security to plump for. The important thing is to understand the issues relevant to this choice and the options available.

This chapter will leave debt instruments aside and focus instead on the issue of equity securities, and primarily ordinary shares.

3.2 Underwriting and placing

In looking at issues of equity securities, we begin with underwriting and placing as these concepts underlie almost all the types of offer considered here.

3.2.1 Underwriting

A company issuing new securities on the LSE or the Alternative Investment Market is looking to raise a fixed amount of money, namely the full value of the securities on offer. Its objective is not just to see how well it can do, and take only whatever it persuades investors to stump up. It has a reason for raising that amount of money, generally to finance identified investment or expansion in particular areas, and anything less than that amount of money will mean that the relevant corporate strategy cannot be implemented.

To avoid this problem, underwriting exists. It is essentially a form of insurance or guarantee. In the event that investors cannot be found to take up all the securities the company is offering, an underwriter agrees to step in and acquire whatever is left. In that way, the company's securities are always paid for by someone, hence securing for the company the total amount of the funds it is looking for from the offer. The quid pro quo is that the underwriter charges a commission for the service, which the company pays whether or not it has to ask the underwriter to take up the shares. An investment bank will normally play the part of underwriter in the offers we look at below (see **3.3.5**).

No underwriter is likely to feel comfortable in taking on the full risk of a multi-million-pound securities offer alone. He therefore lays off the lion's share of his own risk to a series of sub-underwriters, who perform the same service for him as he has undertaken for the company—in other words, to take up an agreed proportion of the company's securities in return for a commission. Sub-underwriters are generally other investment banks or firms of stockbrokers who also have experience of arranging sub-underwritings of their own, or institutional investors such as pension funds, unit trust managers, insurance companies and the like.

3.2.2 Key provisions of an underwriting agreement

Most underwriting agreements contain the following key provisions.

(a) *Conditions*

There will be a clause stating the precise conditions which must be satisfied before the agreement becomes unconditional. These will include:

- the admission of the securities to the Official List and their admission to trading;
- confirmation from the company that there has been no material change in the condition of the company since the execution of the underwriting agreement;
- confirmation that no event has occurred which would make any representations or warranties incorrect in a material respect and that the circular does not contain material inaccuracies or omissions;
- confirmation that the company has complied with all its obligations under the underwriting agreement.

Other conditions will include more practical details such as a provision that the company and/or seller must have delivered certified copies of all the principal documents relating to the offer to the underwriter so that it can check that these are in order. These are usually detailed under the heading 'Obligations of the Company'.

(b) *Allotment and registration*

(c) *The commitment to take shares*

This clause imposes a commitment upon the underwriters either to procure sub-scribers for any shares not taken up (such as sub-underwriters, discussed above) or to subscribe for the shares themselves. This obligation will impose several liability to acquire the shares if bookbuilding is used (**3.2.4**), or possibly joint and several liability on the underwriters if a fixed offer price underwriting method is used. In each case, shares will be acquired at the offer price less any commissions, such as management, underwriting and selling commissions.

(d) *Fees commissions and expenses*

These are made up of a number of elements which are generally calculated as a per-centage of the amount raised. The traditional underwriting commission structure involves the payment by the issuing company of a commission of 2 per cent of the aggregate value at the issue price of the number of shares underwritten for the first 30 days of the underwriting period, together with an additional $\frac{1}{8}$ per cent of such value for each subsequent period of seven days (or part thereof). The underwriting period runs from (and including) the day of announcement to (and including) the day on which sub-underwriters are notified of the number of new shares which they are required to take up. The length of this period depends upon whether an extraordinary general meeting is required and, if so, whether ordinary or special resolutions are to be proposed. If no extraordinary general meeting is required, the total commission payable is likely to be 2 per cent. Where an extraordinary general meeting is required, the likely commission will be $2\frac{1}{4}$ per cent (if ordinary resolu-tions only) or $2\frac{3}{8}$ per cent (if special resolution required).

The 2 per cent commission is typically split as follows:

- $\frac{1}{2}$ per cent to investment bank as underwriter;
- $\frac{1}{4}$ per cent to broker;
- $\frac{1}{2}$ per cent to sub-underwriters as commitment commission for the first 30 days; and
- $\frac{3}{4}$ per cent to sub-underwriters as success commission.

The sub-underwriters' commission (which totals $1\frac{1}{4}$ per cent out of the 2 per cent) is generally split as to $\frac{1}{2}$ per cent commitment commission (i.e. payable in any event) and $\frac{3}{4}$ per cent success commission (i.e. payable only if the issue proceeds). If addi-tional commission is payable because an EGM is required, then this is paid as com-mitment commission to the sub-underwriters.

The Office of Fair Trading has recently concluded that the total 2 per cent fee often amounts to overcharging for underwriting, so having the effect of making raising capital more expensive for UK industry than is necessary. It is difficult for companies to create competition by shopping around for lower fees because of the long-term relationship most companies have with their particular investment bank. The OFT concluded that there was a competition problem but it recom-mended that companies and underwriters took their own steps to tackle it. By the end of 1996, there was some evidence that more competitive structures were devel-oping, involving the use of, for example, tenders. However, the OFT referred the matter to the Monopolies and Mergers Commission (now the Competition Commission) in November 1997.

The Competition Commission found that two complex monopoly situations exist. First, the supply of lead underwriting services at standard fees and, secondly, the supply of sub-underwriting services at standard fees. In relation to lead underwriting services, the Commission concluded that competition among financial advisers and brokers is reasonably vigorous. As a result, the fees retained by the lead underwriter (i.e., the investment bank) and those paid by it to brokers were not viewed as being higher than they would be in the absence of standard fees. Although it was thought that the fees should be more transparent, the Commission did not find that the lack of transparency operated against the public interest. In relation to sub-underwriting, the Commission discussed whether it should make mandatory the tendering of sub-underwriting. However, this was rejected on the grounds that it would restrict market flexibility and the right of companies to choose the share-issuing method they thought was in their best interests. The most appropriate remedies were seen as those which increase transparency and the information available to companies. The main recommendation of the Commission was therefore that the Securities and Futures Authority issue guidance to corporate financial advisers reminding them of the application of the FSA's principle on information for customers and recommending that they should advise their clients of alternatives to underwriting at standard fees. In addition, it was recommended that The Bank of England publish guidance for companies on share-issuing good practice, including encouraging the use of tendering and explaining when deep discounting (see **3.6.4.2**) is likely to be advantageous.

(Commissions on a bookbuilt equity offering (see **3.2.5**) will generally be a higher overall percentage, normally between 3 and 5 per cent. This reflects the fact that the investment bank will usually have to spend a large amount of time marketing. Commissions are split between the managers of the so-called underwriting syndicate so that about 20 per cent of the total commission represents a fee for the management of the underwriting, 20 per cent of the total is a fee for underwriting the issue (agreeing to take securities if there are no interested investors) and about 60 per cent of the total is for selling securities on to interested investors. The total is split between the managers, depending on the separate roles they have performed.)

(e) *Warranties and indemnities*

In an offering of shares, the company and, sometimes, the selling shareholders will be expected to provide comfort to the underwriters relating to the state of the company and the accuracy of information contained in the circular or listing particulars.

Some examples of the most common representations and warranties provided by the company are in respect of:

- the accuracy of the information contained in the listing particulars;
- the accuracy and correct presentation of the financial statements which will form part of the listing particulars;
- the fact that the company is duly incorporated and has the capacity to enter into all relevant agreements and has ensured that all registration requirements have been complied with;
- the fact that there is no material litigation outstanding against the company (other than as may be disclosed in the listing particulars); and
- there having been no material adverse change in the company's circumstances since the date of the last audited accounts.

The company will also indemnify the underwriters for any loss they may incur as a result of any misstatement or omission in the listing particulars or as a result of a breach of any other representations and warranties given by it in the underwriting agreement.

The warranties and indemnities generally provide the major source of discussion during the negotiation of the underwriting agreement. The underwriter will view the warranties and indemnities not only as a protection exercise but also as an important part of the due diligence process. Given the gravity of breaching a warranty, it tends to concentrate the minds of the company—particularly if the directors are also asked to provide additional representations and warranties! There are often instances where discussions over the extent of a particular warranty will lead to additional disclosure in the listing particulars.

(f) *Selling restrictions*

Underwriters will generally only undertake to sell the shares in accordance with the selling restrictions which will be set out in the underwriting agreement. These restrictions set out the circumstances in which the shares may be sold in jurisdictions other than the UK. These provisions are also important for the company as it will not want the underwriters to do anything which imposes liabilities or obligations on the company in other jurisdictions—for example a registration obligation in the US.

(g) *Force majeure clause*

This sets out what will happen in the event that disaster strikes during the underwriting period—for example, war breaks out or there is a stock market collapse. The underwriter will argue that it is being paid its commission for taking a usual 'market risk', but not for agreeing to take shares in all circumstances, regardless of a sudden disaster.

If the underwriter requires the right to terminate its underwriting obligation in such a case, it needs to include a force majeure clause in the underwriting agreement. Such a clause would be subject to negotiation but would generally specify the force majeure events—for example, 'any fundamental change in national or international financial, economic, political, military or market conditions which in the reasonable opinion of the underwriter is likely materially and adversely to affect the financial or trading position or prospects of the company or is likely to have a materially prejudicial effect on the issue or makes the success of the issue doubtful, impracticable or inadvisable to proceed with it'.

3.2.3 Example of underwriting

A company wishes to make an offer of new securities (100 million ordinary shares) at £1.00 each. The company appoints U to underwrite the offer and U appoints 25 sub-underwriters, each of whom agree to sub-underwrite up to 1/25th of whatever is left of the ordinary shares after they have been offered to the public.

Assume the offer is a total failure and not a single share is acquired by a member of the public in the offer. U has agreed with the company to acquire all 100 million shares in this event, but, through its sub-underwriting arrangements, it can require each of the 25 sub-underwriters to take (and pay for) 4 million shares. U has 'laid off' the risk entirely. U and each of the sub-underwriters will receive a commission for their commitment.

If the public had acquired 50 million shares in the offer, leaving 50 million shares to be taken up under the underwriting, each sub-underwriter would have been left with 2 million shares (the appropriate proportion of its 1/25th commitment).

Ordinarily, the underwriter (U) will not lay off all its risk, but, as a sign of its commitment to the offer, will hold some shares back for its own account in the event that not all the shares are wanted by the public.

The important characteristic of underwriting is that it depends entirely on the success of the offer with the general public whether the underwriters and sub-underwriters end up with any of the securities on offer.

3.2.4 Placing

A placing may work in a number of ways, some of which produce results similar to those produced by the underwriting of a public offer.

A company issuing its securities will appoint its investment bank to arrange the placing. As you will see below (**3.3.5**), this means that it is the investment bank's job to identify and target particular potential investors and get them to commit to take some of the securities on offer. These investors are then known as 'placees'. Placees are typically drawn from the same ranks as are sub-underwriters—but do not let this confuse you! In this case, they are the primary investors and are not acting as sub-underwriters. If sufficient interested investors cannot be found, the investment bank may agree to acquire the shares itself—effectively, it underwrites the placing. The company is therefore still guaranteed to get the money it is seeking. This is often referred to as a 'best efforts' placing and is the common form adopted.

Alternatively, and more unusually, an investment bank may agree only to act on a 'reasonable endeavours' basis to secure placees for the offer. This means he will do what he can to find placees, but if he is not successful, then that is the end of his responsibility: he has no further obligation regarding the shares left and does not underwrite the offer. Obviously this is a less attractive option for the company issuing the securities. Notwithstanding these terms of art, the specific obligations of the investment bank will be set out in a placing agreement made with the company.

In a placing with clawback (see **3.6.5.2**), the placees will effectively act as sub-underwriters. This is because the securities are placed conditionally with the placees and offered to other investors first (generally the company's shareholders): the placees only end up with securities if the other investors are not keen on the offer. The merchant bank continues to act as an 'underwriter' in this kind of offer.

Placings are considered in more detail in **3.5.6** below.

3.2.5 Bookbuilding

Bookbuilding is a method of underwriting an offer of securities which is used for international equity offerings and increasingly on large initial and subsequent offerings in the UK market. It is in fact closer to a placing in structure.

With a traditional underwriting, the underwriter approaches sub-underwriters to lay off his risk in advance of the offer, but since the issue price is only determined on the day of the offer, sub-underwriters will only be contractually bound to take the risk they have agreed on the day of the offer itself. When bookbuilding is used, potential investors (usually the same institutions and individuals approached in a placing (see **3.2.4**)) bid in advance of the offer for the securities which are to be issued. Their bid, which is not legally binding, is an indication of the number of shares they would be prepared to take up and the price at which they would do so. The potential investors will assess any bid they make on the basis of a preliminary offer document called a 'pathfinder' prospectus. A pathfinder prospectus is almost identical to the final prospectus which is released, except that the final price and number of shares to be issued are omitted since these figures are not known until the day of the actual offer. This may often indicate the range within which the final offer price will be set.

The level of demand shown by potential investors will eventually determine the issue price of the securities on the day of the offer: effectively the underwriter (known as the manager) has conducted an auction of the securities and 'run a book'—hence bookbuilding—on the interested investors and the price they will pay. The manager continues to act as underwriter of the offer in the event that investors cannot be found or do not pay for the securities they have agreed to purchase. The underwriting agreement is signed following the bookbuilding process and the setting of the issue price just before commencement of dealings. The period of underwriting risk for the investment bank is therefore much shorter than on a traditional underwriting.

The bookbuilding process carries with it a number of advantages. In theory, it generates a higher offer price for the company's securities because the price can be fixed accurately on the basis of demand shown, in contrast with the traditional underwriting where the underwriter may suggest a lower price to sub-underwriters to ensure a successful issue. The bookbuilding route also ensures greater transparency in identifying investors, as they are selected by the underwriter (the manager) rather than the broker (contrast the sub-underwriting process). Since bookbuilding has developed as the typical form of underwriting for international equity offerings (principally because it is the traditional marketing method for securities offerings in the USA), it affords UK companies who conduct their issues through the bookbuilding process an opportunity to access an international investor base. This means a broader range of potential investors and a greater profile, which may be valuable where the company is intending to expand its business overseas.

Section **3.5.4** describes the typical structure for a UK securities offering. This is still the conventional route, but you should be aware that increasing use is being made of the bookbuilding route as an alternative vehicle in the domestic UK market. The underwriting agreement (see **3.5.4.1**) will be very similar in a bookbuilt offering.

3.3 The 'players'

This section is devoted to the 'football team' of participants and advisers in issues of equity securities. The intention is to give you a picture of who is involved and who does what to help you understand what is going on in these transactions.

3.3.1 The company

It is important to remember that the company is a separate legal entity from its directors and other managers. There may be situations in these issues where the directors' interests and the company's are quite different (for example, where the directors are to dispose of or acquire large shareholdings in the course of the offer), in which case separate advice will be needed for company and directors.

There may be a great deal of preliminary legal work needed to get a company ready for an issue of securities to the public. Much of this preparation can be ignored by a company which is already listed on the LSE or has its securities dealt in on the AIM, as it will have taken care of them prior to initial listing or entry onto the AIM. The number of things to deal with will depend largely on the individual nature and circumstances of the company making the issue, hence the following are offered by way of illustration only.

3.3.1.1 Plc status

The company must be registered as a public limited company before it can make an offer to the public (LR para. 3.2 requires this, quite apart from s. 81(1) CA). Time will be needed for the company to register or re-register as a public company (see ss. 117 and 118 CA).

3.3.1.2 Transferability of securities

For a company to have its securities listed, they must be freely transferable (LR para. 3.15). Hence, fully paid shares must be free from all liens and from any restriction on the right of transfer (save for any restriction imposed for failure to comply with a notice under s. 212 CA).

Only in exceptional circumstances will the UKLA allow a company the power to disapprove the transfer of shares, provided that this did not affect the market in such shares.

3.3.1.3 Allotment and issue of securities: statute

The company will need to think about the following requirements of the Companies Act 1985 before it goes ahead with the issue.

(a) *Section 121 CA*

The company will probably need to increase the amount of its authorised share capital to cover the new securities to be issued (s. 121(2)(a)).

(b) *Section 80 CA*

Directors must have authority from the company to exercise the power to allot new securities (see LPC Guide: Business Law).

(c) *Section 89 CA*

The issue of equity securities must be on a pre-emptive basis (i.e., to existing shareholders in proportion to their existing holdings) unless the company has empowered its directors to do otherwise, either by virtue of the articles or by means of a s. 95 CA special resolution disapplying s. 89. The use of the s. 95 special resolution procedure is the normal route (see *LPC Guide: Business Law*).

3.3.1.4 Allotment and issue of securities: regulation

More important for listed companies, in some ways, are the non-statutory restrictions on the allotment and issue of securities which apply to them. These are derived from the Listing Rules (LR, ch. 9), and guidelines issued in 1988 by the Investment Committees (see **2.3.2**). They apply to s. 80 authorities, and s. 89 disapplications (see LR paras 9.18, 9.19, and 9.20).

Breach of the LSE's restrictions will be a breach of its continuing obligations and so subject to the same risks as described in **4.2.10**. Breach of the Investment Committee guidelines runs the risk of incurring the institutional investors' displeasure and so having the offending s. 80 or s. 95 resolution voted down at an annual or extraordinary general meeting. If there is any risk of this, it is therefore vital to discuss the position with the Investment Committees first.

As far as s. 80 authorities are concerned, the Investment Committees guidelines look to restrict them to the lesser of the amount of authorised but unissued share capital of the company, *or* one third of the company's issued ordinary share capital.

As far as s. 89 disapplications are concerned, the non-statutory restrictions affect any disapplication in place on listing—so existing s. 95 resolutions will need to be reviewed carefully in advance of the listing application.

As for the *amount* of a disapplication, the Investment Committee guidelines state that their members should not oppose proposals for non-pre-emptive issues provided that they do not exceed 5 per cent of its issued ordinary share capital at any one time, *or* $7\frac{1}{2}$ per cent of its issued ordinary share capital over a three-year period.

The guidelines also suggest that companies should restrict any *discount* to market price on a non-pre-emptive issue to 5 per cent of the market price immediately before the offer is made.

These guidelines apply only to *listed companies*, and remember that they complement, not replace, the statutory provisions in the CA.

3.3.1.5 Company 'audit'

A great deal of information about the company's activities will need to be researched and prepared, ultimately for disclosure in the prospectus or listing particulars (see **4.2.5.6**).

It is as well to initiate this process as soon as the decision to apply for listing has been taken. It may then be that various disclosures which might otherwise have to be made in the prospectus or listing particulars can be avoided (for instance, if the company has failed to keep its filing of returns under the CA up to date, it may be possible to correct this before the listing process begins). The information to concentrate on includes material contracts, assets and liabilities (particularly any assets which may require valuation, such as real property), any outstanding, pending or threatened litigation and the state of the company's statutory books and registers.

3.3.1.6 Timing notification

Under guidelines issued jointly by the LSE and the British Merchant Banking and Securities Houses Association, the Bank of England should be informed of the launch date (known as 'impact day') for any new issues exceeding £20 million in value. The idea is to avoid clashes in dates between new issues, on the basis that excessive simultaneous demands for new money from investors will mean that one or both of the competing issuers will inevitably lose out. It would be better in these circumstances if the issuers could agree to come to the market at different times.

The system works by means of a notification from the issuer's sponsor to the Bank of England of the proposed timing of the issue. If there is a clash of dates, the sponsor is informed. The issuer may then choose to go ahead with its selected date regardless, and neither the Bank of England nor the LSE has any power to force the issuer to do otherwise, though the Bank will inform the other competing issuer. More often than not, however, the sponsor and issuer will agree a revised date for the launch of their own issue, which is then communicated to the Bank.

3.3.2 The directors

The directors bear a significant risk of liability for misleading statements in their company's prospectus or listing particulars (see **4.2.5.7**). Consequently the directors will take a close interest in the preparation of the prospectus. In any event, some of the information regarding the company's affairs will be known only to them and so they will have an important advisory role as the prospectus or listing particulars are being drafted. There are a number of other considerations to bear in mind.

3.3.2.1 Service contracts

Where a company is coming to the market for the first time, service contracts between the directors and the company will be put in place where none may have existed before. This is done largely to meet market expectations rather than for any compelling business reason, though the professional investment community see it as one way of securing continuity of management, regulating permitted external business interests and providing a clearer basis of remuneration and benefits than would otherwise be the case. The prospectus or listing particulars will have to make various disclosures about directors' remuneration (see, for example, LR para. 6.F.12), as will annual reports and accounts in the future (see LR para. 12.43A), so clarity in this area is important.

3.3.2.2 Non-executive directors

The effect of the Combined Code (see **2.2.3**) is that a company coming to the market for the first time will need to appoint a number of non-executive and independent directors to the board, if it does not already have them. In compliance with the Combined Code, it will also need to establish a series of committees staffed by non-executive directors to review the company's audit procedures, the remuneration of directors and the future nomination and appointment of non-executive directors. The non-executive directors are expected to bring a more objective eye to the company's decision-making process.

3.3.3 Selling shareholders

At the same time as the company issues new securities and applies to have them listed, existing shareholders may decide it is time to realise the whole or part of their shareholding interest in the company. Their securities can then be sold in conjunction with the issue of the new shares (see **3.5.3.1**). If this is to be the case, it needs to be built into the arrangements early on.

3.3.4 Sponsor

The UKLA requires an applicant for listing to appoint a sponsor for its application (LR para. 2.6). Where a company is seeking a listing it must also seek admission to trading from the LSE (LR para. 3.14A). The Stock Exchange Admission and Disclosure Standards ("SEADS") do not require a sponsor but do require companies to select a nominated representative (see SEADS Part 1 para. 2 and Part 2 para. 1.6). It is likely that the sponsor required by the Listing Rules will fulfil this role. The AIM requires the appointment of a 'nominated adviser' (see **4.3.5.1**) which performs the same role as a sponsor. The sponsor must be a person fulfilling the qualification requirements under LR para. 2.4 and approved by the UKLA, as required by s. 88(2) of FSMA. LR para. 2.1. requires sponsors to comply with all listing rules applicable to them. There are over 100 approved sponsors. Often it will be a firm of brokers which is also a member firm of the LSE. It is referred to variously as the issuer's 'sponsor', 'sponsoring member firm', 'brokers' and 'sponsoring brokers'. The sponsor has a number of responsibilities, encapsulated more generally by the undertaking to the UKLA which it has to give. A failure to fulfil such responsibilities may give rise to sanctions such as censure or a ban on future sponsoring (LR para. 2.27 and s. 89 of FSMA). These responsibilities are:

(a) To liaise with the UKLA regarding the listing application (LR para. 2.21(a)), to ensure that it has all the information it needs to consider the application, and to lodge with the UKLA all the documents relevant to the application (LR para. 2.21(b) and see **4.2.6.5**): the sponsor is the UKLA's first port of call if it has any questions or problems relating to the application.

(b) To submit to the UKLA, at an early stage, a declaration of interests in the form of LR sch. 1A, which serves to confirm the independence of the sponsor from the company.

(c) For a new applicant, to satisfy itself that the company has satisfied all relevant conditions and requirements for listing (LR para. 2.9(a)) and then, as required by LR para. 2.12, to complete a declaration in the form of LR sch. 4A, having particular reference to the requirement under LR para. 2.13 that the directors of the company have had explained to them by the sponsor or other appropriate professional adviser the nature of their responsibilities and obligations as directors of a listed company under the Listing Rules, and also saying that everything relevant to a decision regarding the company's suitability for listing has been disclosed to the UKLA (LR para. 2.12 (b)). This may be a responsibility jointly shared with the issuing house where one is appointed (see **3.3.5**).

(d) To ensure the company's directors understand the responsibilities expected of them once the company is listed, and to report this to the LSE (LR para. 2.13).

(e) Where consulted by issuer on the application or interpretation of The Listing Rules, to give proper guidance and advice, exercising due care and skill (LR para. 2.10).

(f) To introduce the company to the market maker(s) who will trade the company's securities on listing.

(g) To advise the company on the appropriate price at which to offer its securities: it will do this jointly with the issuing house where one is appointed (see below).

(h) To secure placees or sub-underwriters for the issue.

(i) In the case of a new applicant for listing or, in exceptional circumstances where the UKLA so requires, of a listed company, the sponsor must obtain written confirmation from the company that the directors have established procedures which provide a reasonable basis for them to make proper judgments as to the financial position and prospects of the company and its group. The sponsor must be satisfied that this confirmation has been given after due and careful inquiry by the company (LR para. 2.15). In all cases where a prospectus or listing particulars are produced, the sponsor must report to the LSE that any profit forecast made by the company has been prepared after due and careful inquiry by the company, and that the company's confirmation that it has sufficient working capital has also been given after due and careful inquiry and has been supported by any institutions providing the finance (LR para. 2.18).

(j) To report on the market's response to the proposed issue of securities for which the application is being made and, in particular, to stimulate market interest by preparing a report (sometimes known as a 'broker's circular') which is circulated to professional investors. This report will contain a detailed analysis of the company's history, performance, products, competitors and future potential. It is not a document required by the listing application, nor is it referred to in the prospectus or listing particulars. It does, however, contain a significant amount of information which will also appear in the prospectus or listing particulars, and it is released to the market prior to the launch of the offer through a controlled distribution process (essentially to the broker's clients, though often also to the media). Consequently, it is important to ensure that what is said in the circular is not significantly at variance with what is said in the prospectus or listing particulars. This is often difficult: the lawyers do not have a role in the production of the circular and often will not see it before it is distributed. As a result, it is important that the circular should contain a disclaimer of liability for the company and its directors.

In addition to the above, if the sponsor is the nominated representative of the company for the purpose of admission to the LSE, it will carry out additional functions. It may liaise with the LSE on regulatory matters, agree the timetable for admission to trading and otherwise deal with the documentation required by the LSE.

Where the company does not also appoint a merchant bank to act for it (see below), the sponsors will also fulfil its functions in addition to any of those mentioned above. LR para. 2.23 permits the sponsor to appoint an agent to discharge all or any of the services in LR para. 2.21.

For more on the sponsor's role in connection with listing, see **4.2.6.2(c)**.

3.3.5 Investment bank

The main business of an investment bank is to provide advice on raising finance and otherwise developing a business through, for example, acquiring other businesses. In a listing, where a company is raising finance through the issues of shares, an investment bank will frequently be involved.

However, not all issues of shares will involve an investment bank. Smaller offers will only need the sponsoring brokers. It is in relation to the bigger issues that the marketing and organisational expertise which a larger organisation like an investment bank can offer is necessary. In addition, the investment bank will often act as underwriter.

In the context of a listing 'issuing house' is the formal term used for the company's investment bank. This is simply because the investment bank is a securities house making an issue of shares on behalf of its corporate client.

Where an investment bank is appointed, a decision should be taken whether it will also be regarded as a sponsor to the issue in the same way as the sponsoring brokers. If so, LR para. 2.22, requires the company to indicate which sponsor has primary responsibility and how the responsibilities referred to in **3.3.4** are to be allocated between them. Hence the investment bank may be referred to, confusingly, as the company's 'sponsors', 'issuing house' or simply as its 'investment bank'. In fact in roughly half of all primary offers, the broker also plays the role of sponsor, while in another third of such offers, the investment bank assumes the role of sponsor alone, leaving the broker to its own functions. Roughly one tenth of these transactions involve the investment bank and broker acting as joint sponsor. The investment bank's responsibilities are as follows:

(a) to fulfil whatever duties under the Listing Rules it agrees with the sponsoring brokers;

(b) to organise the flotation and coordinate the activities of the other parties involved: the company essentially delegates the management of its equity offering to the investment bankers on the basis that they have the experience necessary to make it a success. In particular this means that the investment bankers will be the prime movers behind the preparation of the prospectus or listing particulars;

(c) to advise the company on the appropriate price at which to offer its securities: it will do this jointly with the sponsoring broker (see above);

(d) to act as underwriter and/or placing agent (that is, the agent of the company in arranging the placing): this will involve instructing the sponsoring brokers to secure sub-underwriters or placees and liaising with them on this. Acting as underwriter means that the investment bank will be shouldering the primary risk if the issue is a failure with investors.

3.3.6   Reporting accountants

An issuer must appoint accountants to produce financial information about it (LR ch. 12, and see **4.2.6.3**). Usually the company's existing auditors will play this role unless either they do not have the experience necessary for preparing such a report, or the company's financial affairs require a completely fresh reappraisal (for example, where it has just reorganised its business structure). Accountants appointed for this task will then generally work alongside the company's existing auditors. The responsibilities of whoever plays this role are:

(a) to prepare what is known as the 'accountants' long-form report': this is not required by the UKLA and will not be disclosed in the prospectus or listing particulars. It is a confidential report prepared for the directors, not potential investors, containing a detailed review of the financial information available to the management, including financial controls and reporting systems. It will comment on the adequacy of the company's accounting systems and may suggest improvements. As such it can contain material of a highly sensitive nature which it would not be prudent to reveal to the company's competitors. It will be a valuable source for much of the initial drafting of the listing particulars;

(b) to prepare the financial information for inclusion in the prospectus or listing particulars in accordance with LR ch. 12 (see **4.2.6.3**);

(c) where the company is a new applicant and is presenting its financial information in a comparative table as required by LR para. 12.1 and prepared in accordance with LR para. 12.17 (see section **4.2.6.3**), to file a report with the UKLA that the company's accounts have been audited in accordance with international accounting standards (see LR para. 12.14 (d));

(d) to include a report in the prospectus or listing particulars on the company's profit forecast (or on any profit estimates, which would cover a financial period which had expired but for which the results had not yet been published) in accordance with LR para. 12.24.

(e) to report to the company and its sponsors in the form of a comfort letter that the company has sufficient working capital to meet its needs;

(f) to check any other financial information presented in the prospectus or listing particulars for accuracy and consistency.

3.3.7 Solicitors

What you do as a lawyer in these issues depends to some extent on whether you are appointed to act for the company or the investment bank, although the functions of the two sets of solicitors will often overlap.

Solicitors to the company will be responsible for ensuring the company is ready for the issue, as described above (see **3.3.1**): this will often be the lion's share of their work. They will also spend time advising the company and directors (provided there is no conflict between them) on their liabilities in the issue.

Solicitors to the investment bank (also known as 'solicitors to the issue' or 'solicitors to the offer') will be responsible for preparing the first draft of the underwriting or placing agreement and supervising the sub-underwriting documentation (though this may in fact be produced by the brokers). Of course, this will all need to be negotiated with the company's solicitors. As with the company's solicitors, the investment bank's will need to consider their client's legal liabilities carefully throughout.

The solicitors to both parties spend a significant amount of their time in these issues advising on the drafting of the prospectus and usually take responsibility for preparing some parts of it.

The initial draft of the prospectus is generally prepared by the investment bank, often drawing on the accountant's long-form report for inspiration. Thereafter the prospectus will go through numerous drafts, with the bulk of the attention focused on the description of the company's business. The drafting process is by committee, with investment bankers, representatives of the company, solicitors to both sides and sometimes the accountants and sponsoring brokers present. The solicitors are often relied on for their views on the accuracy or suitability of certain words and phrases in the draft.

The solicitors to the company are very often left to produce the so-called 'back end' or 'boiler plate' of the prospectus or listing particulars, namely the detailed information on the company required by LR ch. 6 (see **4.2.6.3**): particularly, details on the company, its share capital, directors' interests, the terms of material contracts and relevant extracts or summaries from the company's articles of association. This information will be obtained through carrying out the legal due diligence exercise (see below).

In view of the range of potential liabilities which all parties may be exposed to in an issue (see **4.2.5.7**), an elaborate and painstaking ritual has developed to check thoroughly the accuracy of statements made in the prospectus or listing particulars and other documents arising from the issue—this is known as the 'verification exercise' and it is a critical part of the company's solicitor's task to make sure this is done to the highest standards. In carrying out this exercise, the solicitors involved will owe a duty of care to the company and its directors, though the exercise serves everybody's interests.

The purpose is simple enough: by checking the accuracy of every statement in the prospectus or listing particulars, to minimise the risks of any liability for false, misleading or negligent statements made in them or omissions from them. It is important to be clear, and make clear to all parties, that verification is not due diligence. Verification checks the accuracy of information contained in the particulars; due diligence is a more taxing examination of the company to establish whether it is suitable for admission to listing in the first place. Due diligence may very often precede verification; but it is important that the relatively limited scope of the verification exercise is understood.

How is this done? This varies, depending on the practice of the firm of solicitors running the exercise and the particular approach of the individual solicitor who is responsible for it. Broadly, though, the idea is to prepare a document which literally asks a question about every statement in the prospectus. The questions are put to the company's directors for them to answer: in practice, they delegate members of their management team to respond. The questions need to test not only the factual accuracy of statements, but also whether information has been omitted and whether any inferences drawn from statements are correct.

A satisfactory response to a verification question is one which does not simply parrot back the relevant sentence in the prospectus or listing particulars, but which gives detailed reasons for the statement and provides supporting documentation. Specified directors or members of the management team should take responsibility for each verification question. For some questions, for instance on future corporate strategy, the only answer possible will be that the statement in the prospectus or particulars represents the reasonable belief or best judgement of the board (and only the board can confirm this).

Ultimately the completed verification answers must be presented to the board for it to consider prior to approving the draft prospectus or particulars: the directors will need to be completely satisfied that the answers are correct before they can give approval. Since the verification notes are produced by the company's solicitors for the benefit of their client and its directors, they are not public documents, and so are not disclosed during the offer but should be retained by the solicitors at its conclusion.

The same process will be needed for the other public statements made in connection with the issue, particularly any advertisements or publicity material.

The degree of verification required for different issues varies. A company coming to the market for the first time would be expected to go through a rigorous verification exercise. A company making a rights issue and seeking to have the new shares admitted to listing need not be subjected to such an intense examination in view of the amount of information already available to the market: however, a company in financial difficulty attempting a rights issue would need to be vetted much more carefully than on a typical rights issue because of the enhanced risks of possible liabilities arising in the future.

3.3.8   Receiving bank

Where the issue involves an offer to the public as in an offer by subscription or for sale (though not a placing—see **3.5.6**), a receiving bank is generally appointed by the investment bank and the company. It has a number of tasks:

(a) to receive the application forms for securities from the general public: hence 'receiving bank', as most receiving banks are also high-street clearing banks;

(b) to process and clear cheques from applicants;

(c) to allocate securities to succesful applicants and send out share certificates.

The main point of having a receiving bank to do these apparently simple tasks is that, in large issues, the volume of paperwork to be handled in the form of applications, cheques, share certificates and the like is enormous, and the resources of the company and investment bank are simply inadequate.

3.3.9   Registrars

It is usual for a listed company to contract out the task of maintaining its register of members to a firm of professional registrars, which is often a different division of the same organisation which acted as receiving bank for the company. Their task is principally to record share transfers on the register, send out notices to members as required and process dividend payments on behalf of the company. They will usually be appointed to assume their duties when the offer closes and so will need to compile their first register to include all the new investors. Once again, in large offerings, this can be a major undertaking, one for which the company secretary's department is often simply not equipped.

3.3.10   Public relations advisers

Public relations advisers are generally appointed on large public offerings to advise the company on the protection of its image to the investing public to ensure the issue's success. They will supervise the company's advertising and marketing campaigns, and the lawyers will need to work closely with them to ensure that all publicity material is accurate and not misleading, and consistent with the information presented in the listing particulars (not always the easiest of tasks to perform, without killing off a good advertisement).

There may be other parties involved, depending on the nature of the company: property valuers, expert consultants and overseas lawyers are some examples of others who may be brought into play. From a practical point of view, it is vital to make sure that adequate and timely communication takes place between all these parties and that everyone understands what everyone else is doing. This seems trite: but management of the team is as much the key to success in these issues as any other factor.

3.4   Admission to listing and trading

Since 1 May 2000, responsibility for the admission of securities to official listing in the United Kingdom has been vested in the FSA as the UK Listing Authority (see FSMA s. 72). Previously, this was the responsibility of the LSE. However, the LSE retains responsibility for admission of securities to *trading* on the Exchange. There is now a distinction between being admitted to the Official List maintained by the FSA and being admitted to trading on the LSE (or any other recognised investment exchange, within the meaning of FSMA). The consequence is that where a company wishes to have securities admitted to listing and trading, either by way of an initial public offering or otherwise, it has to make two applications: one to the UKLA and the other to the LSE. These applications have to be coordinated such that admission to listing and trading take effect simultaneously, admission to trading being dependent on admission to the Official List.

3.5   Initial public offerings

Initial public offerings are issues of securities by companies coming to the market for the first time, that is, companies which do not already have securities listed on the Official List or which do not already have their securities dealt in on the AIM.

3.5.1   Methods of bringing shares to listing

For companies seeking to have their securities admitted to listing for the first time, LR para. 4.2, sets out the methods which can be used. These are:

(a) an offer for sale;

(b) an offer for subscription;

(c) a placing;

(d) an intermediaries offer;

(e) an introduction; or

(f) such other methods as may be accepted by the LSE either generally or in any particular case.

The structure of each of (a) to (e) above will be described below (see **3.5.4** to **3.5.8**). The most common methods used in 2003 for an initial public offering were placings and introductions. A combination of these methods may also be used.

In 2003, the total amount raised by companies (both UK and international) obtaining listings of their equity securities on the Main Market of the LSE for the first time was around £3.5 billion (source: Table 4 of The London Stock Exchange Primary Market Fact Sheet: 31 December 2003). Of the thirty-nine companies involved, eight companies (20 per cent) used a public offer, seven companies (18 per cent) used a placing, six companies (15 per cent) combined a placing and a public offer, and eighteen companies (47 per cent) used an introduction, as the method by which their shares were admitted to listing. The increasing significance of AIM is shown by the fact that in 2003 over four times as many new companies obtained listings on AIM as obtained listings on the Main Market (source: Table 4 of The London Stock Exchange Primary Market Fact Sheet: 31 December 2003). The value of the money raised was almost £1.1 billion. Of the 162 companies involved, only one company (1 per cent) used a public offer, sixty-nine companies (43 per cent) used a placing, seventeen companies (10 per cent) combined a placing and a public offer; and 75 companies (46 per cent) used an introduction, as the method by which their shares were admitted to listing.

Prior to 1 January 1996, companies seeking to have their securities admitted to listing for the first time could use placing only in small-scale offers. These restrictions have now been entirely removed. Companies can use whatever method of marketing they prefer, whether it be an offer for sale, a placing or intermediaries offer. The only general requirement which still applies is that the securities must be sufficiently widely held such that their marketability when listed can be assumed (see **3.5.2**). There has been criticism that this will work against the interests of wider share ownership, in that companies will prefer to use placings rather than offers for sale (and placings inevitably concentrate shares in the hands of fewer investors).

3.5.2   Marketability of shares when listed

Whatever method is chosen for an initial listing, the securities must be sufficiently widely held that their marketability when listed can be assumed. Prior to the UKLA considering an application, the sponsor must submit a statement summarising shareholdings in the company for which listing is sought. The statement, in the form set out in LR sch. 2, must include details of the percentage of shares in public hands. One of the conditions for the listing of shares is that 25 per cent of the shares to be listed must be in the hands of the public no later than the time of admission to listing (LR paras 3.18 and 3.19). There are circumstances in which a percentage lower than 25 per cent will be allowed (LR para. 3.19). Circumstances in which shares *will not* be regarded as being in public hands are set out in LR para. 3.20.

3.5.3 Principal or agent

Whether it is a placing or an offer for sale or subscription which is being used, the company will appoint an investment bank (in larger offerings) or a broker (in smaller offerings: see **3.3.4** and **3.3.5** for a description of their respective roles) to arrange and effect the offer of securities. In this section, they are both referred to as 'the sponsor' for convenience. The legal relationship of the sponsor in the offer is central to the way it is structured.

The sponsor is an intermediary between the company and the investors. The immediate assumption is therefore likely to be that the sponsor will, on a legal analysis, always act as the company's agent in organising the offer. But consider the effect of the underwriting or 'best efforts' placing described in **3.2.3**: the sponsor agrees to take on to its own shoulders all the primary risk of the issue failing. Of course, as we have seen, it takes steps to cushion itself from that risk by sub-underwriting in the case of the offer for sale or subscription— but the ultimate risk is still the underwriter's in the event that one of the sub-underwriters is unable to honour its commitment.

An alternative approach to the sponsor acting as agent in this role as intermediary would be for the sponsor to acquire all the shares from the issuer in the first place, and then sell them on to the investing public as principal. The sponsor can still arrange a sub-underwriting to protect itself if the offer to the public does not succeed. All the sponsor has done is to convert its conditional primary risk when an agent to an unconditional primary risk when it acquires the securities outright—but it has not changed its fundamental risk at all. Nor does the sponsor thereby change its costs or benefits: the sponsor will still charge the same commission even if it acts as principal.

3.5.3.1 What is the legal effect of the sponsor acting as principal rather than agent?

(a) If there is a false or misleading statement in the listing particulars, the sponsor is at no greater risk of liability under the principles derived from *Hedley Byrne & Co. Ltd* v. *Heller and Partners Ltd* [1964] AC 465 or *Caparo Industries plc* v. *Dickman* [1990] 2 AC 605 (see **4.2.5.7**) than if acting as an agent. Under s. 150 FS Act, the sponsor's risk of liability is likely to be greater if it acts as principal (see **4.2.5.7**) because it will issue the listing particulars in its own name.

(b) Of course the investor acquires its shares from the sponsor and its contract is with the sponsor, hence it is the sponsor and not the company whom the investor will sue under s. 2(1) Misrepresentation Act 1967 and for breach of contract. The sponsor is therefore in theory marginally more exposed as principal than agent.

(c) Where some or all of the company's existing shareholders are to sell their securities as part of the offer (the rest of it being made up of the company's issue of entirely new securities) and they appoint the sponsor to act as their agent in doing this, there is the theoretical risk that different investors could end up with different roots of title to their securities, depending on whether they acquired them from the company or its shareholders. This could be important where there is a question over the legitimacy of a selling shareholder's entitlement to the securities being disposed of. This risk will only arise if the sponsor acts as agent; if the sponsor is a principal, all investors buy from the same seller and so a common root of title prevails.

(d) The other potential difficulty for the investor where the sponsor is the selling shareholders' agent is that the agency may terminate if the shareholder goes bankrupt, dies or becomes insane in the interim—all of which are such unlikely eventualities, and can in any event usually be accommodated through devices such as taking powers of attorney from the selling shareholders, that the risk is generally regarded as sufficiently remote not to affect the decision whether to act as principal or agent.

The trend of the argument is broadly that, where there are selling shareholders, there is a good case (in the interests of general convenience) for the sponsor to act as principal provided it is happy to carry the additional legal risk this brings.

3.5.3.2   What is the tax effect of the sponsor acting as principal rather than agent?

The principal tax issues to consider are stamp duty ('SD') and stamp duty reserve tax ('SDRT'). To understand these in this context, it is worth recapping on the nature of the two taxes.

(a) SD is chargeable on documents conveying or transferring property (including shares) on sale, not on transactions.

(b) SDRT is imposed on transactions, not on documents. Those transactions are where A agrees to transfer to B chargeable securities for consideration in money or money's worth. Chargeable securities for our purposes include shares and loan capital.

Both SD and SDRT attract a $\frac{1}{2}$ per cent charge on the value of the shares being transferred.

Applying these to an offer for sale and offer by subscription, we see the following results:

(a) Where the investment bank acts as agent, no SD or SDRT is payable. The shares are never transferred to the investment bank as agent—they are simply issued direct into the hands of the investors.

(b) Where the investment bank acts as principal, neither SD nor SDRT is payable on the issue of shares to the investment bank (this is an issue and not a transfer), but when the investment bank sells the shares on to the investors, then the sale attracts both SD and SDRT. The SDRT charge is treated as 'franked' by the SD, and so only the SD is payable.

There is an exemption available under s. 89A Finance Act 1986 which allows the investment bank acting as principal to be treated in exactly the same way as if it were acting as agent, provided the securities are to be listed on the LSE and the investment bank is making an offer to the public. (The exemption is therefore effectively not available for an AIM offering or a private placement.)

(c) Where selling shareholders are involved, the tax analysis is more complex as there will be SD and SDRT on the transfer of the existing shares from selling shareholder to investment bank. The SDRT charge can be relieved through the 'franking' exemption.

These tax issues apply equally in the context of secondary offerings (see **3.6**).

The conclusion from this tax analysis is that, provided the 'public offer' exemption is available, there is no difference in tax treatment between the investment bank acting as principal and agent.

Assuming the decision of principal or agent can then be resolved, how do the offering structures actually work? You will find the following descriptions are simplified accounts of typical transactions. In real life, they may look quite different from this—but these, if you like, are the 'role models'.

Whether the company is coming to the LSE or the AIM, these offering structures will be equally relevant, as they are determined by market considerations and not regulation.

3.5.4 Public offers for sale or subscription (LR para. 4.2(a) and (b))

In an offer for sale, the public is invited to purchase securities which have already been issued or allotted by the company (LR para. 4.4).

An offer for subscription is one in which the public is invited to subscribe for new securities of the company (LR para. 4.5).

These methods are often combined: selling shareholders use the prospect of listing as an opportunity to realise their investment by offering their shares to the public whilst the company seeks to increase its share capital by offering the public new shares.

Figure 3.1 assumes an investment bank has been appointed as well as a broker. The following description is based on **figure 3.1**:

(1) The company (and in this case the selling shareholders as well) appoint the investment bank to arrange the offer and act as underwriter to it. This appointment and the investment bank's responsibilities will be recorded in an underwriting or offer for sale agreement. It is usually known as an underwriting agreement where the investment bank is acting as agent and as an offer for sale agreement where the bank is a principal, but terminology can vary so it is important to analyse the text of the agreement to determine the precise role of the investment bank. Sometimes the appointment is also reflected in an engagement letter or a letter of appointment, though this is not always the case.

Any underwriting agreement is likely to be negotiated fiercely by the parties to it. The 'typical agreement' set out here will therefore vary with the respective bargaining power of the parties. For instance, in privatisations, HM Government (the selling shareholder of the relevant state enterprises) has forced underwriting commissions down to well below the 'market norm' because of the size of such offerings and its own negotiating strength.

To recap, the main terms in the underwriting agreement deal with the following matters:

(a) The investment bank agrees with the company and the selling shareholders to underwrite the issue and sale of securities.

(b) The agreement is conditional on the securities being admitted to listing or the AIM, on approval, registration and distribution of the prospectus listing particulars (see **4.2.5.4**) and on passing of any necessary shareholders' resolutions.

(c) The company (and sometimes the directors) warrant to the investment bank that:
(i)   the prospectus or listing particulars (including the profit forecast) are true and accurate in all material respects,
(ii) the company's latest accounts present a true and fair view of its financial position,
(iii) the company has the constitutional power and authority to enter into and effect the issue, and
(iv) the company has taken on no onerous liabilities or been threatened with any material litigation otherwise than as reported in the prospectus,

and indemnifies the investment bank against any loss resulting from breaches of these warranties.

(d) The investment bank may terminate the agreement (usually, at any time up to admission) if:
(i) the company materially breaches any provision in the agreement, including the warranties; or

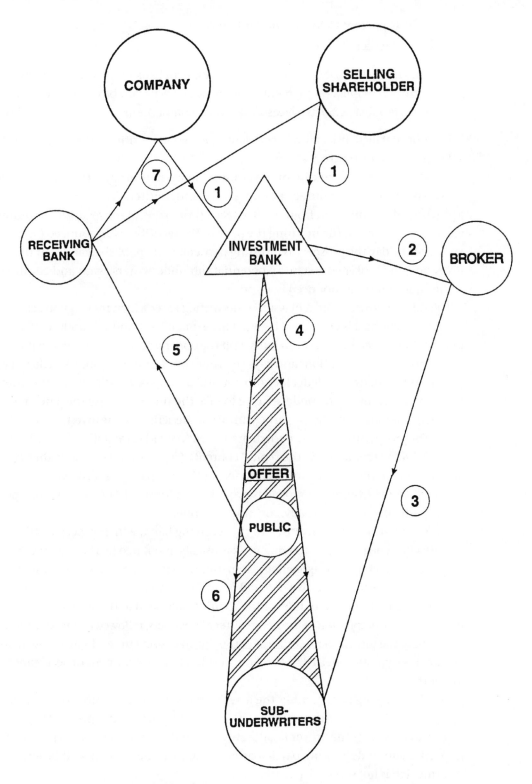

Figure 3.1   Offer for sale or subscription.

        (ii) there are changes in the UK or international financial, economic or political conditions which may have a material adverse impact on the success of the offer (the *force majeure* provision, often hotly contested).

    (e) Commissions payable to the investment bank and other parties are set out: these are usually percentages based on the market value of the underwritten securities, paid out in the following proportions:

        $\frac{1}{2}$ per cent to the investment bank in its capacity as underwriter,

$1\frac{1}{4}$ per cent to the sub-underwriters,

$\frac{1}{4}$ per cent to the brokers,

amounting to 2 per cent in total. The investment bank may receive an advisory fee on top of its commission payment. Commissions will usually be payable even if the agreement terminates *unless* by reason of *force majeure* or the investment bank's own default.

For more detailed discussion of the clauses of an underwriting agreement see **3.2.2**. Returning to the **figure 3.1**:

(2) The investment bank appoints the broker its agent to arrange the sub-underwriting.

(3) The broker will contact potential sub-underwriters by telephone and extract a provisional commitment from them to take a proportion of the securities if the investors are not interested. On the morning the price of the securities is announced ('impact day') (and also the day the prospectus or listing particulars are published and sent to potential investors), the broker contacts the potential sub-underwriters again and confirms their commitment at the announced issue price.

The sub-underwriters are sent a sub-underwriting letter which they sign in acknowledgement and a contract is concluded between investment bank and sub-underwriter. The sub-underwriting letter must be on all fours with the underwriting agreement—that is, must be subject to the same conditions and have the same commissions payable. You do not want to find the sub-underwriting letter failing because of unfulfilled conditions but the investment bank still liable under the underwriting to take the shares because the agreement is not caught by the same condition—particularly if you are acting for the investment bank!

(4) The prospectus or listing particulars are sent or made available to potential investors (see **4.2.6.4** for a summary of the typical content of a prospectus). Legally, they constitute an invitation to those investors to subscribe for the company's securities at the advertised price. Interested investors complete the application form contained in the prospectus or listing particulars (which, legally, constitutes an offer).

(5) The offer is sent by investors to the receiving bank, which processes all the forms and attached cheques. The receiving bank is usually appointed by the investment bank in a separate receiving bank agreement. Sometimes applications have to be scaled down or eliminated because of excessive demand for available securities. Successful applicants are sent an interim document of title for the securities allocated to them which they can trade in the market. Compilation of the new register of members, followed by preparation and distribution of the formal share certificates, usually takes some time—hence these temporary documents (typically referred to as renounceable letters of allotment or acceptance—RLAs for short).

(6) The receiving bank notifies the investment bank of the number of securities taken up by the public. If there are securities left outstanding in the offer (the 'stick'), the investment bank instructs the broker to allocate these to the sub-underwriters pro rata to their respective sub-underwriting participations. The investment bank will be left with any securities it has not sub-underwritten.

(7) The proceeds from the issue (less commission and fees) pass up to the company and selling shareholders: the offer has completed its course, and the company's securities are now publicly traded.

3.5.5 Tender offers

The foregoing description assumes an offer of securities at a fixed price. An issuer may choose to offer its securities to the highest bidders on an auction basis. The same structure as above applies, but investors are invited to bid for shares at or above a 'minimum tender price', and the underwriting and sub-underwriting take place at this price. Securities are allocated to those with the highest tenders at the price at which they bid, and so on down, until the point at which all the securities have been taken up. The purpose behind this is to realise maximum value from the offering. Sometimes a common striking price is selected (the highest price common to all bids at which the entire issue will succeed), and this is the price which everyone ends up paying for their securities. The important point to note is that in all other respects, this method replicates the offer for sale or subscription route. It is also possible to have a partial tender whereby a proportion of the shares to be sub-underwritten are put out to competitive tender. Basically, sub-underwriters are allocated a sub-underwriting participation at the usual commission level. Part of this allocation is firm in the usual way; however, the balance is subject to clawback under the tender process. Sub-underwriters are then invited to tender for the available shares at or below the usual commission level. The tender forms set out bands of commission levels (ranging, say, from $\frac{1}{8}$ per cent to $1\frac{1}{2}$ per cent) and, when submitting their tender forms, sub-underwriters have to specify the number of shares (if any) that they wish to bid for against each band. The tender process does not have to be limited to existing sub-underwriters. The opportunity to tender could be opened up to all institutions and not just sub-underwriters who had taken an initial allocation.

3.5.6   Placings (LR para. 4.2(c))

LR para. 4.7 describes a placing as 'a marketing of securities . . . to specified persons or clients of the sponsor . . . which does not involve an offer to the public'. In legal terms, it may in fact be an offer to the public (see LR paras 3.19 and 3.20). In concept though, it is not an offer by general invitation but to selected persons, usually institutional investors.

The investment bank is faced with the decision in a placing whether to act as agent or principal, in exactly the same way as for the offers considered above. The same legal and practical considerations apply. There is no difference in terminology here, however, between placings for sale or subscription.

A company coming to the market for the first time is typically faced with the choice of launching itself through an offer for sale or subscription, or a placing. To understand how it makes this decision, let us look first at how a placing works. **Figure 3.2** assumes an investment bank has been appointed alongside a broker.

(1) The company (and in this case the selling shareholders as well) will appoint the investment bank to arrange the placing. Invariably, where these placings are in connection with an application for a full listing or admission to the AIM, the investment bank will be acting on a 'best efforts' basis and so will be underwriting the offer of securities. As with the offer for sale or subscription, the investment bank's responsibilities may be recorded in an engagement letter, and will always be set out formally in a placing agreement.

The terms of the placing agreement will closely resemble what you will find in an underwriting agreement (see **3.5.4.1**). Obviously any descriptions of the mechanics of the offer will vary to reflect the placing's differences. The parties to the agreement will be the same: the company and the investment bank, with the selling shareholders and the directors parties to some (or perhaps all) of the warranties.

The major difference between the underwriting and placing agreements is in the commission payable:

$\frac{1}{2}$ per cent to the investment bank,

$\frac{1}{2}$ per cent to the placees (as compared with $1\frac{1}{4}$ per cent to the sub-underwriters),

$\frac{1}{4}$ per cent to the broker.

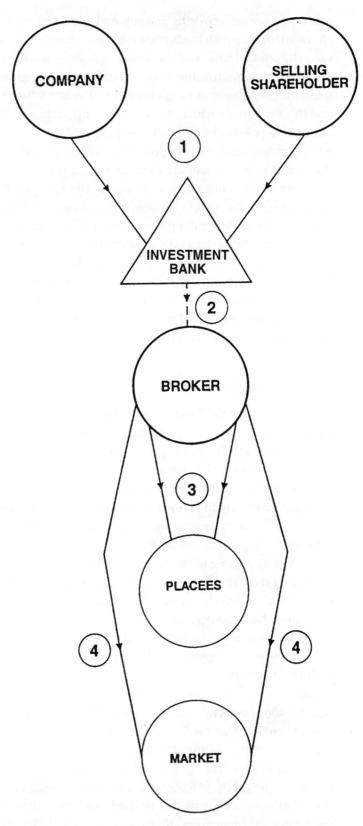

Figure 3.2 Placing.

The higher commission paid in an offer for sale or subscription is because of the open-ended nature of the risk which sub-underwriters take on. Placees are able to decide definitively in advance how many securities they are prepared to take.

(2) The investment bank appoints the broker its agent to arrange the placing.

(3) Usually the broker will have solicited informal indications of interest in the company's securities from potential placees before the placing is launched. When the placing is announced, the broker will renew contact with the potential placees over the telephone, announce the price at which the securities are to be issued and then confirm the placees' interest. The broker will follow up this conversation with a placing letter, which will be accompanied by a placing memorandum (though the placees will have already seen a draft version of this).

A placing letter resembles a sub-underwriting letter. The placee agrees to subscribe for or buy the securities at the issue price, on conditions that are identical to those contained in the placing agreement (for example, that the securities are admitted to listing). Legally, the placing letter constitutes the offer of securities to the individual placee.

A placing memorandum is the term, in the context of a placing, for the offer document, which will also invariably be the listing particulars or prospectus. As with the offer for sale or subscription, this will be an invitation to treat.

The placee signs the letter of confirmation attached to the placing letter, indicating acceptance of the offer, and returns it with payment to the broker. Occasionally, the proper contractual analysis is that the contract with the placees has been concluded in the telephone conversation between broker and placee, with the exchange of letters merely confirming an existing agreement.

The securities are then allotted in the name of the placee, and documents of title are sent to him in exactly the same way as described in **3.5.4** for offers for sale or subscription.

(4) If potential placees contacted by the broker over the telephone are not willing to take up securities in which they originally expressed interest, the broker's task is to identify other investors in the market who would be prepared to take up shares as part of the placing syndicate. If this fails, the investment bank is of course the ultimate back-stop.

What, then, are the principal distinguishing features of a placing and what are its merits?

(a) A placing is clearly more appropriate where the company wishes not to throw itself into the arms of the public at large, but rather to persuade the professional investing community to take a more serious interest in the company. There are all kinds of circumstances where this may make commercial sense.

An example is where the company's business is relatively high-risk (for instance, businesses with high environmental exposure, such as waste management operations, will be perceived as risky). The general public is unlikely to be attracted to such investments.

Where the conditions for launching new issues are volatile or poor, it will be much harder to secure the success of an offer for sale or subscription than a placing.

A placing is cheaper, and this may be compelling particularly where the total value of the offering is relatively low and the company therefore wishes to keep the costs of the issue down.

(b) Since the number of investors taking up securities will be significantly less than for an equivalent offer to the general public, there is no need for a receiving bank. The broker is able to handle the applications for securities from the placees.

(c) The marketing of the securities is essentially performed by the broker over the telephone with its contacts. There is no need for a campaign to raise investor awareness of the issue.

(d) The commissions payable to placees are less than those the sub-underwriters in an offer for sale or subscription would normally expect to be paid (see **3.5.4**).

This amounts to a cheaper offering. The placing is therefore most attractive to companies anxious to bear down on the costs of the offering.

Before we leave the placing, it is worth re-emphasising that many primary offerings are a mix of offer for sale or subscription and placing. In other words, a portion of the securities to be offered are kept aside for the institutions to acquire through a placing, and the rest are sold to the general public through an offer for sale or subscription. Technically, the public offer and placing structure and mechanics will simply work alongside but apart from each other (though both offers will use exactly the same prospectus or listing particulars). Sometimes arrangements are made which allow for securities allocated to the placing to be 'clawed back' in favour of the public offer if demand there is higher than anticipated.

3.5.7 Intermediaries offer (LR para. 4.2(d))

The intermediaries offer is available as an alternative to an offer for sale or subscription or a placing. The way the offer works is that securities are allocated to intermediaries, who then sell them on to their own clients (at a commission) (see LR para. 4.10). Intermediaries for this purpose are LSE member firms and other securities houses selected by the sponsoring broker. The idea is that this achieves a wider spread of investors than would be the case with a placing: you can imagine that the offer structure looks something like **figure 3.3**, with the securities passing down the pyramid.

In terms of mechanics, the intermediaries offer otherwise works very much like a placing (see **3.5.6** and **figure 3.2**), with the sponsoring broker initially making informal contact with the potential intermediaries (who are here the equivalent of the placees) and then making the allocations to them when the offer is announced. The UKLA may require a list of the names of the intermediaries to whom shares were allocated and the names and addresses of the clients to whom each intermediary passed shares (LR para. 4.11).

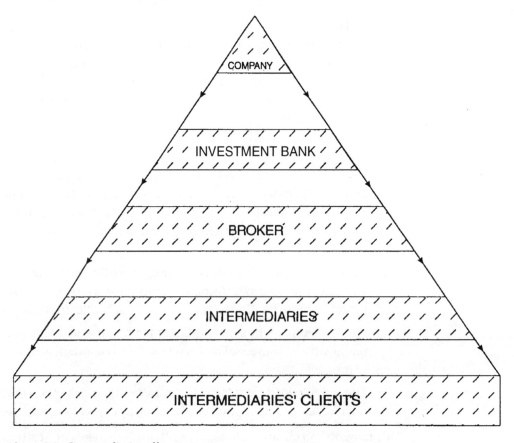

Figure 3.3 Intermediaries offer.

Depending on the scale of the transaction, there may or may not be an investment bank coordinating the transaction and acting as co-sponsor with the brokers. The issuer and the sponsor will enter into an offering agreement which sets out the sponsor's responsibilities and contains some of the standard warranties from the company we have seen in the context of underwriting agreements (see **3.5.4.1**). There have been comparatively few of these offers so far.

3.5.8 Introduction (LR para. 4.2(e))

A company may also obtain a listing on the Official List (and also technically on the AIM, though this would be very uncommon) by means of an introduction. To call this an issue of securities is something of a misnomer, as no issue of securities is actually involved. An introduction is an acknowledgement, as the Listing Rules say at para. 4.12, that 'the securities are already widely held by the public'—it is simply that they have not been formally listed.

When will this be the case? There are two likely situations. The first is where the company has an overseas listing so that its securities are already being traded internationally, and the second is where the company's securities are being dealt in on the AIM and the company wishes to transfer to a full listing.

The process of seeking an introduction involves an application for admission to listing of the company's securities (as with any other offer), save that this application relates only to securities already in existence. The application will of course require the production of a prospectus or listing particulars.

The company, as with other offers, needs to appoint a sponsor, which will handle the mechanics of the introduction, and the sponsor will need to identify potential market makers who will be prepared to buy and sell the company's securities on the LSE.

No actual offer or issue of new securities takes place: on admission of the securities to listing, it becomes possible to trade the securities on the LSE in exactly the same manner in which they were traded up to that time on the AIM or the overseas stock exchange. In a sense, a new market has been opened up to existing investors in the company.

3.6 Secondary issues

We mean by this expression issues of securities by companies already listed or whose securities are already being dealt in on the AIM. Further issues of securities take place to raise extra working capital, fund acquisitions, finance growth, and so on. Once again, there are some commonly accepted offering structures for these kinds of issues, which will be used on whichever market the issue takes place. The full range is set out in LR para. 4.1. This section will look at the most common of them. Before we do, there are two preliminary points to observe.

3.6.1 Pre-emption rights

You will be familiar with s. 89 Companies Act 1985, which requires offers of new securities to be made on a pre-emptive basis to the company's existing shareholders in proportion to their existing holdings. You will also have encountered the additional layer of regulation which listed companies face when contemplating further issues of securities (see **3.3.1.4**).

It is worth noting that the UKLA supports s. 89 by making it a basic condition of listing that issues for cash of securities having an equity element must, unless shareholders otherwise permit, be offered in the first place to the existing equity shareholders in proportion to their holdings (LR para. 9.18). The same condition applies to AIM companies.

The presumption, then, is that a company seeking to raise further capital through an issue of securities will do so through an offer to its existing shareholders.

One of the consequences of this presumption is that companies frequently use their annual general meetings each year to obtain and then renew disapplications of s. 89 under s. 95 (within the restrictions laid down by the Investment Committees). This then confers on them the flexibility to launch a non-pre-emptive issue in the ensuing year and still operate within the UKLA's basic conditions.

3.6.2 Prospectus requirements

Section 84 of FSMA requires as a condition for admission the publication of a prospectus where securities are offered to the public in the UK for the first time before admission. This applies where there is a subsequent issue of shares, even though that class of shares is already listed.

There are a series of exemptions in Sch. 11 to FSMA which will take the offering outside the requirement for a prospectus. These include:

(a) Where shares are offered to no more than 50 persons (FSMA Sch. 11, para. 4).

(b) Where securities are offered to persons whose ordinary business activities involve them in buying, selling and managing investments (FSMA Sch. 11, para. 3).

(c) Where securities are offered to a restricted circle of persons who are sufficiently knowledgeable to understand the risks involved in accepting the offer (FSMA Sch. 11, para. 6).

(d) Where the issue is raising less than 40,000 euros in total (FSMA Sch. 11, para. 9).

There is no specific exception for offers to existing members of the company. Therefore a rights issue by a company already listed will normally give rise to the need for a prospectus, rather than listing particulars.

The Listing Rules apply to a prospectus in exactly the same way as they apply to listing particulars, but as if references to listing particulars were a reference to a prospectus. Accordingly, the contents requirements for the document will stay exactly the same, and will depend on the type of transaction (see **4.2.6.3** for the contents requirements).

The Listing Rules contain a list of exemptions from the requirement to issue full listing particulars (see LR paras 5.23A and 5.27). These are referred to in **4.2.5.5**. These exemptions do not apply to prospectuses, only to listing particulars. The key test is to ask whether or not there is an offer of shares to the public within the meaning of s. 84(2), as defined in Sch. 11 to FSMA. If there is, then the prospectus requirements apply. If not, because one of the exemptions applies, then the provisions relating to listing particulars under The Listing Rules automatically bite. Listing particulars will therefore need to be published in accordance with the Listing Rules. Accordingly, it may be possible, in these circumstances, to take advantage of the exemptions set out in **4.2.5.5** from the requirements to issue full listing particulars.

3.6.3 Placing

The placing is widely used in both initial public offerings and secondary issues. As we saw in **3.5.6**, the placing is relatively cheap and straightforward as an offering structure.

The structure and mechanics of a placing by way of a subsequent offering mirror those for an initial public offering. In addition, if the securities being placed are of a class already listed, the company will have to observe LR paras 4.8 and 4.9, which regulate the price at which the securities can be placed.

3.6.4   Rights issue

3.6.4.1   Introduction

As **3.6.1** above will have made plain, the rights issue is the offering structure for new issues of securities preferred by the UKLA and the Investment Committees (see LR para. 9.18).

The rights issue is an offer of **new** securities to **existing** shareholders **in proportion** to their existing holdings. The new securities may be different in nature to those already held by shareholders. It is possible, for instance, to offer ordinary shareholders new redeemable preference shares by way of a rights issue.

To encourage shareholders to take up the new securities being offered, they are offered at a discount to the market price of the existing securities (assuming they are of the same class and type). Unless the securities are cheaper than those currently available in the market, what point is there in shareholders subscribing to the offer? Discount to nominal value is obviously not acceptable (see s. 100 CA).

What shareholders are offered is the *right* to take up new securities (hence 'rights issue'). If they choose not to take up the new securities themselves, they are entitled to sell on that right to interested buyers. The listing regulations relating to rights issues are contained in LR paras 4.16 to 4.21.

3.6.4.2   Procedure

The description below refers to **figure 3.4**.

(1) There is no question with a rights issue of shareholders selling their stake in the company: the issue is by the company alone of new securities.

The issue of whether the investment bank is to act as principal or agent is also irrelevant. The offer is by the company to its own existing shareholders, so the investment bank can only act as the company's agent in arranging and facilitating the offer.

The investment bank's duties will be defined in the same way as for an offer for sale or subscription: there may be a letter of engagement and there will usually be an underwriting agreement with broadly the same terms and conditions as in the offer for sale agreement (see **3.5.4.1**). The only difference will be in the description of the mechanics of the offer. The commissions will be as for offers for sale or subscription.

Deep discount rights issue: the circumstance where there would be no underwriting agreement is where the company decides to offer the new securities at such a discount to the market value of the existing securities that there is perceived to be no danger of the issue failing (known as a 'deep discount' issue). This would only happen where the company either is desperate to save the expense which the underwriting commissions otherwise incur or where it needs the money very quickly and cannot afford to wait for the investment bank to arrange an underwriting.

Underwritten rights issue: assuming this is not a deep discount issue, the investment bank will agree, exactly as for an offer for sale or subscription, to underwrite the entire issue if it fails.

(2) The investment bank appoints the broker as its agent to arrange the sub-underwriting.

(3) The broker arranges the sub-underwriting exactly as for an offer for sale or subscription (see **3.5.4**).

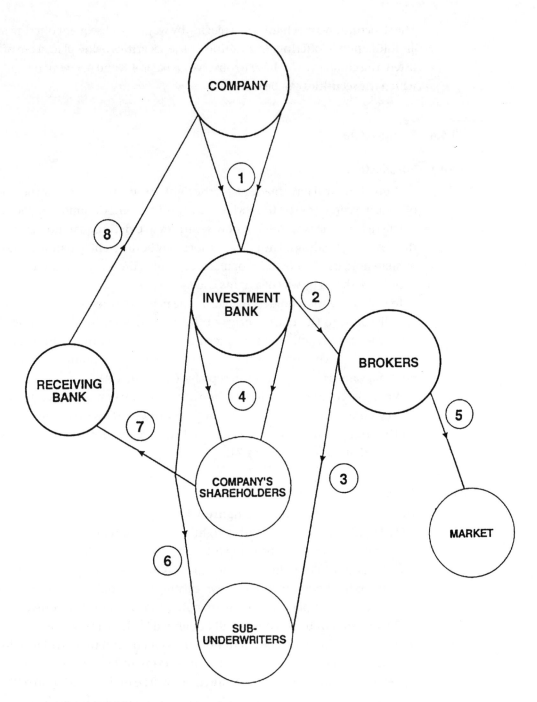

Figure 3.4   Rights issue.

(4) The shareholders are sent a circular, usually consisting of a letter from the company's chairman explaining the reasons for the rights issue, and the additional information to be included in the prospectus (see **3.6.2**). The circular sets out the terms and conditions which form the basis of the offer made to the shareholders.

With the circular is a document known as a provisional allotment letter, or 'PAL' for short. This offers the shareholders the right to subscribe for the new securities which have been provisionally allotted to them already. The shareholders must have a minimum of 21 days within which to accept the offer (s. 90(6) CA).

If shareholders choose to pay the subscription price, the securities are theirs upon notification of acceptance and payment to the receiving bank. The PAL will be their temporary document of title until a definitive share certificate can be dispatched.

A shareholder who chooses not to pay the subscription price can either do nothing, in which case the PAL is said to 'lapse' (see stage (5) below), or sell the PAL (and hence the right to subscribe for the new shares).

(5) When the 21-day offer period closes, the broker is responsible for attempting to sell the 'lapsed' securities (collectively known as the 'rump') into the market to any interested buyers (usually other professional investors). If the broker can agree a price at a premium to the subscription price, the premium belongs to the 'lapsed' or 'lazy' shareholders, and the rest is obviously the company's.

(6) If the broker cannot sell any of the lapsed shares, the so-called 'stick' (i.e., what is left of the unsubscribed PALs) is taken up by the sub-underwriters in the normal way.

(7) The receiving bank is appointed as most listed or AIM companies have large numbers of shareholders and so only an organisation of the bank's capacity and experience is likely to be able to manage the volume of PALs, cheques and share certificates effectively.

(8) Commissions and fees are deducted before the cash passes up to the company.

3.6.4.3 Effects of disapplication of pre-emption rights on the rights issue timetable

We have discussed the pre-emption requirements of s. 89 CA in **3.6.1** and the additional restrictions for listed companies in **3.3.1.4**. A company need not always offer new securities on a pre-emptive basis so long as it has disapplied s. 89 and complies with Investment Committee Guidelines when making the offer. In addition, there are significant benefits in offering shares by way of rights when s. 89 has been disapplied.

Disapplication of s. 89 CA

Often, as mentioned in **3.6.1**, a company may use its annual general meeting to disapply the s. 89 pre-emption rights by a special resolution in accordance with s. 95 CA. Where s. 89 has been disapplied, the offer of the new shares by way of rights need only remain open for a minimum period of 21 days from the date of posting of the circular and provisional allotment letters to (and including) the final date for acceptance and payment, i.e. the rights issue timetable will run for 22 days (including day of dispatch—'impact day'). Note the underwriting period also begins on impact day.

Section 89 not disapplied

An offer which complies with the pre-emption rights in s. 89 must remain open for acceptance for a minimum of 21 days (excluding the day on which the provisional allotment letters are deemed to have been received in the normal course of post and the final day for acceptance and payment). For normal UK first class post the provisional allotment letters will be deemed to have been received the next business day after dispatch: i.e. the rights issue timetable runs for 24 days (including impact day).

EGM required to disapply s. 89

If a general disapplication of s. 89 (e.g. passed at the AGM) is not in place and the company is not able to comply with the statutory pre-emption requirements, it will be necessary to call an EGM to pass a special resolution in order to disapply s. 89 (together often with a s. 121 ordinary resolution to increase share capital and a s. 80 ordinary resolution to allot the shares). This will significantly extend the timetable for the rights issue, since shareholders must be given 21 days' notice of an EGM proposing to pass a special resolution. Therefore the rights issue circular and the EGM notice would be posted on impact day, the EGM would be held approximately 23 days later after which the PALs would be posted and the 21-day offer period would run and the offer would close 45 days after impact day. This would be a very long (and expensive) underwriting period! However, even if the company does intend to comply with s. 89 rights, it may still need to call an EGM to pass a s. 121 ordinary resolution to increase share capital and a s. 80 ordinary resolution authority to allot shares if it lacks sufficient share capital to effect the rights issue. In this case, the timetable will still be extended but to a lesser extent as shareholders need only 14 days' notice of an EGM proposed to pass ordinary resolutions. Disapplying s. 89 rights carries particular advantages in relation to two specific areas: fractional entitlements and overseas shareholders.

(a) *Fractional entitlements*

Where s.89 has been disapplied, fractional entitlements of qualifying shareholders will typically be aggregated and sold in the market for the benefit of the company. If s.89 has not been disapplied, such entitlements will be rounded down to the nearest whole number of new shares and the fractions of new shares shall be disregarded.

(b) *Overseas shareholders—Gazette route*

If s. 89 has been disapplied, the company will have the flexibility of not having to offer the rights to certain overseas shareholders. This may be preferable in certain cases to avoid breach of the local securities laws (usually US and Canada) and instead those holders will receive the money's worth of such rights by the company aggregating their entitlements and selling them in the market, nil paid, and then remitting the net proceeds to them.

If s. 89 has not been disapplied, the statutory pre-emption procedure requires that the offer is made to these overseas shareholders. However, to send a circular and PAL into certain jurisdictions may breach their securities laws. Therefore, the way around this is to publish a notice in the London Gazette (the 'Gazette notice') in accordance with s. 90(5) making the offer to overseas shareholders (or stating where the PALs can be obtained). The Gazette notice will be published the day after the PALs are posted and s. 90(6) requires the offer to remain open for not less than 21 days, which would take the rights issue timetable to 23 days. So the fact that there are overseas shareholders does not extend the rights issue timetable beyond that of a standard pre-emptive offer.

3.6.4.4   Trading in PALs

There is one particular problem to watch out for. As the PALs are effectively tradeable documents of title, it is important that they can only be traded when all the conditions to the offer have been satisfied—otherwise there is the danger of the offer terminating and all the sales of all the PALs having to be reversed (which may in practical terms be very difficult). Hence (save in rare cases), sending out the PALs will need to await any EGM resolutions which the offer requires (for instance, giving the directors s. 80 CA authority to allot the securities or disapplying the statutory pre-emption rights contained in s. 89 CA). This is done in order to deal with fractional entitlements, the issue of overseas shareholders and to ensure that the offer period is no longer than 21 days (see the effect of s. 90(2) CA). The only condition which is an exception to this is admission of the securities to listing or admission to the AIM, as this almost always takes place within 24 hours of dispatch of the PALs and is a virtual formality by that stage.

3.6.4.5   Effect of CREST on rights issue

The advent of CREST (see **1.6.3**) will have an effect, in a rights issue, on those members who hold shares in uncertificated, dematerialised form. These members will not receive PALs but will have their nil paid rights credited to their CREST accounts. Instead of the ability to trade their PALs, they will be able to trade the nil paid rights through CREST. They should be able to do this from the morning after the PALs are posted to certificated shareholders.

3.6.5   Open Offers

Contrary to the impression given by its title, an open offer is not 'open' to anyone, but is similar to a rights issue in that it is made on a pre-emptive basis to existing shareholders 'to subscribe or purchase securities in proportion to their holdings. . . .' (LR para. 4.22). There are, however, certain major differences between an open offer and a rights issue which arguably make an open offer less attractive than a rights issue to shareholders but more attractive to the company. The terms of an open offer are such that, although similar to a rights issue, the offer itself cannot comply with the s. 89 statutory pre-emption rights. Hence, an important point to note is that on an open offer to shareholders for cash, there must be in existence the requisite s. 95 disapplication of those rights obtained before or at the time of the offer.

3.6.5.1   Disadvantages (in comparison to a rights issue) for shareholders

There are two key disadvantages:

(a) An open offer does not include any arrangements to sell shares (which were not taken up by shareholders under the offer) for the benefit of such shareholders (compare **3.6.5.2(5)** for rights issues). Therefore a 'lazy' shareholder who does nothing will not receive any money in respect of the shares for which he is entitled to apply and once the offer closes his entitlement lapses. Whereas in a rights issue if a shareholder does nothing the lapsed securities will be sold into the market and if the broker can agree a price at a premium to the subscription price, such a premium will go to the 'lazy' shareholder.

(b) The second difference is that application forms rather than provisional allotment letters are used. These are non-renounceable (LR para. 4.22) and so cannot be traded nil-paid, i.e. either the shareholder accepts the offer and purchases shares at a discount or not. He is not able to trade the 'right' to buy shares at the offer price.

3.6.5.2   Advantages of an open offer for the company

As far as the company is concerned, there are generally more advantages in conducting an open offer rather than a rights issue for the following reasons:

(a) Because the application forms cannot be traded, there is no concern about them being conditional and so the timetable for an open offer and for satisfaction if the conditions (including, for example, the passing of requisite resolutions at an EGM) can run concurrently rather than consecutively as in a rights issue. If an EGM is required (say, to increase the company's authorised share capital or to disapply the s. 89 pre-emption rights), application forms can be posted at the same time as the EGM notice. For a rights issue, provisional allotment letters can only be posted after the EGM because the UKLA does not allow shares to be allotted provisionally on a conditional basis. Because the notice of EGM and offer period run concurrently for an open offer, the timetable is reduced and the company gets its money sooner and the underwriting commission is less.

(b) The offer period itself for an open offer is shorter than that of a rights issue. The application forms are usually posted on Impact day together with the circular and EGM notice (if applicable). The offer period is usually a minimum of 15 business days which is shorter than the 21 minimum days required for a rights issue.

(c) Shares in an open offer are offered at a finer discount that on a rights issue. The maximum discount is 10 per cent to the middle market price of the securities at the time of announcing the offer. The only way this discount can be increased would be if the company can satisfy the UKLA that it is in severe financial difficulties or that there are other exceptional circumstances. (LR para. 4.26).

In summary, open offers are generally cheaper for the company (the discount on the current share price is finer and the underwriting commission is less due to the reduced offer period). However, an open offer is less flexible for shareholders which is why the Association of British Insurers (ABI) prefers rights issues to open offers if the increase of the share capital is more than 15–18 per cent or the discount greater than 7.5 per cent.

3.6.5.3   Effect of CREST on an open offer

An information pack is available from CRESTCo which contains specimen wording for inclusion in open offer documentation. This will detail the procedures to be followed where entitlements to apply for open offer shares are to be held as separate participating securities in CREST in which case the applications for open offer shares must accordingly be made using the CREST system.

3.6.6   Vendor placing

One of the possible uses of the funds raised by a rights issue will be to finance an acquisition of another company or business. The vendor placing has developed as an acquisition-financing technique which combines both the raising of finance and the acquisition itself, and rather neatly confers a number of advantages in the process.

What is a vendor placing? LR para. 4.29, defines a 'vendor consideration placing' as a 'marketing, by or on behalf of vendors, of securities that have been allotted to them as consideration for an acquisition'. To explain in more detail, let us start with a situation and a problem arising from it.

Buyer plc, a listed company, wants to buy Target Ltd, and Seller Ltd, which owns all the shares in Target, has agreed to sell it. Seller wants cash for the sale. Buyer has no cash available and would like to give Seller some of its own securities as consideration for the purchase. How is this mismatch resolved?

If Buyer agrees to appoint an investment bank to arrange for its securities to be placed into the market (and, let us say, listed and traded on the LSE alongside its other securities), then Seller agrees to have the securities allotted to it as consideration for the sale of Target and sells them to the investment bank to be placed. The placing produces cash. This would ordinarily pass into the company's coffers, but here it passes to Seller as its consideration for the transfer to Buyer of Target.

Result: Buyer issues its securities, Seller gets its cash, and Target is sold to Buyer.

If it sounds complicated, it is! The basic idea, though, is very simple. A vendor placing is a placing of securities to raise cash to finance an acquisition—nothing more nor less.

How does it work in more detail? **Figure 3.5** describes a typical transaction. If we ignore the reference to buyer's shareholders for the moment:

(1) The securities which are the consideration for the acquisition are allotted by Buyer to Seller. These two parties also enter into an acquisition agreement which records their deal to sell Target to Buyer. One of the conditions which must be fulfilled before the ultimate transfer of Target is that the securities which are to be placed in the market are admitted to full listing or to the AIM. It would be a disaster if the Seller took the securities as consideration and then discovered they were unmarketable, as they would be impossible to place.

(2) Now that the consideration has technically been paid, Target transfers to Buyer, though this will be conditional on the securities being issued in consideration by the Buyer being admitted to listing or the AIM, as appropriate, and satisfaction of the other conditions to the placing.

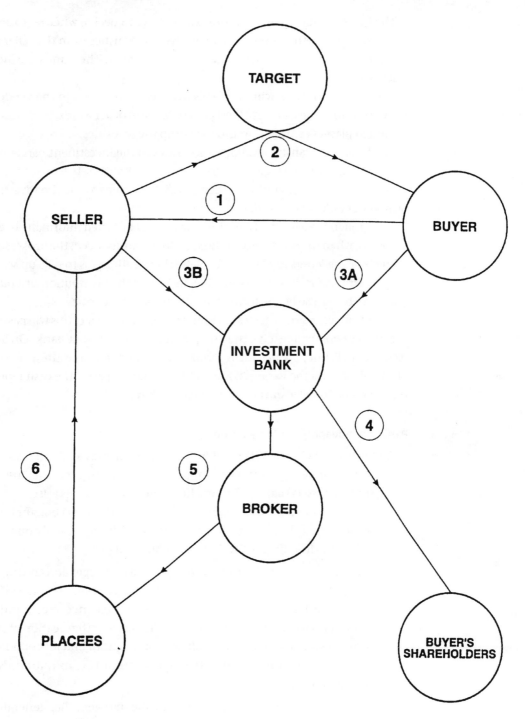

Figure 3.5   Vendor placing.

(3A) Buyer will have appointed an investment bank to arrange the placing, usually by a vendor placing agreement. This will contain similar terms and conditions to those found in an underwriting agreement (see **3.5.4.1**), though descriptions of the mechanics will vary. Commissions will be payable as in an ordinary placing.

One of the conditions to the vendor placing agreement will be that the conditions in the acquisition agreement have been satisfied! Although this seems like circularity, this is intended to avoid putting the placing into effect only to find that a vital regulatory approval for the transfer of Target has not been obtained. Hence, when Target is transferred, this will only be after all conditions to the transfer have been satisfied (with the exception of the securities being admitted to listing and the LSE or the AIM, as appropriate).

The investment bank in this context will have to decide whether to act as principal or agent, that is, whether it buys the newly issued securities from the seller in its own name or simply acts as agent of the seller in placing them. The same considerations arise as discussed in **3.5.3**.

The investment bank will invariably agree with the Buyer in the vendor placing agreement to arrange the issue on a 'best efforts' basis: in other words, to underwrite the placing if enough placees cannot be found to take up the securities.

(3B) Seller will transfer its allotted securities to the investment bank under a sale agreement, in which the seller gives the investment bank authority to place the securities.

(4) Clawback, an offer of the securities by the company via the investment bank to its own shareholders. See **3.6.6.2**.

(5) Through the agency of a broker, placees are contacted informally to establish interest and then, when the exact price of the securities is announced, the brokers arrange for them to sign placing letters to confirm formally their willingness to take up securities. This will work exactly as for an ordinary placing, including the distribution of a placing memorandum which will also be the listing particulars for the securities.

(6) The placees pay up their cash to buy the securities. In fact this will pass up back through the broker (who will receive the cheques) to the investment bank. On admission of the securities to listing, the placing is formally unconditional, as is the acquisition agreement. The bank deducts the various commissions and then passes the cash representing Seller's consideration to Seller and any surplus back to Buyer.

3.6.6.1   Particular advantages of the vendor placing

(a) Section 89 CA rears its head only where securities are being issued for cash. The particular beauty of the vendor placing is that the securities are being issued for shares or assets (namely Target), hence no s. 89 concerns arise.

A consequent problem is that a valuation of the assets bought for the issue of the securities may be required under s. 103 CA, although usually one of the exceptions to s. 103 will apply (see **2.1.2**). See s. 103(3) and (5).

(b) A vendor placing will often permit the use of merger accounting, where Buyer is using shares to buy at least 90 per cent of Target's share capital. The advantage of this is that Buyer and Target can merge their balance sheets and profit and loss accounts as if they had been one entity. This avoids the creation of goodwill and the consequent need to write that off against the profit and loss or other accounts and so is generally a more attractive option from the accountant's point of view (see **8.6.3.5**).

(c) Even if merger accounting is not available, merger relief generally will be under s. 131 CA. This means there will be no need to set up a share premium account in respect of any premium at which the securities are issued. As a share premium account ties up capital which might otherwise be put to use, that is a benefit (see **8.6.3.7**).

(d) The discount to market price at which securities are issued in rights issues varies (and there are in any event the Investment Committee guidelines to consider), but normally the range is anywhere between $12\frac{1}{2}$ per cent and 20 per cent (more than this in deep discount issues). The discount in vendor placings is usually finer than this (the exception is open offers—see **3.6.5.2**—where the level of discount tolerated by the Investment Committees is between 15 and 18 per cent). This is because LR para. 4.30(b) makes a discount of more than 10 per cent subject to UKLA permission and, since a placing is a selective marketing to institutions rather than an offer to shareholders whose mood may be unpredictable, there is not the need to be quite so generous with discounts to ensure its success.

The benefit of this is that fewer securities need to be issued to raise the same amount of money, hence it is cheaper for the company.

(e) In recent years it has become standard practice for a new structure to be adopted for a vendor placing arrangement. In this, rather than the Buyer's securities being issued to the Seller of the target, and then sold on in the placing, the securities are issued directly to the placees (or, in the case of clawback, the Buyer's shareholders—see **3.6.6.2**).

The principal reason for this is that it saves stamp duty and stamp duty reserve tax when the securities are transferred by the Sellers. Accordingly, it is a cheaper method of finance-raising.

The effect of these advantages is that the vendor placing is a more attractive route for a company when funding an acquisition than a rights issue.

3.6.6.2   **Clawback**

To return to figure 3.5 and, in particular, arrow 4, the concept of clawback is that, instead of placing the securities into the market, the company offers them, via the investment bank, to its own shareholders. The broker still identifies placees in the usual way, but their commitment is conditional on the company's shareholders not taking up the offer made to them: in a sense, then, the placees stand almost in the position of sub-underwriters. The only differences in terms of the structure of the offer are that there is an offer of securities to the company's shareholders and, given the likely scale of the offer, it may also be necessary to bring in a receiving bank to handle acceptances and payment from the shareholders.

Why do this when it is not strictly required by s. 89 (see **3.6.6.1**)?

Partly this is due to the influence of the Investment Committees, and partly what the LSE says in its continuing obligations for listed companies (LR para. 9.18). The presumption is that further issues of new securities will be to existing shareholders in proportion to their existing holdings *unless shareholders otherwise permit*. It follows that it is very difficult for a listed company to avoid returning to its shareholders to explain why it is proposing to exclude them from its latest issue of securities, and even harder to come up with a very good reason when it does try to explain.

So how is the offer made to shareholders? There are two basic variations.

(a) *Rights offer*

This works almost exactly like a rights issue. The shareholders are offered the securities, in proportion to their existing holdings, on a PAL which they can trade, allow to lapse or take up as they see fit. If the issuer is a listed company, the listing particulars prepared for this offer need only comply with the The Listing Rules' requirements for rights issues. This is the route preferred by the Investment Committees, as it gives shareholders the most favourable deal.

(b) *Open offer*

This looks like a rights issue, but it is subtly different as described in **3.6.5**. Shareholders are offered new securities in proportion to their existing holdings, but not on a PAL. They get a letter of entitlement which entitles them to a minimum number of securities. They can apply for more if they choose. The letter of entitlement is not tradeable, so all that the shareholders can do with it is to let their entitlement lapse or take it up.

For listed companies, UKLA listing requirements are similar for open offers and rights issues. The rationale for this is that, essentially, both are pre-emptive issues to shareholders. Requirements for rights issues are set out at LR paras 4.16–4.21 and requirements for open offers are set out at LR paras 4.22–4.26.

As between these two, there is likely to be some preference on the company's part for doing an open rather than a rights offer, despite the attitude of investors. The reason lies in the letter of entitlement. As it is non-tradeable, there are none of the fears of issuing the letter before all the conditions to the issue have been satisfied—unlike a PAL (see **3.6.4**). Consequently an open offer is speedier than a rights offer, which in turn means that the company obtains its cash faster. The UKLA reinforces this by only requiring that the timetable for an open offer is approved by the relevant recognised investment exchange (e.g., the LSE) on which the company's securities are traded (LR para. 4.24). The LSE requires that an open offer be open for at least 15 business days from the posting of application forms. This compares to the 21-day requirement for rights issues.

With vendor placings, it is important to look out for variations. The transactions are complex and refinements are being devised all the time. Just remember the basic theme of placing a buyer's securities (or offering them to its shareholders) as a way of providing cash to buy shares or an asset from a seller.

3.7 Timetable

The timetable set out below is provided only to be indicative of the typical path of an offer for sale or subscription, where the company is a new applicant seeking an initial listing from the UKLA and admission to trading on the LSE. That is, it is intended to show the general order of events over an acceptable timescale for a specific transaction. Circumstances may require significant variations in particular cases, where, for example, there are overseas regulatory requirements to take into account. The other transactions described in this chapter will also differ in certain aspects from the model below; for example, post-impact matters on a placing will generally occur within a shorter period of time.

The timetable assumes that any approvals required from shareholders for the issue will be obtained before the run-up to the offer itself. This is usual, and part of the process of preparing the company for the issue (see **3.3.1**). Approvals required include those under the Companies Act 1985, such as an increase in authorised capital (s. 121), or obtaining authority to allot for the directors (s. 80), or under ch. 10 of the Listing Rules (see **5.6.4**).

Remember that the applications to the UKLA and the LSE have to be coordinated (see **3.4**).

Date	Events
By 12 weeks before impact day	Appointment of advisers. Company's solicitors review issuer's constitution. Agree timetable and list of documents.
By 8 weeks before impact day	First draft of prospectus circulated. First drafting meeting (all parties). Accountants' long-form report available. Company's solicitors finalise changes to constitution. Company's solicitors prepare tax clearances.
By 5 weeks before impact day	Drafting meetings on prospectus continue: early draft submitted to LSE for comments. Tax clearances received. Opening meeting on underwriting agreement.

	Accountants initiate work on statements of indebtedness and working capital. Company's solicitors submit new or revised constitution to UKLA for comments.
By 3 weeks before impact day	Drafting meetings on prospectus continue. Submit draft prospectus to UKLA (at least 20 clear business days before publication). Initial publicity in newspapers (sometimes earlier). Public announcement of offer (sometimes earlier). Accountants finalise long-form report and working capital projections. Company's solicitors prepare first draft of verification notes.
By 2 weeks before impact day	Drafting meetings on prospectus continue. Negotiations on underwriting agreement continue. Accountants finalise short-form report for prospectus and statement of indebtedness.
By 1 week before impact day	All documents substantially agreed with UKLA. Verification meetings to finalise verification notes. Drafting meetings on prospectus continue.
By 2 days before impact day	Profit forecast finalised. Prospectus finalised (subject to minor amendments). Documents submitted to UKLA and LSE.
By 1 day before impact day	Price of securities finalised. Underwriting agreement finalised. Issuer's board meeting approves issue and all documents (underwriting agreement held in escrow).
Impact day	Underwriting agreement released from escrow. Sub-underwriting letters sent to sub-underwriters. Press conference and price announced. UKLA approves prospectus. Prospectus registered at Companies House. Prospectus bulk-printed.
By 1 day after impact day	Application lists open.
By 3 days after impact day	Newspaper publicity. Presentations ('roadshow') to institutions.
By 5 days after impact day	Applications for listing and admission to trading heard.
By 7 days after impact day	Close application lists (sometimes earlier). Clear cheques from applicants. Allocate shares.
By 8 days after impact day	Allocations made to sub-underwriters.
By 12 days after impact day	Letters of acceptance or rejection posted to investors. Underwriting and sub-underwriting commissions paid.
By 14 days after impact day	Admissions to the Official List and to trading effective. (n.B. The need to obtain admission to CREST.) Dealings in shares commence.
By 6 weeks after impact day	Share certificates posted.

3.8   Documents

This is a summary only of the documents most commonly of importance in these transactions.

3.8.1   UKLA documents

Prospectus or listing particulars, prospectus, mini-prospectus, circular to shareholders.
Application form(s) for listing.
Derogation and non-applicables letter.

Advertisement for the securities.

Working capital letter.

Profit forecast reports.

Memorandum and articles of association (primary offers only).

Directors' declarations (only primary offers).

Sponsor's declaration.

Temporary and final documents of title (i.e., PALs, letters of entitlement).

3.8.2 LSE documents

Prospectus or listing particulars, mini-prospectus, circular to shareholders.

Application for admission to trading.

Copy board resolution allotting the securities or authorising the issue.

3.8.3 Agreements

Underwriting or placing agreement.

Sub-underwriting or placing letter.

Acquisition agreements (for vendor placings with or without clawback).

3.8.4 Supporting documents

Verification notes.

Completion board minutes.

Material contracts.

Accountants' reports (long and short-form).

Brokers' circular.

Notices and resolutions for any general meetings.

3.9 Checklist

This checklist is no more than a summary of the most important questions you need to ask yourself when acting on an issue of equity securities.

3.9.1 For companies with their registered office in the UK

Q1   Has the company considered its obligations under ss. 80 and 89 CA, and the requirements of s. 121 CA?

See relevant sections in *LPC Guide: Business Law* and (if the company is listed on the Stock Exchange) **3.3.1.4**.

Q2   Have the directors of the company considered whether they are exercising their power to issue securities for a proper purpose?

See relevant sections in the *LPC Guide: Business Law*.

Q3   Is the company public or private?

IF PRIVATE, does it wish to make an offer to the public?

NO: see **4.3.1** and no further questions; the company may be able to issue shares privately to interested institutional shareholders provided the restrictions of s. 81(1) CA (restriction on public offers by private company) and s. 21 FSMA (restrictions on financial promotion) are observed.

YES: see **4.3.1** and then Q5.

IF PUBLIC, see Q4.

Q4   If the company wants to make an offer to the public, does it already have securities listed on the Official List, or are its securities admitted to the AIM?

NO: see Q5.

YES: see **3.6.1** and **3.6.2** and then Q5.

Q5   Has the company appointed advisers for the offer yet?

NO: see **3.3** and then Q6.

YES: establish which ones and then see Q6.

Q6   Has the company notified the Bank of England of the proposed date of the offer?

See **3.3.1.6** and Q7.

Q7   Are the securities to be listed on the Official List?

NO: see Q8.

YES:

   (a) If they are already admitted to the AIM, or a foreign stock exchange, and the company wants in future to have them on the Official List and traded on the LSE instead of or in addition to these other markets, see **3.5.8** and no further questions.

   (b) If (a) is not true of the company, see **4.2** and then Q9.

Q8   Are the securities to be admitted to the AIM?

NO: see Q9.

YES: see **4.3** and Q9.

Q9   Is the company planning to issue an advertisement for the securities?

NO: see Q10.

YES: see **1.5.1.4** and then Q10.

Q10   Is the company making an acquisition at the same time as the offer?

NO: see Q11.

YES: see **3.6.5** and then Q11.

Q11   What marketing structure is the company proposing to use for the offer?

See **3.5** or **3.6**.

3.9.2   For companies incorporated overseas

Q13   Does the company want to have its securities publicly traded in the UK?

NO: no further questions; it can, like UK private companies, seek to raise capital from interested investors privately.

YES: see Q14.

Q14   Does the company have a listing on a recognised overseas stock exchange?

NO: see Q5.

YES:

(a) Does the company want to issue new securities and have them listed on the Official List? See **4.2.9** and **4.2.10.5**.

(b) Does the company want simply to have listed on the Official List its securities already in issue? See **3.5.8**.

Regulation and liability in securities offerings

4.1 A public market for securities

The regulation of the securities offerings we have been looking at in **Chapter 3** varies, depending on whether the issuer's securities will be traded on a market or not at all. There are three options available:

(a) the company is public and wants its securities listed on the Official List and traded on the LSE (see **4.2**);

(b) the company is public and wants its securities admitted to the AIM (see **4.3**);

(c) the company is private and so is not free to make an offer to the public (s. 81 CA) but may still find ways of offering its securities through private subscriptions.

Traditionally the LSE was the only official market on which securities could be publicly traded and prices quoted for them (see **1.6.2**).

The AIM was formed in 1995 as a successor to the Unlisted Securities Market (USM). AIM is based on the highly successful NASDAQ market in the United States. The objective is to attract new companies and investors at the junior end of the market through a relaxed regulatory regime and with a low cost base. Whereas the USM was seen as a 'feeder' market for listings on the Official List, the AIM is seen as a quite separate market from which companies may choose never to move, though they will be free to graduate to the Official List and LSE if they choose to do so.

The regulatory regime which applies to the AIM is described in **4.3**.

4.2 Listed securities on the LSE

4.2.1 What does 'listed' mean?

When securities (see **3.1**) are 'listed', this means they have been admitted to the Official List of the UKLA (see FSMA s. 74)and admitted to trading by the LSE (see SEADS part 2 para. 2). A price at which those securities can be bought and sold will be quoted by those who deal, or 'make a market', in them. Those securities can then be bought and sold on the stock market, i.e., through the LSE's trading procedures and in accordance with its rules. A listing therefore allows a company's securities to be freely traded and publicly priced. It opens up the company's securities to anyone interested in buying shares—the general public and the professional investing community.

4.2.2 Why obtain a listing?

Obtaining a listing is difficult and expensive. A company wanting a listing has a complex series of requirements to satisfy—they are described in **4.2.6**. Once listed, a company has to pay an annual listing fee to the UKLA to stay on the Official List (see LR para. 1.3. and LR Sch. 13) and to the LSE under SEADS Part 2 para 3.12 to stay admitted to trading (this rises as the value of its listed securities increases) and is subject to the UKLA's Continuing Obligations (LR chapter 9) and the LSE's Disclosure Standards (see **4.2.10**). So what are the advantages?

4.2.2.1 Access to capital

One of the objects and requirements of listing is to attract new investors to the company, and their acquisition of the company's securities makes new money available to the company. If the company needs further capital in the future, it has a larger shareholder base from which to obtain those additional funds. In 2003, around £129 billion was raised by UK companies alone (both joining and already on the LSE and the AIM), from a combination of equity and debt finance. (source: LSE Primary Market Fact Sheet: 31 December 2003)

4.2.2.2 Liquidity

As a listing means public trading, the company hopes this will generate demand for its securities. The average value of securities bought and sold on the LSE's UK domestic equity market every day in 2003 (source: *Exchange the magazine of the LSE*, 31 December 2003) was over £7 billion—again, the size of the potential market is huge. As demand grows, the company will find it easier to make further issues of its securities, hence raising more capital. Increased demand should also enhance the company's share price, which in turn improves the company's buying power if it is using its own securities as an asset in making acquisitions (see **Chapter 8** and **3.6.5**).

4.2.2.3 Prestige

The LSE trades more equity securities by volume than any other stock exchange in Europe (there were 32,500,000 equity bargains between January 2004 and June 2004 (source: *Exchange-the magazine of the LSE*: 30 June 2004). Although New York trades more securities by value than London, London quotes more securities than any other major exchange worldwide. A quotation in London does not thereby change a company's fortunes overnight, but belonging to a market of this importance raises a company's profile in the eyes of the domestic and international investment community.

4.2.2.4 Investor relations

A listed company must inform the market of its financial performance, business developments and any activities affecting its securities so that investors can constantly appraise the company's value (see **4.2.10.1**). Though onerous, these duties are also an opportunity for the company to secure the future commitment and confidence of its investors. These are in turn vital in the context of access to capital and liquidity.

4.2.3 How does a company go about obtaining a listing?

4.2.3.1 Application for admission to the Official List

A company's application to be listed on the Official List must be made through a sponsor by means of the UKLA's Form—Application for Admission of Securities to the Official List (see LR sch. 3A and see **3.3.4** on the role of a sponsor). It is the company's responsibility to appoint a sponsor (LR para. 2.6). The sponsor in turn needs to be satisfied it is dealing with a company and directors who understand the obligations and commitments expected of a company seeking listing (LR paras 2.10 and 2.13). Although the relationship between company and sponsor is sometimes represented by a formal agreement in the shape of an engagement letter, there is no legal or UKLA obligation to do this.

Assuming the company's application presents no problems (on which, see below), the company's securities will eventually be admitted to listing when this is announced to the market as a whole by means of a notice disseminated by the electronic systems used by the UKLA for communications with the public (see LR, para. 7.1). Once a company is listed, the sponsor is expected to advise and assist the company in complying with its continuing obligations (see **4.2.10**).

4.2.3.2   Application for admission to trading on the LSE

In order to have securities admitted to the LSE's markets for listed securities, companies must follow a two-stage admission process. In addition to applying for admission to the Official List (see **4.2.3.1**), a company must also seek admission to trading on the LSE. This is done by means of the Stock Exchange Form—Application for Admission of Securities to Trading (Form 1 appended to the LSE's Admission and Disclosure Standards). There is no LSE requirement to appoint a sponsor; however, it does recommend that a company appoint a nominated representative from an outside organisation to assist in the admission process. This representative will most likely be the sponsor required by the UKLA.

Admission to trading will occur simultaneously with admission to listing. It becomes effective only when the decision to admit the securities to trading has been announced by the LSE (see SEADS Part 2, para. 2.1).

4.2.4   What requirements must a company fulfil to obtain a listing?

A company must comply with:

    (a) Part VI of FSMA (see **4.2.5**);

    (b) the Listing Rules' provisions on:

        (i)   general conditions for listing (see LR ch. 3, and **4.2.6.2**),

        (ii) specific contents of prospectus or listing particulars (see LR ch. 6, and **4.2.6.3**),

        (iii) application procedure (see LR ch. 7, and **4.2.6.5**),

        (iv) publication of prospectus or listing particulars (see LR ch. 8, and **4.2.6.5**); and

    (c) The LSE's Admission and Disclosure Standards (see **4.2.7**).

4.2.5   Part VI Financial Services and Markets Act 2000

This section is a description of the legal framework around which a company seeking a listing of its securities and its advisers must work. Any lawyer working in this field must be familiar with this framework; in the actual handling of an issue of securities, however, attention tends to be focused on the detailed requirements laid down by the Listing Rules as to listing (see **4.2.6.2** and **4.2.6.3**), as these will determine the structure of an offering and what can actually be written into the offering and listing document read by investors.

4.2.5.1   Background

The FSMA currently governs the admission of securities to listing. Since 1 May 2000, the FSA, acting as the UKLA, has been the 'competent authority' under the Act, with a general duty to make listing rules (s. 73). The rules it has created are set out in the Listing Rules.

4.2.5.2 Why must a company seeking a listing comply with Part VI's requirements?

Under s. 75 FSMA, a company may only apply for listing in accordance with the Listing Rules. The UKLA cannot admit securities to listing unless the Listing Rules have been fulfilled in respect of those securities.

4.2.5.3 What are the UKLA's listing powers under FSMA?

The UKLA is the competent authority with power to make listing rules. In practice, it issues occasional amendments to the Listing Rules, usually after prior consultation with affected parties together with their financial and legal advisers.

It is empowered to grant dispensations to its listing rules (s. 101(2): see **4.2.6.1**), and in practice exercises considerable flexibility in the interpretation and application of the rules. The curious result of this is that, though the rules have the effective force of law, they often work in reality more like the rules of the City Code on Takeovers and Mergers: in other words, it is as important to understand the spirit behind the rules as it is to know their letter.

The UKLA has power to refuse an application for listing (s. 75(5) and (6)). If an application is refused, the applicant may appeal to the Financial Services and Markets Tribunal, established under Part IX of FSMA. If it grants approval, its decision is not justiciable (s. 76(7)).

The UKLA is entitled to suspend a listing temporarily or to discontinue a listing altogether (s. 77: this is generally referred to as 'de-listing'). This is the ultimate sanction for companies which fail to comply with the Continuing Obligations in the Listing Rules or commit any other breaches of the rules (for instance, when making a further issue of shares at some future date). Decisions to de-list securities are thought to be susceptible to judicial review applications (for example, by shareholders, see *R* v. *International Stock Exchange of the United Kingdom and the Republic of Ireland Ltd, ex parte Else (1982) Ltd* [1993] QB 534). The chances of success are always likely to be slim in view of the need for the UKLA to act quickly and decisively, and the courts' general reluctance to interfere with the decisions made by securities markets regulators (see **8.8.7**).

It is vital, therefore, when acting in a transaction where a company is seeking admission of its securities to listing, to ensure that the company understands what its Continuing Obligations will be (see **4.2.10**), and at no stage prejudices its relationship with the UKLA.

4.2.5.4 The need for listing particulars or a prospectus

As the competent authority, the UKLA can impose requirements on companies seeking admission to the Official List in its Listing Rules. In particular, it requires as a condition of admission the publication of listing particulars (which are the particulars required by the Listing Rules).

Section 84 FSMA requires as a condition for admission to listing the publication of a 'prospectus' where securities are offered to the public in the UK for the first time before admission.

There are several exemptions to the requirement to publish a prospectus where there is an offer to the public. These are listed in Sch. 11 to FSMA. The principal exemptions cover the following circumstances:

(a) where shares are offered to no more than 50 persons (FSMA Sch. 11, para. 4);

(b) where securities are offered to persons whose ordinary business activities involve them in buying, selling and managing investments (FSMA Sch. 11, para. 3);

(c) where securities are offered to a restricted circle of persons who are sufficiently knowledgeable to understand the risks involved in accepting the offer (FSMA Sch. 11, para. 6);

(d) where the issue raises less than 40,000 euros in total (FSMA Sch. 11, para. 9).

If the offer falls within one of these exemptions, the need for a prospectus falls away; the need for listing particulars will still exist by virtue of the Listing Rules. Where, however, the exceptions do not apply, it will be necessary to prepare a prospectus rather than listing particulars. The Listing Rules apply in relation to a prospectus in exactly the same way as they apply in relation to listing particulars, but as if references to listing particulars were a reference to a prospectus. Accordingly, the contents requirements for the document will stay exactly the same (see **4.2.6.3**), and will depend on the type of transaction. It is just the name of the document that will change.

There are exemptions to the need to produce listing particulars (see **4.2.5.5**). These exemptions are not available where the document is a prospectus.

In practice, an offer for sale will almost certainly require publication of a prospectus. In contrast, a placing will normally be exempt on the grounds that securities are offered only to a restricted group of people who are in the investment business or who are sufficiently knowledgeable. By the same token, an intermediaries offer is also likely to be exempt from the prospectus requirements.

Where a company's securities are already listed, and it is undertaking a subsequent offering, the prospectus requirements will also apply. These are described in **3.6.2**.

4.2.5.5   When are listing particulars not required?

LR para. 5.23A indicates that issuers may be exempted from the obligation to publish listing particulars, provided an application for admission of the securities to listing is made, where:

(a) an equivalent document has been published in the previous year as a result of the securities in question having been the subject of a public issue, or issued in connection with a takeover or merger (LR para. 5.23A (a));

(b) the securities have been listed in another Member State of the European Union for the past three years (or, if for less, the relevant local stock exchange has confirmed the issuer has complied with its rules since being listed) (LR para. 5.23A (b)); or

(c) the securities have been traded on the AIM for at least two years prior to the issue (LR para. 5.23A (c)).

In these cases the issuer must produce an exempt listing document. In the case of (a), this should contain details of any material changes since the equivalent document was published, a statement as to the securities being listed, and the directors' responsibility statement (LR ch. 5, app. 2, para. 1). In practice, this kind of exempt listing document is rarely possible, because the changes which occur to any listed company in any twelve-month period are usually significant enough to merit large-scale revisions to the information presented in the original document.

In the case of (b), the exempt listing document which is required is discussed in more detail in **4.2.9.2**. (see LR ch. 5, app. 2, para. 2).

In addition, LR para. 5.27 sets out a number of categories of issues for which listing particulars are not required. These include the situations where the new securities would increase a company's listed securities of the relevant class by less than 10 per cent (LR para. 5.27 (e)) and where shares of a class already listed are allotted to employees (LR para. 5.27 (f)). In the cases described in LR para. 5.27, LR paras 5.28 to 5.30 prescribe certain information which must be published in printed form.

4.2.5.6   What should prospectuses and listing particulars contain?

The detailed requirements for the contents of prospectuses and listing particulars are set out in **4.2.6.3**. In addition, s. 80 FSMA also imposes a general obligation to disclose in the prospectus or listing particulars facts material to an investment decision about the company's securities. These are also considered in **4.2.6.3**.

4.2.5.7   What are the risks of civil liability in preparing prospectuses or listing particulars?

Prospectuses and listing particulars make a series of statements about the company's assets, liabilities, financial position, profits and losses, its prospects, the rights attaching to its securities and other assorted details about the company and its performance. These are all made ultimately with a view to attracting investors to acquire those securities. There are the usual risks of civil liability associated with such statements with which you will already be familiar:

(a) *Negligent misstatement*

Liability under the principles derived from *Hedley Byrne & Co. Ltd* v. *Heller and Partners Ltd* [1964] AC 465 and *Caparo Industries plc* v. *Dickman* [1990] 2 AC 605 will arise if the maker of the statement owes a duty of care to the reader and that duty is breached. The law implies a duty of care where the maker possesses special skills or knowledge and knows or ought to know that the reader will rely for a particular purpose on that skill or knowledge. The reader will, though, have to be within the contemplation of the person making the statement. In the case of prospectuses and listing particulars, new investors will in law be relying on the document. A duty of care may extend to purchasers of the company's securities in the 'after market' where the document specifically or implicitly contemplates this (*Possfund Custodian Trustee Ltd* v. *Diamond* [1996] 2 All ER 774). It is important to be conscious of this risk when drafting the document.

Prospectuses and listing particulars are prepared with the clear intention of encouraging people to invest in the company which issues them, so the investor will have little difficulty in showing reliance if they contain a misstatement. If there has been a failure to exercise due care (as described above) in making that statement, the maker will be liable to the investor for any foreseeable loss resulting from it. Liable parties include:

(i)   The company itself: the company issues the prospectus or listing particulars and it will clearly be reasonable for an investor to assume the company's expertise in relation to its own affairs!

(ii) The directors of the company: the directors are required to assume responsibility for the contents of a prospectus or listing particulars by virtue of the Listing Rules (LR para. 6.A.3). Directors, both in practice and law, can usually be taken to possess a reasonable degree of expertise in relation to the affairs of their company, on which an investor will almost certainly be entitled to rely, and the responsibility statement makes it clear that the directors have authorised the statements contained in the prospectus or listing particulars: hence they will find it very difficult to avoid liability.

(iii) If the misstatement is contained in financial information supplied or verified by the company's auditors (such as the company's latest audited results), the auditors or the accountants reporting on the financial information would almost certainly be liable.

(iv) The investment bank appointed by the company to advise it on the offering (see **3.3.5** for a more detailed description of the merchant bank's activities) will probably also be at risk of liability. To some extent, this will depend on the structure adopted for the offering (see **3.5.3.1** on this point).

In all cases, however, the UKLA makes it clear (LR para. 2.13) that the investment bank (or 'issuing house') has a responsibility as sponsor to ensure that the directors understand and fulfil their own responsibilities properly, and must be satisfied that the company is suitable for listing. This may not amount to issuing direct statements on the face of the prospectus or listing particulars to this effect; but certainly the professional investment community places considerable importance on the quality of the 'name' sponsoring the company. An investor may therefore be able to show that the bank is so intrinsically associated with the contents of the prospectus or listing particulars that it is legally responsible for misstatements in them.

Quite apart from this, an issuing house as sponsor is required (LR para. 2.15) to state publicly in respect of any profit forecast made in the prospectus or listing particulars that it is satisfied the forecast has been made after due and careful enquiry: profit forecasts are probably among the most exposed of any statements made (and have been the subject of negligence actions involving investment banks in a different context (*Morgan Crucible Co. plc* v. *Hill Samuel & Co. Ltd* [1991] Ch 295). An investment bank therefore needs to be particularly careful here.

(v) Other advisers: any other party which is responsible for a statement in a prospectus or listing particulars which turns out to be false or misleading (for example, a firm of surveyors producing a valuation report for a property investment company) will also be exposed to liability. Solicitors also fall into this bracket, though it is almost unknown for a firm of solicitors to authorise a statement: their task is confined to that of advising their clients (typically the company or investment bank) on the legal accuracy of a statement—hence their liability, if any, will be to their own clients, not investors.

(b) *Misrepresentation*

Misrepresentations in a prospectus or listing particulars will give rise to the following remedies:

(i) *Rescission*

An investor will be entitled to rescind his contract with the company where he is induced to invest by statements of fact made in the prospectus, or listing particulars which are untrue. In some issues, the contract will in fact be with the company's investment bank, in which case the right of rescission is obviously against the bank.

The right applies whether the misrepresentation in the prospectus or listing particulars was fraudulent, negligent or entirely innocent, although the misrepresentation must be material and must be as to fact rather than opinion (for example, production figures for the past year, not the company's prospects in the ensuing 12 months).

Of course the usual limitations as regards the right to rescind apply: in particular, it will not survive if the investor affirms the contract (e.g., by trying to sell the shares), nor will it extend beyond a reasonable period of time following discovery of the misrepresentation by the investor. The courts have in the past held that a two-week delay between discovery and seeking rescission was too long a period.

It is worth bearing in mind that the court may refuse rescission and grant damages instead (Misrepresentation Act 1967, s. 2(2)), though not for consequential losses.

(ii) *Damages*

If the misrepresentation was fraudulent, the investor may sue for all the loss flowing directly from the misrepresentation (whether foreseeable at the time of the misrepresentation, or not), as in any action in deceit. The investor will need to show he was induced to acquire the securities by the fraudulent misrepresentation. The right to sue for damages lies against any person responsible for the misrepresentation (on which, see above).

If the misrepresentation is negligent or innocent, the investor may sue under s. 2(1) Misrepresentation Act 1967, as the company (or investment bank, as the case may be) will have a contract with the investor. There have been two traditional benefits of pursuing this remedy in preference to an action based on *Caparo Industries plc* v. *Dickman* principles, as far as the investor is concerned. The first has been that the skill or knowledge of the maker of the statement does not have to be established, and the second that the maker has to show that he had an honest and reasonable belief that his statement was true.

The damages for a claim under the Act return the victim of the misrepresentation to the position he was in before the misstatement. *Royscot Trust Ltd* v. *Rogerson* [1991] 2 QB 297 has made it clear that, as far as the measure of damages is concerned, the maker of a negligent or innocent misstatement is liable to the same extent as for a fraudulent misrepresentation—that is, for all the loss flowing directly from the statement whether foreseeable or not at the time the statement was made. This may therefore confer another advantage on investors pursuing a claim for negligent misstatements under the Act rather than *Caparo Industries plc* v. *Dickman*, as damages in tort for misstatements are recoverable only if they are foreseeable.

(c) *Breach of contract*

Damages arising from actions in misrepresentation will put an investor in the position he was in before the misstatement. An investor may in addition seek to recover damages for his loss of bargain, that is, what the securities would have been worth had the misstatement made in the prospectus or listing particulars been correct. This assumes that the misstatement has become a term of the contract, but an investor who takes securities on the strength of what is in the prospectus or listing particulars should be able to treat all material statements in the particulars or prospectus as contractual representations.

The old rule that a shareholder could only sue for damages for breach of contract if he had rescinded his contract of allotment in the first place has been removed by s. 111A CA.

As with rescission, in some offers, the investor's contract will be with the investment bank and not the company—hence it may be the investment bank and not the company which will be the defendant in these circumstances.

(d) *Financial Services and Markets Act 2000*

Although there is no doubt that investors will continue to rely on the various heads of liability described above when suing for misstatements in prospectuses or listing particulars, s. 90 FSMA is likely to be the most powerful weapon in the investor's armoury, because it suffers from none of the constraints of other remedies (for example, the need to show reliance under *Hedley Byrne & Co. Ltd* v. *Heller and Partners Ltd* or inducement in misrepresentation). Having said this, it has yet to be tested in the courts. It makes the 'persons responsible' for listing particulars or prospectuses liable to pay compensation to any person who has acquired any securities, and suffered loss as a result of any untrue or misleading statement in the particulars or prospectus or any omission from them of anything which s. 80 FSMA would require (the general duty of disclosure—see **4.2.5.6**).

Note there need be no reliance on the misstatement, only a causal connection between it and the loss suffered. Note also that a misstatement includes an omission—but an omission which would fall foul of s. 80: hence an omission of detail required by the Listing Rules (see **4.2.6.3**) will not of itself give rise to liability under this section. The remedy is available to subsequent purchasers of the securities as well as the original investors (it will be more difficult for subsequent purchasers to argue this in a claim in negligence), although proving the loss was caused by the misstatement will become more difficult the longer the time elapsed since publication of the particulars or prospectus.

The persons responsible for listing particulars and prospectuses are defined in reg. 6 of the Financial Services and Markets Act 2000 (Official Listing of Securities) Regulations 2001 (SI 2001/2956). They are:

(i)   the issuer of the securities to which the particulars relate (reg. 6(1)(a));

(ii) where the issuer is a body corporate, each person who is a director of that body at the time when the particulars are submitted to the competent authority (reg. 6(1)(b));

(iii) where the issuer is a body corporate, each person who has authorised himself to be named, and is named, in the particulars as a director or as having agreed to become a director of that body either immediately or at a future time (reg. 6(1)(c));

(iv) each person who accepts, and is stated in the particulars as accepting, responsibility for the particulars (reg. 6(1)(d));

(v)   each person not falling within (i) to (iv) who has authorised the contents of the particulars (reg. 6(1)(e)).

Where a person accepts responsibility for particulars under (iv) above or authorises their contents under (v) above, they may state that they do so only to a specified extent. Their liability will then be limited to the extent specified (reg. 6(3)(a)). They will also only be liable if the material in question in the particulars is included in the same or substantially the same form and context as agreed by the relevant person (reg. 6(3)(b)).

Parties who authorise the contents, or elements, of listing particulars or prospectuses will include auditors and/or reporting accountants in respect of the financial information which they approve. It will also extend to the merchant bank where the listing particulars contain a profit forecast and the bank has to report that it is satisfied that the forecast has been prepared after due and careful enquiry. Where an investment bank issues particulars in its own name (in, for example, an offer for sale) it is likely to be treated as having authorised the document. Surveyors who produce a valuation report on assets held by a company will be taken to have authorised part of the relevant document.

The regulations state that a person shall not be held responsible for any particulars by reason of giving advice as to their contents in a professional capacity (reg. 6(4)). This will exclude any liability for solicitors, provided that they advise only in a professional capacity.

The FSMA provisions on market abuse (see **1.5.1.3** (b)) may also give rise to liability should there be evidence of behaviour likely to give a regular market user a false or misleading impression as to the supply of, or demand for, or as to the price or value of, the shares being issued (see FSMA s. 118).

To summarise, civil liability for a prospectus or listing particulars may arise through:

(a) negligent misstatement (*Hedley Byrne & Co. Ltd* v. *Heller and Partners Ltd*);

(b) misrepresentation;

(c) breach of contract; and

(d) FSMA provisions on liability and market abuse.

4.2.5.8   What are the risks of criminal liability when preparing listing particulars or prospectuses?

(a) *Financial Services and Markets Act 2000*

The financial promotion provisions of FSMA s. 21 (see **1.5.1.3**) do not apply to non-real time communications (i.e., any communication not being a personal visit, telephone conversation or other interactive dialogue) included in listing particulars, prospectuses, supplementary listing particulars or supplementary prospectuses. This is as a result of reg. 71 of the Financial Services and Markets Act 2000 (Financial Promotion) Order 2001.

A real-time communication within the context of a listing has the potential to fall within the financial promotion provisions of FSMA.

Section 98(1) FSMA states that no advertisement or other information of a kind required by listing rules may be issued in the United Kingdom unless its contents have been submitted to the UKLA and the UKLA has approved the contents or authorised their issue without such approval. Section 98(2) states that it is an offence to fail to submit advertisements or information which fall within s. 98 to the UKLA.

In addition, those preparing listing particulars or prospectuses need also to consider the effect of s. 397 FSMA. This section makes it an offence for a person to make misleading, false or deceptive statements, promises or forecasts, or dishonestly to conceal facts, for the purpose of inducing someone to acquire investments (s. 397(1), (2)). The section also extends the offence to any conduct which creates a false or misleading impression as to the market in or price of any relevant investments.

(b) *Theft Act 1968*

Section 15 Theft Act 1968 makes it an offence to dishonestly obtain by deception property (including cash) belonging to another. Deception takes place when a person attempts to pass off a statement which is or may be false as being true. Dishonesty is a question left to juries to decide. The same statement may also give rise to liability under s. 397(1) FSMA.

Section 19 Theft Act 1968 makes it an offence for an officer of the company (or person purporting to act as an officer of the company), for example, a director, to publish or concur in publishing a written statement or account which to his knowledge is or may be materially false, misleading or deceptive, if he intends to deceive the company's members or creditors in the process.

Other more minor offences also exist, such as failure to deliver prospectuses or listing particulars to the Registrar of Companies under s. 83 FSMA.

4.2.5.9   Supplementary prospectuses and listing particulars

At any time following the preparation of a prospectus but before dealings start in the relevant securities, a supplementary prospectus will have to be published if there is a significant change affecting any matter mentioned in the original prospectus, or a significant omission appears in the original prospectus (s. 81 FSMA). This and the following provisions apply equally to listing particulars, so prospectus and listing particulars should be read interchangeably in this section.

What is significant? Significance is to be measured against the test of disclosure in s. 80 FSMA—in other words, it depends whether the change significantly affects the information an investor would reasonably require in order to make an informed assessment about the company (See also LR paras 5.14 and 5.15).

A supplementary prospectus carries exactly the same risks of liability as the original (including the possibility of compensation under s. 90 FSMA).

What form does a supplementary prospectus take? LR para. 5.16 gives you the answer. It contains a directors' responsibility statement (LR para. 5.16(b)). It states it is to be read in conjunction with the original prospectus. It details the significant changes which have arisen since the original prospectus was submitted to the LSE and indicates that the directors are aware of no other significant changes on which the company should be reporting (LR para. 5.16(c)).

In practice, everything possible is done to minimise the prospect of having to publish a supplementary prospectus. Partly this is because of the additional work and time involved, not to mention the cost of producing another document. Largely, though, it is because the need to publish a supplementary prospectus is often taken as a sign that all is not well with the issue, and this may affect its success. This may only be a matter of perception, but if the supplementary prospectus was required because the company and its advisers were unable to anticipate new developments or resolve outstanding issues adequately prior to publication of the original prospectus, this may cause them considerable embarrassment.

Submission of the original prospectus for approval by the UKLA will precede commencement of dealings in the securities only by a matter of days, hence the time in which the potential obligation to prepare a supplementary prospectus exists is very short—in practice, therefore, a supplementary prospectus is rarely required.

If the change (or new matter) arises after dealings have commenced, that will not require a new prospectus. The change will, though, affect the price at which the securities trade on the market—and it might give rise to questions of liability as discussed in **4.2.5.7** above if it adversely affects the value of the securities.

4.2.6 The Listing Rules

As we have seen, Part VI of FSMA gives the UKLA the power to make Listing Rules. The Listing Rules requirements apply equally to prospectuses and listing particulars. References in this section to prospectuses therefore apply to listing particulars as well. The Listing Rules contain provisions on the following:

(a) the general conditions to be satisfied by any issuer (LR ch. 3, see **4.2.6.2**);

(b) the specific contents requirements for prospectuses (LR ch. 6, see **4.2.6.3**);

(c) the process through which companies must go to obtain a listing for their securities (application procedure, LR ch. 7, see **4.2.6.5**);

(d) the requirements applying to the constitutional documents of companies seeking listing for their securities, i.e., articles of association (LR paras. 13.1 (a) and 13.9, see **3.3.1.2**);

(e) continuing obligations which listed companies must observe once listed (LR ch. 9, see **4.2.10**);

(f) rules applying to listed companies involved in acquisitions, sales and takeovers once listed (LR, ch. 10; these are *in addition* to the City Code on Takeovers and Mergers, and are dealt with in that context—see **5.6.4**);

(g) rules applying to the listing of the securities of overseas companies (LR ch. 17, see **4.2.9**);

(h) rules applying to the listing of eurobonds and other euro-currency debt securities (LR ch. 23; not covered in this book);

(i) some specific rules applying to certain types of companies seeking listing of their securities, such as property companies, investment trusts, public sector issuers and innovative high growth companies (LR chs 18–22 and ch. 25; not covered in this book).

4.2.6.1   Status and interpretation of the Listing Rules

The natural tendency of the lawyer is to treat a book of rules as an inflexible and unyielding set of limitations and prescriptions, particularly when, as here, the rules have been prepared under a statutory power. While an applicant must always assume that compliance with the rules is required, the UKLA is prepared to be flexible in its interpretation and application of the rules (though this may not always be to the applicant's advantage). Hence if a company finds it is unable to comply with a rule, the right course is not to assume that it is automatically disbarred from seeking a listing: its sponsor should discuss the point with the UKLA first to see whether there is scope for relaxing the rule in this case.

The Listing Rules expressly indicate where the UKLA is prepared to deviate from the stated rule, for example, where disclosure of information in the prospectus otherwise required by the Listing Rules would be contrary to the public interest (see LR para. 5.18 (b)).

In any event, the UKLA has the power to grant dispensations from the general duty of disclosure under s. 80 FSMA by virtue of s. 82 FSMA, where enforcing it would be contrary to the public interest (s. 82 (1)(a)), or seriously detrimental to the company (s. 82 (1)(b)).

The process of seeking 'derogations' from the rules is governed by LR para. 5.21. It is generally handled by the sponsors in writing, though may also be done by another adviser, such as the lawyer. They will prepare a list of derogations wanted by the company, which they submit to the UKLA for approval during the application process. On occasion, the UKLA is not prepared to make a concession and a compromise is needed. Generally, though, requests for derogations with suitable reasons will be received reasonably favourably.

In addition, when checking listing particulars against the UKLA's specific requirements (see **4.2.6.3**), requirements which are not relevant to the company should be listed in a letter to the UKLA. This 'non-applicables' letter is usually prepared by the sponsoring brokers. It is a quite normal part of the procedure (see LR para. 5.17).

Hence it is important to look at these requirements as a perimeter fence which the UKLA carefully polices but is prepared in appropriate circumstances to snip away at.

4.2.6.2   Conditions for listing

The general conditions for listing are set out in LR ch. 3. These conditions are prefaced by the UKLA's 'health warning' in para. 3.1 that it may apply special conditions to particular issuers where it considers this appropriate in the interests of protecting investors. The Listing Rules are therefore not a comprehensive guide to all the factors which decide suitability. Essentially the UKLA wants to preserve some element of flexibility in its admissions process.

The conditions for listing set out in LR ch. 3 are split into two main sections. The first section includes the conditions relating to the applicant (i.e. the company) and the second section details the conditions relating to the securities which are to be listed. The main conditions in each section are set out below.

(a) *Conditions relating to the company*

   (i)   *Incorporation*   The company must be duly incorporated and be operating in accordance with its memorandum and articles of association (or other constitutional documents if not a UK company). It must be a public company (LR para. 3.2 says that it may not be a private company or an 'old public company', which is one existing prior to December 1980 which has neither been reregistered as a public company or become a private company under. ss. 1–3 Companies Consolidation (Consequential Provisions) Act 1985).

   (ii)   *Accounts*   The company should have a three-year trading record and should present audited accounts for the latest three years (LR para. 3.3(a)). This is one of the requirements which the UKLA will relax in particular cases. Financial information submitted must be prepared and audited in accordance with UK, US or international accounting standards (LR para. 3.3(c)).

   (iii)   *Auditors*   The company's auditors must be independent and must supply written confirmation that they comply with guidelines on independence issued by their national accountancy bodies (LR para. 3.5).

   (iv)   *Type of business*   LR para. 3.6 requires a company either to be carrying on its main activity itself or through a subsidiary for the period covered by the accounts required in LR para. 3.3 or, if it is an investment company, it must comply with the conditions in LR ch.21. LR para.3.6A allows the UKLA to approve companies for listing which are outside the conditions in LR para.3.6 if it is satisfied that listing is in the interests of the company and its investors.

   (v)   *Directors*   The directors and senior management of the company must have the appropriate expertise and experience to run the company's businesses (LR para. 3.8) and such expertise must be disclosed in any listing particulars which are produced (LR paras 6.F.1, 6.F.2). A director may not have any actual or potential conflicts between his duty to the company and his private interests unless it can be shown that arrangements are in place to avoid detriment to the company. Any potential conflicts must be flagged up to the UKLA as soon as possible (LR para.3.9).

   (vi)   *Working capital*   In listing particulars arid certain circulars to shareholders, LR para. 3.10 requires the inclusion of a working capital statement (as detailed in LR paras 6.E.16 or 6.L.10) which confirms that the company has sufficient working capital for at least 12 months. This must also be confirmed by the company's sponsor in accordance with LR para. 2.18. Some companies with insufficient working capital may still be allowed to list their securities if the UKLA approves the proposals for any additional working capital required, which must be detailed in the listing particulars or circular. Assuming certain criteria are met as set out in LR para. 3.11, which satisfy the UKLA, banking, insurance or financial services companies are not required to include a working capital statement.

   (vii)   *Controlling shareholder*   The UKLA needs to be satisfied that the company is an independent entity and that it has no conflicts of interest with substantial shareholders. Where a shareholder has more than 30 per cent of the votes in the company, clearance will be needed before listing can proceed (LR paras 3.12 and 3.13).

(b) *Conditions relating to the securities to be listed*

   (i)   *Transferability*   The securities for which listing is sought must be freely transferable (LR para. 3.15). i.e. pre-emption rights on transfer of shares will have to be removed.

    (ii) *Market capitalisation* The minimum expected market value of equity securities for which listing is sought is £700,000 (LR para. 3.16(a)). In practice, companies seeking listing will require a market capitalisation significantly in excess of this in order to meet typical investor demand and satisfy the required advertising costs—a more usual value would be at least £5 million. There is, however, a provision under LR para 3.17 that the UKLA may admit securities of a lower value if it is satisfied that there will be an adequate market for them.

    (iii) *Twenty-five per cent of shares must be in public hands* At least 25 per cent of any class of shares for which listing is sought must (by the end of the offering) be in the hands of the public, i.e. not directors, major shareholders of the company or people connected with them, unless widespread distribution of the shares would still be possible with less than 25 per cent in the public's hands (LR paras 3.18 to 3.20). If the percentage of a class of shares in public hands, once listed, falls below 25 per cent the UKLA allows a 'reasonable' time to restore the percentage. However, if this does not happen there is a risk of suspension or cancellation of the listing (LR para.3.21).

    (iv) *Whole class* LR para. 3.22(a) requires that where there is an application for listing of securities, all the securities in that class must be listed.

    (v) *Electronic settlement* LR para. 3.27 requires that all new listed shares in UK companies must be eligible for electronic settlement. The UKLA does have the power to waive this requirement in exceptional circumstance, but this would be unusual. Electronic settlement is not a requirement for overseas companies (LR para. 17.14).

Additional conditions are contained in LR paras 3.23–3.28 which relate to warrants or options to subscribe for shares or for convertible securities. LR para 3.29 requires full disclosure of any non-cash fees paid to directors or advisers in connection with a listing, and the conditions required where an application is made to list certificates representing shares ars set out in LR paras 3.31–3.37.

(c) *Role of the sponsor in connection with the conditions required for listing*
    The main responsibilities of a sponsor are discussed at **3.3.4**. They are the 'middle-man' between the UKLA and the company. The UKLA expects them to be fully conversant with the rules and requirements in place for an application for listing and it is the sponsor's job to keep the company fully informed of such requirements and to explain the listing process to them, ensuring the smooth running of the listing application! However, there are a number of specific requirements that a sponsor must consider in connection with a listing of securities which are set out in LR Ch. 2 and these are considered below.

    (i) *Satisfaction of conditions* A sponsor must be sure that the issuer has satisfied all applicable conditions for listing and any other relevant requirements (LR para. 2.9(a)).

    (ii) *Schedule 1A* If the sponsor or any of its directors, partners or employees have any interests in the issuer, these must be declared to the UKLA on a Schedule 1A declaration (which is attached to the Listing Rules).

    (iii) *Schedule 4A* The sponsor must give confirmation to the UKLA in the form of a Schedule 4A declaration (which is appended to the Listing Rules) that all relevant documents in respect of the application for listing have been or will be supplied to the UKLA, all matters which should have been disclosed to the UKLA in respect of the application for listing have been disclosed in the listing particulars or in writing to the UKLA and that any other relevant requirements of the Listing Rules have been complied with. In addition, the sponsor must confirm in the Schedule 4A declaration that there has been compliance with specific paragraphs of the Listing Rules, a summary of this is set out below:

Directors   The sponsor must be sure that the directors of the issuing company understand their responsibilities and obligations as directors of a listed company and that these have been clearly explained to them by the sponsor or other applicable advisor (LR para. 2.13).

Financial reporting procedures   The directors of the company must give written confirmation to the sponsor that they have established procedures which enable them to make proper judgements of the financial position of the company and its prospects. The sponsor must be satisfied that the directors have given this confirmation after due and careful enquiry (LR para. 2.15).

Accountants' report   If no accountants' report is published in the case of a primary listing, the sponsor must be satisfied that such a report is not required (LR paras 2.16 and 12.7).

Financial information   The sponsor must obtain written confirmation that relevant financial information published in the listing particulars has been properly extracted from the company's accounting records and must be satisfied that such confirmation has been given after due and careful enquiry by the company (LR para. 2.20).

Working capital statement/profit forecast   Also in certain circumstances where a working capital statement or profit forecast is included in the listing particulars, the sponsor must be satisfied that the written confirmations from the company in these respects have been given after due and careful enquiry. (LR paras 2.18, 2.19).

The sponsor has additional responsibilities in relation to non-financial operating data for innovative high growth companies which are detailed in LR, Ch 25.

4.2.6.3   Specific requirements

The specific contents requirements for a prospectus or listing particulars are set out in LR ch. 6. The UKLA will require copies of the prospectus or particulars marked in the margin to indicate where particular items from LR ch. 6 have been dealt with (see LR para. 5.11). Partly for this reason and partly to be absolutely sure that the Listing Rules have been complied with, at some stage in the preparation of the prospectus or listing particulars, they will need to be cross-checked rigorously against LR ch. 6 to be certain that nothing is missing. The sponsoring brokers will prepare the marked-up draft for the UKLA, but it is sensible for the solicitors to check the document as well.

It is not possible to list all the specific contents requirements: only the main features have been covered. There are a number of points to bear in mind before studying the list below:

(a) Section 80 FSMA requires that, in addition to the information the Listing Rules demand, a prospectus shall contain 'all such information as investors and their professional advisers would reasonably require, and reasonably expect to find there, for the purpose of making an informed assessment of—

   (i)   the assets and liabilities, financial position, profits and losses, and prospects of the issuer of the securities; and

   (ii)   the rights attaching to those securities.'

(b) Section 80 thus imposes a general obligation to disclose in the prospectus or listing particulars facts material to an investment decision about the company's securities. It is an overriding duty *to which the detailed contents requirements in the Listing Rules are themselves subject.* The basic rule is: if it is material, it should be disclosed, whether LR ch. 6 requires it or not. When preparing a prospectus or listing particulars, it is therefore vital always to have the words of s. 80 in mind.

(c) Not all the specific contents listed in LR ch. 6 are required for every prospectus or set of listing particulars. The contents requirements are more relaxed for rights issues, other secondary issues and debt securities issues (see LR ch. 5, app. 1).

(d) Specific exemptions from the requirement to publish a prospectus or listing particulars may apply (see **4.2.5.5**).

(e) As mentioned in **1.5.1.3(a)** and **4.2.5.8(a)**, the financial promotions provisions in s. 21 FSMA state that a person must not, in the course of business, communicate an invitation or inducement to engage in investment activity (s. 2l(1) FSMA), unless that person is an authorised person or the content of the communication has been approved for the purposes of s. 21 by an authorised person (s. 21(2) FSMA), or the communication is exempt. A sponsor, as a person approved by the FSA, will be an authorised person and so may approve the issue of, or itself issue, any financial promotion. It must take care to comply with the FSA's Conduct of Business Rules which require the authorised person to be able to show that the communication is fair and not misleading. Details of the exemptions are set out in the Financial Services and Markets Act 2000 (Financial Promotion) Order 2001 (SI 2001/1335) as amended, (the 'FPO'). Article 6 FPO explains the definition of a communication for the purposes of financial promotion and makes the distinction between a communication being *made* to a person directly (e.g. in a telephone call or a letter) and a communication being *directed* at people generally (e.g. in a television broadcast). The exemptions relating to promotions in connection with a listing application and listing particulars are set out in arts 70 and 71 FPO respectively which, in the case of listing particulars, state that the financial promotion restriction does not apply to any non-real time communication which is included in them. Note that the distinction between real time and non-real time communications is set out in art. 7 FPO and the distinction between solicited and unsolicited real time communications is discussed in art. 8 FPO.

There are further exemptions applying to certain communications made *by* an exempt person (art. 16 FPO) or to communications made *to* investment professionals (art. 19 FPO).

(f) Companies and sponsors should also be aware of s. 98 FSMA when preparing for listing and should be careful to make sure any promotional information concerning the listing has been duly authorised before being released. Section 98 states that where listing particulars are to be published in connection with an application for listing, no advertisement or other information of a kind specified by the listing rules may be issued in the UK unless the contents of the advertisement or other information have been submitted to the competent authority which has approved the contents or authorised the issue of the advertisement without such approval.

There is no need to follow the order in which the requirements are listed in LR ch. 6, when preparing the prospectus or listing particulars.

The specific contents requirements are divided into a number of parts:

(a) *Part A: the company, its directors and professional advisers*
   (i)   Name and address (LR para. 6.C.1) of company, date (LR para. 6.C.3) and country of incorporation (LR para. 6.C.2);

(ii) names and functions of directors (LR para. 6.F.1(a));

(iii) names and addresses of the company's auditors (LR para. 6.A.4), bankers, sponsor (LR para. 6.A.8)—this requirement leads to the typical display of the team of advisers at the front of the prospectus or particulars;

(iv) directors' responsibility statement (LR para. 6.A.3). This should read:

> 'The directors of [the issuer], whose names appear on page [ ], accept responsibility for the information contained in this document. To the best of the knowledge and belief of the directors (who have taken all reasonable care to ensure that such is the case) the information contained in this document is in accordance with the facts and does not omit anything likely to affect the import of such information.'

This statement should also be given by those intending to become directors upon listing;

(v) statements of consent from experts (LR para. 6.A.9); where the prospectus or listing particulars contains a report from an expert, that expert must state his consent to its inclusion, and authorise the relevant part of the prospectus or listing particulars for the purposes of reg. 6(1)(e) Financial Services and Markets Act 2000 (Official Listing of Securities) Regulations 2001 (see **4.2.5.7**):

(b) *Part B: the company's securities, and the terms and conditions of any recent marketing of securities*
This is principally a description of the securities for which admission is being sought, their price and their rights (see, for example, LR para. 6.B.7).

(c) *Part C: general information about the company and its share and loan capital*

(i) Details of the share capital of the company (LR paras 6.C.9 and 6.C.10);

(ii) the company's group structure, if relevant (LR paras 6.C.17, 6.E.11 and 6.E.12);

(iii) substantial and controlling shareholders in the company (LR paras 6.C.16 and 6.C.15);

(iv) all material contracts entered into within the last two years will need to be disclosed (including consideration and terms and conditions) (LR para. 6.C.20); this does not extend to contracts entered into in the ordinary course of business;

(v) list of documents available for public inspection (LR para. 6.C.7): this includes the material contracts (LR para. 6.C.7(c)), the last two years' accounts (LR para. 6.C.7(g)), directors' service contracts (LR para. 6.C.7(c)) and the memorandum and articles of association of the company (LR para. 6.C.7(a)).

Derogations from the need to put the material contracts on display are quite often sought. The UKLA does countenance this under LR, para. 5.22. It will rarely permit a company to exclude a particular contract altogether, but may allow it to delete from the public eye any sensitive or confidential commercial information, in particular the amount of consideration passing under a contract.

(d) *Part D: information on the company's activities*

(i) A description of principal activities (LR para. 6.D.1);

(ii) an analysis of sales by geographical area and product group (LR para. 6.D.3);

(iii) details of land, buildings and principal establishments (LR para. 6.D.4);

(iv) policy on research and development (LR para. 6.D.7);

(v) number of employees (LR para. 6.D.10);

(vi) material investments in other companies (LR paras 6.D.12 and 6.D.13);

(vii) information on any pending or threatened legal proceedings which may yet, or in the past year did, represent a significant liability (LR para. 6.D.8).

(e) *Part E: financial information*

This information is to be provided for the entire group of companies to which the issuer belongs (LR para. 6.E.3). An accountants' report on a new applicant for listing is not required, unless the last three years' audited accounts no longer present a complete picture because of material changes (LR paras 6.E.9 and 12.1). A comparative table for the last three financial years can be used instead. The table should compare profits and losses, assets, cashflow, accounting policies and notes for those three years (LR paras 12.17 and 12.19). If an accountants' report is not needed, the sponsor will need to confirm this in writing to the LSE (LR para. 2.16), and the reporting accountants will have to confirm that the three years' accounts were satisfactorily prepared, and that the comparative table is a proper extract from them (LR paras 12.17 (c) and 12.18). The detailed provisions on these accounts and tables is contained in LR, ch. 12. The solicitors' function is to check that everything required by ch. 6, part E, and ch. 12 has been included. The information required by Part E, whether in the form of a comparative table or an accountants' report, is:

(i)   statement of any significant change in the financial position of the company or group since its last financial statement;

(ii) statement of current indebtedness;

(iii) statement of company or group's contingent liabilities.

Part E also requires the directors to state that the company's working capital is sufficient (LR para. 6.E.16). Working capital is available cash and facilities less immediate cash requirements (e.g., salaries). The accountants will invariably produce a report on the adequacy of the working capital to give the directors the comfort they need before making this statement, though this report will not be reproduced in the listing particulars: it is a private document addressed to the directors of the company alone. The investment bank or sponsoring member firm will also have to confirm to the UKLA (LR, para. 2.18) that the working capital statement has been arrived at by the directors after due and careful inquiry and the person or institution providing the finance has confirmed that the finance exists.

(f) *Part F: the management*

(i)   directors' remuneration for the previous and coming years (LR paras 6.F.3 and 6.F.11);

(ii) details of directors' existing or proposed service contracts (LR paras 6.F.12 and 16.11);

(iii) directors' (and their families') interests in the company's securities (LR paras 6.F.4 and 6.F.5);

(iv) details of employee share option schemes (LR para. 6.F.8).

(g) *Part G: information on recent developments and prospects of the company's group*

If the company wishes, it may choose to include a profit forecast in the listing particulars. If it does, that profit forecast is required by LR para. 6.G.2 to contain:

(i)   a report by the accountants on the accounting policies and calculations used in arriving at the forecast (LR para. 12.24);

(ii) the assumptions on which the forecast is based (for example, that inflation will not rise above 5 per cent next year) (LR para. 12.27); and

(iii) a statement from the sponsor that the forecast was made by the company after due and careful enquiry (LR para. 2.19).

Trends affecting the company or group over the next year (in terms of prices, demand for its products, costs, new factors affecting its particular trading activities) will in any event have to be reported on (see LR para. 6.G.1).

4.2.6.4 Typical layout of a prospectus or listing particulars

A prospectus or listing particulars does not have to follow a regimented pattern, only to 'provide factual information in words and figures, in as easily analysable and comprehensible a form as possible' (LR para. 5.7). In addition, the Listing Rules restrict the use of some techniques for presenting information: for instance, the prospectus or particulars should not contain pictures, graphs or illustrations unless the UKLA is satisfied this is the only way to present the information (LR para. 5.7). There are also restrictions on the use of text and illustrations on the cover of the document (LR para. 5.8).

In spite of the relative latitude which issuers have in the construction of their prospectus or listing particulars, they do typically follow a particular order.

Front page

'Headline' for the offer and number of shares to be issued.

Statement that an application for listing has been made to the UKLA.

Responsibility statement.

Statement that the prospectus or listing particulars has been delivered to the Registrar of Companies under s. 83 FSMA.

Other wording required to satisfy US securities legislation (if there are US shareholders or any likelihood of the offer being made in the US).

Following pages

Contents, definitions.

Share capital statement—this must appear on the first page.

Indebtedness statement—this must appear on the first page.

Expected timetable.

Directors and advisers.

Key information: this is a summary of the key commercial and financial facts about the issuer, the reasons for the offer and its structure.

Commercial information: the issuer's industry, history, performance and trading record, and strategy.

Management team.

Reasons for the offer and offer structure.

Profit forecast, followed by accountants' and issuing house's letters on the forecast.

Accountants' report.

Information required by the Listing Rules and not included elsewhere (generally referred to as 'additional information' or 'statutory and general information'): details about the company's share capital, subsidiaries, constitution, directors and their interests, share schemes, pensions, premises, and arrangements for the offer; most importantly, statements regarding material contracts, litigation, sufficiency of working capital and documents available for inspection.

Terms and conditions for applying, and public application form.

4.2.6.5 What happens to the prospectus or listing particulars?

This section covers the procedure an issuer must go through with its prospectus or listing particulars and related documents to apply for listing. Most of what follows is derived from LR ch. 7, and assumes that the company is not yet listed. If the company already has a listing, the application process is somewhat more relaxed.

There are a number of stages any applicant must go through:

(a) *10-day documents*

LR para. 5.9 lists the documents which must be submitted to the UKLA at least 10 clear business days before the date of intended publication of the particulars (which will be the date the offer is actually launched). However, where a new applicant is seeking a listing or there are complex issues to be resolved, the draft prospectus should be submitted at least 20 clear business days before intended publication (LR para. 5.10). The most important of these are:

(i)   the draft prospectus or set of particulars (LR para. 5.9 (a));

(ii) in the case of a new applicant, letters from the reporting accountants that the company's accounts have been audited in accordance with international accounting standards or standards applied in the UK or the US, and that the comparative table (if relevant) is properly extracted from the audited accounts (LR paras 5.9(n) and 12.18), and, if there is one, reporting on the profit forecast (LR para. 12.24);

(iii) the derogation and 'non-applicables' letters (LR paras 5.9(j) and 5.17) (see **4.2.6.1**).

If, as is usually the case, revised drafts of the particulars are produced after the original draft has been lodged with the UKLA, the UKLA should be sent the new drafts, marked up to show the changes (LR para. 5.11).

(b) *48-hour documents*

At least two business days before the company's application is heard by the UKLA, a number of documents should be sent to it. The most important are:

(i)   the AFA form required by LR para. 7.5(a) (application for admission to listing: LR sch. 3A);

(ii) final copies of the prospectus or listing particulars (LR para. 7.5(b)) (one copy signed and dated on behalf of the directors);

(iii) the form in which the prospectus or listing particulars is to be published in the press (LR para. 7.5 (c)) (see below).

The full list of 48-hour documents is at LR para. 7.5. Paragraph 7.5(g) requires additional documents to be submitted by new applicants.

(c) *Approval*

The prospectus or particulars must be formally approved by the UKLA before publication. LR para. 5.12, contains another list of documents which must be submitted to the UKLA in final form before formal approval will be given. They include, by virtue of LR para. 5.12 (b)(i), a declaration by the sponsor in the form set out in LR sch. 4A. In this, the sponsor is required, *inter alia* to declare that the directors of the company have had their responsibilities explained to them (see LR para. 2.13). In addition, in the case of a new applicant, the sponsor must declare (if relevant) that an accountants' report is not required (LR para. 2.16) and that it has received written confirmation that the directors have established procedures which provide a reasonable basis for them to make proper judgements as to the financial position of the company (LR para. 2.15).

At the hearing of the application for admission, permission for listing is granted and the UKLA stamps and dates the prospectus or listing particulars. As discussed in **4.2.3**, listing becomes effective (usually the next day) when admission is notified through the electronic systems used by the UKLA for communicating with the public (LR para. 7.1).

(d) *Registration*

This is not required by the UKLA, but by s. 83 FSMA, which makes it a criminal offence not to have a prospectus or listing particulars registered by the Registrar of Companies on or before publication. Therefore, as soon as you have your UKLA approval, you race the prospectus or particulars to Companies House as they will be formally published the next day. Also note that the prospectus or particulars itself must say it is to be registered in this way.

(e) *Publication*

LR para. 8.1, states that a prospectus or listing particulars must not be published until it has received the formal approval of the UKLA. Once approval has been given the publication requirements of the Listing Rules must be observed (LR para. 8.2). The prospectus or particulars must be made available to the public at the UKLA Document Viewing Facility and also at the registered office of the company for 14 days after admission of the securities to listing (LR paras 8.4 and 8.5). Thereafter, the requirements depend on the type of offering which the company is making.

The basic requirement is that companies whose shares are not already listed must publish a formal notice in one national newspaper (LR para. 8.7) A formal notice (known in practice as a 'box advertisement') contains brief details of the issue. LR para. 8.10, details the required content of a formal notice.

If the company is not already listed and is marketing its securities by way of an *offer for sale* or an *offer for subscription*, it may elect instead to publish an offer notice, mini-prospectus or full listing particulars in a national newspaper (LR para. 8.7). An offer notice (LR para. 8.11) is a formal notice together with an application form attached. A mini-prospectus (LR paras 8.12 and 8.13) is essentially a set of summary listing particulars which can be used in addition to a full prospectus or set of particulars. In practice, they have only been used in major offerings such as privatisations.

If the company is already listed, the publication requirements are as stated in the first paragraph above, save that, for offers to existing shareholders, the prospectus or listing particulars should be circulated to them (see LR para. 8.14).

LR paras 8.23 to 8.25 also require an issuer to obtain the approval or authorisation of the UKLA for any other advertisements it produces as part of the offer.

(f) *Documents to be lodged later*

The UKLA also requires an issuer to follow up admission of its securities to listing with a final bundle of documents (LR para. 7.8), principally a declaration from the company in the form of LR sch. 6, that all legal requirements in connection with the issue have been satisfied.

The process is therefore this:

(a) 10-day documents or 20-day if a new applicant;

(b) 48-hour documents;

(c) approval;

(d) registration;

(e) publication;

(f) documents to be lodged later.

You should refer to the timetable in **3.7** to see how the whole process fits together. At the end of this long and arduous route through the maze of the Listing Rules, the prospectus or listing particulars will be in the hands of potential investors. The regulatory purpose is now over: the securities will have been admitted to listing and dealings will have commenced, and the marketing function—selling the shares to investors— now begins.

4.2.7   Admission to trading on the LSE

Whilst a company and its advisors are carrying out the processes detailed above to obtain admission to the Official List, they also need to take steps to obtain admission to trading on the LSE. The route to admission to trading is set out in the LSE's Admission and Disclosure Standards (see SEADS Part 1, para. 2). Companies are encouraged to approach the LSE at the earliest possible stage to discuss their application and, in any event, no later than when they first contact the UKLA as regards their application for listing.

New applicants are required to provide the LSE with a company contact, a senior director or employee, and are encouraged to appoint a nominated representative from another organisation (this is likely to be the sponsor). These parties will liaise with the LSE throughout the process.

A timetable for admission must be agreed with the LSE. This must operate such that admission to trading occurs at the same time as admission to the Official List.

The company must submit the following documents to the LSE no later than two business days (except in the case of new applicants who are listing shares, who are required by SEADS Part 2, para 2.5 to submit Form 1, the Application for Admission of Securities to trading, at least ten business days before the day on which the application for admission to trading is due to be considered) prior to the day on which the application for admission to trading is to be considered:

(a) the application form for admission to trading signed by a company officer (SEADS Part 2, para. 2.6(a));

(b) two copies of the prospectus or listing particulars (SEADS Part 2, para. 2.6(b)); and

(c) a copy of the board resolution allotting the securities or authorising the issue (SEADS Part 2, para. 2.6(c)).

There is a fee payable for admission (SEADS Part 2, para. 2.4), calculated on a scale in accordance with the securities being issued. Following admission, the LSE must be provided with a statement of the number of securities issued (SEADS Part 2, para. 2.7).

The company is subject to a number of continuing requirements under the LSE's Standards (SEADS Part 2, para. 3), which are the equivalent to the continuing obligations in paras 9.1 to 9.9 of the Listing Rules (see **4.2.10**). Should a company fail to comply in any respect with the Standards, the LSE has powers of private and public censure (SEADS Part 2, para. 3.21 (a)), suspension of trading (SEADS Part 1, para. 3, and Part 2, para. 3.14) and cancellation of trading (SEADS Part 1, para. 3, and Part 2, para. 3.21(b)).

4.2.8   Shelf registration

This system was introduced in 1999. The detailed procedure for shelf registration is set out in paras 5.35–5.41 of the Listing Rules. Shelf registration allows a company that has been listed for at least twelve months to publish on an annual basis a shelf document (LR para. 5.35), which contains much of the information required in listing particulars.

If a company, during the next twelve months, wishes to issue and list further shares, all that is then required is the publication of a short issue note (LR para. 5.36). The shelf document and the issue note together comprise the prospectus and listing particulars for the purpose of the new issue. The required respective content of the shelf document and issue note is set out in Table 1A in the appendix to ch. 5 of the Listing Rules. This table, as with the other tables in this appendix, makes reference to the relevant paragraphs of LR ch. 6, which describe the content of a prospectus or listing particulars.

Three copies of a shelf document must be submitted to the UKLA at least ten clear business days before the relevant intended publication date (20 clear days if there are any complex issues to be resolved) (LR para. 5.38). As with a prospectus or listing particulars, the draft must be annotated as required by LR para. 5.11. The shelf document must be formally approved before publication. The UKLA publishes the document on its website for so long as the document remains current. A shelf document will remain current until the earlier of:

(a) the publication of the issuer's next annual report and accounts (LR para. 5.35 (a));

(b) twelve months from the date of publication on the website (LR para. 5.35 (b)); or

(c) the date at which the issuer requests that the document be removed from the website (LR para. 5.35 (c)).

When an issue of shares is to be made, the issue note must be submitted at least ten clear business days before the intended publication date (LR paras 5.40 and 5.9). It must also be annotated in accordance with LR para. 5.11. Assuming it is approved by the UKLA (LR para. 5.12), the issue note must then be published in accordance with LR ch. 8, in the same way as a prospectus or listing particulars. Again, admission of the shares to trading will have to be sought from the LSE.

4.2.9 Overseas companies and the listing requirements

The basic conditions required for listing (see **4.2.6.2**) apply equally to overseas companies (i.e., companies incorporated outside the UK), subject to the modifications contained in LR ch. 17.

General conditions (described in LR paras 17.2 to 17.4) are essentially that the company is listed overseas and that its accounts have been prepared in accordance with appropriate accounting standards. Its listing particulars may incorporate other documents by reference, such as the overseas equivalent of listing particulars, provided they are in English or are accompanied by a translation into English (LR para. 17.5). The specific requirements thereafter depend on whether the listing in London for the overseas company will be its main (or primary) listing, or secondary to its overseas listing. For a company seeking its main or primary listing in London, the specific requirements are much as for other issuers (see LR paras 17.11 to 17.13). For companies whose main listing is overseas and which want a secondary listing in London, the specific listing requirements are modified (see LR paras 17.14 to 17.21A). The principal differences are that the sponsor does not have to report on the company's working capital position (LR para. 17.15), and the subsequent continuing obligations are adjusted significantly (LR paras 17.22 to 17.67). Any company (UK or foreign) with its primary listing overseas must additionally show that it is in compliance with the requirements of the relevant stock exchange (LR para. 17.19 (a)(i)) and competent authority or equivalent regulatory body which regulates it (LR para. 17.19 (a)(ii)) if it is seeking a listing in the UK as well.

The essential point to note is that, subject to these modifications, the general conditions and specific requirements for a prospectus or listing particulars otherwise apply as for UK companies. In addition, the overseas company's listed securities must be admitted to trading by the LSE (LR para. 17.67A).

4.2.9.1   Mutual recognition

Mutual recognition of prospectuses and listing particulars is now required throughout the EU. This means that listing particulars or a prospectus produced and approved in one EU Member State for a securities offer must be accepted as listing particulars or a prospectus in any other EU Member State, provided they are translated and produced within three months of the listing in the first Member State (see LR paras 17.68(b), 17.68(e), 17.72(b) and 17.22(d)). It is now possible to use the mutual recognition procedure even where no application for listing in the UK is intended, so that a UK-approved prospectus can be used in other Member States. The conditions for mutual recognition are set out in LR para. 17.68.

Thus the LSE must accept as listing particulars or a prospectus a document in English for a Greek-registered company approved as such by the Paris Bourse, so long as the particulars or prospectus are not out of time. It is not then relevant how far the document complies with the specific requirements of LR ch. 6: the fact of its approval as listing particulars or a prospectus in another Member State is generally enough. The only exception is where derogations obtained by the company in its first Member State (of which the UKLA must be informed) are not available in the UK (see LR para. 17.68 (f)).

Paragraphs 17.69, 17.70, and 17.71, and also 17.73, 17.73A and 17.74 of the Listing Rules also set out the application procedure for companies taking advantage of entry to the market in this way. In essence they need to produce 10-day documents consisting of evidence of approval from the other EU Member State, and copies of the approved prospectus or listing particulars together with details of derogations obtained (see LR paras 17.68(f), 17.70, 17.73 and 17.73A).

4.2.9.2   Exempt listing documents

Where securities have been listed in another Member State of the European Union for the past three years, or where the securities have been listed for less than three years but the relevant local stock exchange confirms the issuer has complied with its rules during that time, the LSE will grant a listing in London under LR para. 5.23A(b) and ch. 5, app. 2, on production by the issuer of an exempt listing document in English.

The exempt listing document must include any equivalent to a prospectus or listing particulars produced by the issuer in the past year (LR ch. 5, app. 2, para. 2 (c)), the latest published accounts (LR ch. 5, app. 2, para. 2 (a)), together with information about the management structure (LR ch. 5, app. 2, para. 2 (h)(i)), securities and capital (LR ch. 5, app. 2, para. 2 (h)(ii)), and major shareholders (LR ch. 5, app. 2, para. 2 (h)(iii)).

There can be no marketing of the securities through an exempt listing document—in other words, the listing works like an introduction (see **3.5.8**). The exempt listing document will need to be published in the same way as a prospectus or listing particulars (see **4.2.6.4**) (LR para. 5.25).

4.2.10   Impact of European legislation

The European Council adopted the Financial Services Action Plan ("FSAP") in 1998 with the aim of creating a pan-European market developing open and secure markets for retail financial services and eliminating the tax obstacles to financial market integration. It hoped that this would then promote competitiveness within the European economy and at the same time lower the cost of raising capital for all types of companies. The FSAP is due to be implemented in Member States by 2005.

The report produced by the Lamfalussy Committee (which was established in 2000 to assess the regulation of securities markets in the European Union) recommended the development of new European legislation which would reshape the structure of the capital markets throughout Europe.

Four major areas of legislation to be adopted following the Lamfalussy report are:

(a) the Prospectus Directive: a directive detailing the contents of a prospectus to be published when securities are offered to the public or admitted to trading;

(b) the Transparency Directive: updating the rules of disclosure of information by companies whose securities are traded on regulated markets;

(c) the Market Abuse Directive: a directive on combating insider dealing and market manipulation;

(d) the IAS Regulations: regulations on the application of International Accounting Standards.

4.2.10.1   EU Prospectus Directive

The Prospectus Directive was adopted by the European Commission in July 2003 and was published in the Official Journal on 31 December 2003. Under this Directive, the European Commission is seeking to create a single market for financial services. The primary aim of this Directive is to allow companies to offer their securities throughout the European Union using a single prospectus approved by one regulator, without needing additional approvals or clearances in other countries. Once a prospectus meeting these requirements has been approved in one EU Member State, the same document may then be used in any other state for issues there.

The Directive is a maximum harmonisation directive which means that Member States may not impose any additional requirements than those stated in the directive. There has been a certain amount of concern within the UK (which operates one of the more stringent regimes within the EU) that the minimum requirements which must be included in a single European prospectus may not be considered sufficient for the UK regime. Recommendations have been issued by the Committee of European Securities Regulators to the European Commission comprising the proposed minimum disclosure obligations for various types of companies and securities, including those listing shares. However, it is likely that the final form of these disclosure requirements will be subject to further consultation before they are introduced into law in Europe.

The proposed rules include lesser requirements for companies raising smaller amounts of capital, following concerns regarding the costs of meeting the standard of disclosure required. Overall, however, the intention is that the Directive should provide not only an integrated market but lower the costs of raising capital by simplifying the legal system for doing so within the EU.

Member States must bring the required laws into force by 1 July 2005 and the contents requirements for listing particulars contained in the Listing Rules will have to be amended to reflect the requirements of the Prospectus Directive.

4.2.10.2   The Transparency Directive

The Transparency Directive is a minimum harmonisation directive, which means that it sets out minimum requirements, which must be observed. A Member State is then able to impose additional requirements if it feels these are necessary within its regime. These are called 'super-equivalence' provisions.

Areas covered by this Directive include the minimum requirements for periodic disclosure of financial information, disclosure of significant interests in shares, the dissemination of information to shareholders and others and giving companies a choice as to the language in which they make disclosure.

There has been much focus on the requirement for companies to disclose financial information. The initial draft required quarterly disclosure, but this has since been diluted and now requires a company to publish interim management statements between the annual report and half-yearly report which should include a narrative description of the financial position of the company and the impact of material events on such financial position.

Once the final Transparency Directive is published, the UK will be required to amend continuing obligations requirements in the Listing Rules to reflect the provisions of the Directive (see **4.2.11.11** below).

4.2.10.3   The Market Abuse Directive

This Directive, which was adopted in April 2003, is required to be implemented into the laws of Member States by 12 October 2004. In June 2004 HM Treasury and the FSA published a joint consultation document ('MAD JCD') on proposals to implement the Market Abuse Directive in the UK. This contains draft regulations (at Annex A of MAD JCD) and states that sections of the FSA Handbook would be amended including the Code of Market Conduct, the Price Stabilising Rules, the UK Listing Rules and the Conduct of Business Sourcebook (see Annexes C and D of MAD JCD). Paragaph 1.13 of MAD JCD adds that HM Treasury and the FSA are aiming to finalise the legislative and rule changes required by the end of November 2004. Once they are finalised, industry will be given approximately three months to adapt to the changes before they are enforced. Under this Directive, listed companies will be under an obligation to ensure that people with access to inside information are aware of, and acknowledge, the legal and regulatory duties as well as the sanctions that may be incurred through the misuse or unauthorised disclosure of such information. The Directive requires listed companies to establish and keep up to date a list of all persons who have access to inside information whether on an habitual basis or on an occasional basis. This list must be a complete record for the past five years.

4.2.10.4   The IAS Regulations

These Regulations will require listed companies that currently prepare consolidated accounts to prepare audited accounts in accordance with International Financial Reporting Standards from 1 January 2005 (with some exceptions until 2007). In conjunction with the Transparency Directive, listed companies will also be required to prepare half yearly financial information in accordance with International Financial Reporting Standards issued by the International Accounting Standards Board.

4.2.11   Continuing obligations

Continuing obligations are the obligations which a company listed on the Official List must observe. Failure to comply may lead to a suspension of listing. The obligations are contained in LR ch. 9 and equivalent provisions form part of the LSE's Admission and Disclosure Standards. The UKLA also publishes a Continuing Obligations Guide at Appendix 3 to its Listing Authority Guidance Manual. The Continuing Obligations Guide ('COG') is designed to assist companies, sponsors and directors to better understand and meet their obligations under the Listing Rules and highlights key obligations. One of the principal objects of the Continuing Obligations, as the Listing Rules make clear, is 'the maintenance of an orderly market in securities and to ensure that all users of the market have simultaneous access to the same information'. This is so that investors may deal in shares with the benefit of up-to-date information on a company and its securities whilst also ensuring even and fair treatment towards all investors.

The principal requirements of the continuing obligations are outlined below.

4.2.11.1   Avoidance of a false market—disclosure obligations

In particular, this requires the prompt disclosure to a Regulatory Information Service (as defined in LR sch. 12) of information necessary for the appraisal of the company's value (LR para. 9.1). It is supported by a wide range of separate provisions requiring announcements on (for example) acquisitions and disposals, major new operational developments, board decisions changing the general character or nature of the company's business, dividends, annual profits, any changes in capital structure, and interests in the company's securities. LR para. 9.2 imposes a requirement to make an announcement if there is a change in the company's financial condition or performance or in the company's expectation of its performance, and that change is likely to lead to a substantial movement in the company's share price. This obligation to disclose is satisfied by dispatching an announcement to an RIS. The RIS is responsible for receiving and publishing all announcements it receives from listed companies and can receive announcements electronically, ensuring they are processed quickly. LR para 9.15 and para 2.9 COG give guidance as to what to do if an RIS is not open at a time when disclosure is required.

Subject to certain exceptions (see reference to LR paras 9.4 and 9.5 below) no information requiring public disclosure pursuant to a continuing obligation may be disclosed to any third party in advance of its public release (LR para 9.6). However, LR paras 9.4 and 9.5 allow a company to give price sensitive information to certain recipients without notifying an RIS—usually in the course of negotiation of transactions. These recipients include the company's advisors, people with whom it is negotiating, trades union representatives, government departments or other statutory bodies. The UKLA and the LSE can require a company to issue an announcement where it is apparent that leaked information has resulted in sharp movements in its share price. The LSE can also halt trading in the shares and, if the company fails to make an announcement in good time, the LSE may make its own announcement or suspend the shares from trading altogether. Accordingly, it is good practice for a company to issue a holding announcement as soon as there appears to be a leak about a transaction or development relating to the company, even if the company is not ready to issue a full and detailed announcement.

It is possible for a company to be granted a dispensation by the UKLA from disclosing certain information to an RIS if such disclosure might prejudice the company's legitimate interests (LR para. 9.8).

The UKLA has published a Price Sensitive Information Guide ('PSI Guide') as Appendix 2 to its Listing Authority Guidance Manual. The PSI Guide is designed to assist companies, directors and others dealing with price-sensitive information to understand the scope of the disclosure requirements, identify price-sensitive information, develop a framework for handling such information in various situations and make decisions on how and when to disclose price-sensitive information.

In addition to the general obligation, the Listing Rules specify a number of other matters requiring public disclosure. Examples of these can be seen in LR para. 9.10 in relation to notifications concerning the company's capital. These include:

(a) LR para. 9. 10 and para. 6.21 COG:
- alterations to share capital;
- new issues of debt securities;
- changes of rights attaching to securities;

- redemption or drawing of listed securities;
- basis of allotment of any publicly offered securities;
- temporary documents of title;
- issues affecting conversion rights;
- results of new issues.

(b) LR para.9.11 and 9.12:

- information disclosed to the company relating to major interests in its share capital under ss. 198–208 CA (also see para. 4.15 COG);
- information received pursuant to s. 212 CA regarding interests in the share capital which had not been disclosed under ss. 198–208 but ought to have been (also see para. 4.16 COG).

The prevention of a false market in the company's securities also requires equivalence of information about the company as between different exchanges on which the company is listed, and equality of treatment for holders of securities of the same class (LR para. 9.9) also see Part 2, COG.

4.2.11.2   Informing the shareholders about the company and its securities

The company must communicate with its shareholders about, amongst other things, the allocation and payment of dividends and the issue of new securities. For example, a company must obtain shareholder consent before any major subsidiary undertaking of the company makes any issue for cash of equity securities so as materially to dilute the company's percentage interest in the subsidiary (LR para. 9.22). It should also notify a RIS of circulars and notices issued to shareholders and resolutions passed by them, of dates and decisions of board meetings, of any changes to the rights of securities and of the results of any new issue of securities.

A listed company is required to inform all its shareholders of the holding of meetings which they are entitled to attend. The company must also ensure that shareholders are given the opportunity to vote in person or by proxy. Any information or facilities necessary to enable shareholders to exercise any other rights, including those in respect of the payment of dividends and the issue, exchange or repayment of securities, must also be made available by the company (LR para. 9.24).

4.2.11.3   Other miscellaneous continuing obligations

These include:

(a) *Further issues of shares*   When further shares of the same class as the shares already listed are allotted by a listed company, application for listing of the new shares must be made before, or not more than one month after, allotment (LR para. 9.33).

(b) *Controlling shareholder*   Where a listed company has a controlling shareholder, it must always carry on its business independently of such shareholder and all transactions between them must be at arm's length on a commercial basis (LR para. 9.34).

(c) *Shares in public hands*   At least 25 per cent of any class of listed equity shares must be in the hands of the public, and the company must inform the UKLA in writing as soon as it becomes aware that such percentage ever falls below 25 per cent (LR para. 9.37 and paras 6.19, 6.20 COG).

4.2.11.4   Transactions by listed companies—LR ch. 10 and Part 7 COG

The Listing Rules govern the acquisition and disposal of shares and assets by listed companies. It classifies these transactions according to the comparative size of the transaction to the company itself, using a number of 'percentage ratio tests' known as 'Class Tests'. Such tests are based on assets, profits, turnover, consideration to market capitalisation and gross capital of the company which is the subject matter of the transaction (LR para. 10.5). Depending on the ratio, the company may have to send a circular to shareholders and may need to convene a meeting to obtain shareholder approval or issue an announcement. LR ch. 10 gives details of the calculation of each of the class tests and also sets out the requirements of the company depending on which class a transaction falls under. Also see **5.6.4.** and Part 7, COG. Where any acquisition amounts to a reverse takeover (i.e. the ratio amounts to 100 per cent or more) of another unlisted company, trading in the company's securities will be suspended. The company must prepare a Class 1 circular and obtain shareholder approval and then a new application to list must be made.

4.2.11.5 Related party transactions—LR ch. 11

The Listing Rules also govern transactions with related parties. A related party is:

(a) a shareholder who controls or controlled within the last twelve months the exercise of 10 per cent or more of the voting shares at a general meeting ('substantial share- holder');

(b) a director or shadow director (either currently or within the last twelve months) of the company or its subsidiaries; or

(c) an associate or (a) or (b) above (LR para. 11.1(b)).

In relation to a substantial shareholder or director who is an individual, 'associate' covers (i) family members, (ii) the trustees of any trust of which that individual or his family members are beneficiaries, and (iii) any company in which such individual or his family are able to exercise 30 per cent or more of the voting rights at a general meeting or have the ability to appoint or remove directors holding a majority of voting rights at board meetings (LR para. 11.1(d)).

In relation to a substantial shareholder which is a company, "associate" covers subsidiary and parent companies and any company whose directors are accustomed to act in accordance with the substantial shareholder's directions.

If a company (or any member of its group) proposes to enter into a transaction with a related party then the company must obtain the approval of its shareholders prior to entering into the transaction (or if it is expressed to be conditional on such approval), prior to completion of the transaction and ensure that the related party abstains from voting on the relevant transaction (LR para. 11.4).

4.2.11.6 Accounts

There are detailed provisions on information which the company's annual accounts, preliminary and interim results must contain. The accounts must be audited by inde- pendent accountants of good standing and the auditors' report which must be annexed to the accounts should confirm that a true and fair appraisal of the state of affairs, profit and loss and changes in the group's financial position has been presented in the accounts. The provisions to be contained in the results and accounts are set out in LR paras 12.40 to 12.59 (also see Part 6, COG). These include explanations of material differences between published results and forecasts, explanations of any significant departures from applica- ble accounting standards (see **2.4.3**), and interests in the company or its securities held by any director or substantial shareholder (see **2.2.1**).

The company must publish half-yearly reports for the first six months of a financial year. These must contain, among financial details such as turnover, profits, dividends, tax and extraordinary items, information to enable investors to make an informed assessment of the trend of the group's activities and profits, and a reference to the group's prospects for the full financial year. The basis used for the presentation of half-yearly reports must be consistent with that used for the annual accounts. The half-yearly report must be published within 90 days of the half-year and must also:

(a) include an explanatory statement relating to the group's activities and profit or loss during the period;

(b) enable a comparison to be made with the corresponding period of the previous financial year; and

(c) as far as possible refer to the group's prospects in the current financial year.

The interim statement does not, however, need to be audited, though that fact must be stated.

4.2.11.7   Directors' obligations and the Model Code (LR ch.16 and Part 3 COG)

(a) *Directors' responsibilities*   Directors and proposed directors are responsible, under FSMA, for information contained in their company's listing particulars or supplementary listing particulars and must make a statement that they accept responsibility for such information (LR para. l6.1 and para. 3.1, COG). A listed company must ensure its directors individually and collectively accept responsibility for the company's compliance with the Listing Rules (LR para. 16.2 and para. 3.2, COG).

(b) *Directors' details*   A company must include details of each of its directors and, where relevant, members of its senior management in any listing particulars it publishes. It must also notify an RIS of various directors' details as set out in LR para. 16.4 and para. 3.4, COG as well as any changes to the board of the company. Each director's service contract must be made available for inspection at the AGM and at the company's registered office. Such contracts will include details of the director's remuneration, profit sharing arrangements and other relevant benefits.

(c) *Notification of directors' interests*   A company must notify an RIS of any information disclosed to it in accordance with s. 324 CA (director's duty to disclose shareholdings in his own company). In addition there are a number of other continuing obligations under the Model Code which is set out as an appendix to LR ch. 16 and which constrains the freedom of directors and those associated with them to deal in their company's shares. The Listing Rules require companies to adopt a dealing code for their directors at least as strict as the Model Code. A more detailed discussion of the provisions of the Model Code can be found at **2.2.2.1**. Also see Part 5 COG.

4.2.11.8   Circulars

Companies are required to send explanatory circulars to, and, depending on the size of the transaction, obtain the approval of, shareholders when large acquisitions or disposals, takeovers or mergers are proposed. Details of the required contents of such circulars are contained in LR ch. 14.

4.2.11.9   Corporate governance

A number of committees have investigated corporate governance issues in recent years. Higgs is the latest in January 2003 and that committee took the opportunity to agree with the Smith report (on audit matters, January 2003) at the same time. Higgs was preceded by Hampel (January 1998), Greenbury (July 1995) and Cadbury (December 1992). The resulting 'Combined Code' on corporate governance is appended to the Listing Rules and applies to listed companies incorporated in the UK. FSA Consultation Paper CP203 (the review of the listing regime, published in October 2003) has proposed that the Listing Rules be amended to extend compliance with the Combined Code to all overseas companies with a primary listing in the UK.

The Combined Code   The Listing Rules require that a UK listed company provides in its annual report and accounts a narrative on how it has applied the principles of good corporate governance set out in the Combined Code and a statement as to whether or not it has complied with the Combined Code provisions (LR para. 12.43A). The requirements of the Combined Code are set out in more detail at **2.2.3**.

4.2.11.10 Overseas companies

The continuing obligations regime is modified for foreign companies whose primary listing is not in London. The detailed provisions are in LR paras 17.22 to 17.67. They cover the same areas as for the ordinary obligations (for example, avoiding a false market, public announcements, accounts), except that they are adapted to fit in with the foreign company's domestic regulations—so, for instance, details of directors' and major shareholders' interests in shares are those required by the law of the company's country of incorporation (see LR para. 17.33(a)).

4.2.11.11 Review of the listing regime

When the UKLA became the competent authority for listing in May 2000, it was agreed with HM Treasury that the FSA would conduct a review of the listing regime which has resulted in a consultation paper, CP203 published in October 2003 (see **4.4**). This considers a number of prospective changes to the listing regime and accordingly a number of the continuing obligations set out in the Listing Rules may well also be subject to change. The consultation period for CP 203 ended in January 2004 and the Financial Reporting Council ('FRC') published its proposals for changes to the Listing Rules on 13 October 2004. These should be read in the light of the new EU legislation in the form of the Prospectus Directive, the Transparency Directive and the Market Abuse Directive (see **4.2.10**).

4.2.11.12 Continuing obligations as part of the seamless web

Although this sounds rather grandiose, the point is that the listed company cannot look just to the continuing obligations and believe this is where its obligations begin and end. There is the whole range of additional statutory and regulatory provisions to observe as well—the Companies Act 1985, the rest of the Listing Rules, the City Code and so on (see **chapter 1**). In particular, while the Listing Rules requirements regarding the avoidance of a false market are vital, they must be read alongside s. 118 (market abuse) and s. 397 (misleading statements) FSMA, breach of which may give rise to much more serious problems for the company and/or its directors.

4.3 Offers of unlisted securities

All public offers of unlisted securities are now governed by the Public Offers of Securities Regulations 1995, which have replaced Part III of and Sch. 3 CA.

The Regulations apply to any investment which is not admitted to listing or the subject of an application for listing on the Official List. Accordingly, they apply to securities traded on the AIM or for which application is being made to admit to the AIM.

Over 900 companies were quoted on the AIM by the end of September 2004, with a total market capitalisation of over £25 billion (source: LSE AIM Market Statistics: 30 September 2004). For a new market, this is a successful beginning, enabling embryonic UK companies to find their money to expand from investors other than the commercial banks. Since AIM commenced, over 50 companies have now moved on to a listing and trading on the Stock Exchange.

4.3.1 Offer to the public

The Regulations require a prospectus to be issued whenever securities are offered to the public in the UK. 'The public' includes any section of the public, whether members of the company or institutional investors (see reg. 6).

4.3.2 Exemptions

Regulation 7 of the Regulations lists a series of exemptions from the need to publish a prospectus. Some of the most important are:

(a) Where shares are offered to no more than fifty persons (reg. 7 (2)(b)).

(b) Where securities are offered to persons whose ordinary business activities involve them in buying, selling and managing investments (reg. 7 (2)(a)).

(c) Where securities are offered to a restricted circle of persons who are sufficiently knowledgeable to understand the risks involved in accepting the offer (a 'professionals' exemption) (reg. 7 (2)(d)).

(d) Where securities are offered by a private company to its existing members or employees (reg. 7 (2)(f)(i)).

(e) Small issues of under 40,000 euros in total (currently about £27,000) (reg. 7 (2)(h)).

4.3.3 Contents

What has to be included in the prospectus if the offer does fall within the Regulations? Schedule 1 to the Regulations sets out the contents requirements. These track in broad respects the requirements for listing particulars under Part VI of FSMA. The prospectus requirements, in summary, are as follows:

(a) *General requirements*
These include the name of the issuer (Sch. 1, para. 2), the names and functions of the directors (Sch. 1, para. 4), and the date of publication of the prospectus (Sch. 1, para. 5).

(b) *The persons responsible for the prospectus and advisers*
This requires a declaration by the issuer's directors that 'to the best of their knowledge the information contained in the prospectus is in accordance with the facts and that the prospectus makes no omission likely to affect the import of such information' (Sch. 1, para. 10 (1)).

(c) *The securities to which the prospectus relates and the offer*
This should include a description of the securities being offered (Sch. 1, para. 11), including the rights attaching to them regarding voting (Sch. 1, para. 11 (a)(i)) and dividends (Sch. 1, para. 11 (a)(ii)). The prospectus must also state the number of securities being issued (Sch. 1, para. 18), the names of underwriters (Sch. 1, para. 22), and the expenses of the offer (Sch. 1, para. 23).

(d) *General information about the issuer and its capital*

This should include a summary of the memorandum of association (Sch. 1, para. 32), the structure of the issuer's share capital (Sch. 1, paras 34, 35, 36 and 37), the organisation of the group of companies of which the issuer is a member (if relevant) (Sch. 1, para. 39), and any information about those who could or do exercise control over the issuer, including the percentage of share capital they hold (Sch. 1, para. 40).

(e) *The issuer's principal activities*

This should provide information about the issuer's corporate operations (Sch. 1, para. 41), and in particular any information on legal or arbitration proceedings which are having or may have a significant effect on the issuer's financial position (Sch. 1, para. 44).

(f) *The issuer's assets and liabilities, financial position and profits and losses*

The issuer will need to set out its annual accounts for the last three years (Sch. 1, paras 45(1)(a) and 45(2)(a)). Where more than nine months has elapsed since the end of the last financial year, the prospectus should also include interim accounts since the end of the last financial year (Sch. 1, para. 45 (10)).

(g) *The issuer's administration, management and supervision*

This should include directors' service contracts (Sch. 1, para. 46), remuneration paid to directors (Sch. 1, para. 47 (1)) and interests of directors in the share capital of the issuer (Sch. 1, para. 47 (2)).

(h) *Recent developments in the issuer's business and prospects*

This should identify significant recent trends concerning the development of the issuer's business since the end of the last financial year (Sch. 1, para. 48), and information on the issuer's prospects for the current financial year (Sch. 1, para. 49).

In addition, reg. 9 contains a general duty of disclosure in broadly similar terms to that set out in s. 80 FSMA. Thus, a prospectus must contain all such information as investors would reasonably require, and would reasonably expect to find there, for the purpose of making an 'informed assessment' (see reg. 9 (1)) of the assets and liabilities, financial position, profits and losses and prospects of the issuer (see reg. 9 (1)(a)), and the rights attached to the securities (see reg. 9 (1)(b)).

Regulation 10 requires a supplementary prospectus if there is a significant change affecting any matter contained in the prospectus after it has been issued and before the offer closes.

The Regulations permit exceptions for the contents and prospectuses for companies traded on the AIM, where the issuer is making a rights issue or the offer is for less than 10 per cent of the existing share capital (see reg. 8 (5)). These are contained in the AIM Rules.

4.3.4 Liability

The extent of liability for prospectuses is identical to that for listed securities set out in Part VI of FSMA. Those responsible for the prospectus are liable to pay compensation to any person who has acquired the securities to which the prospectus relates if it is found to be untrue or misleading (reg. 14). *Possfund Custodian Trustee Ltd* v *Diamond* [1996] 2 All ER 774 indicates that this limits compensation to those who subscribe for the shares in the offer and rules out subsequent purchasers.

The persons responsible for the prospectus are set out in reg. 13. They include the issuer (reg. 13 (1)(a)); the directors of the issuer (see reg. 13 (1)(b)); each person who accepts, and is stated in the prospectus as accepting, responsibility for, or for any part of, the prospectus (reg. 13 (1)(d)); and each person who has authorised the contents of, or of any part of, the prospectus (reg. 13 (1)(g)). They also make liable any person offering securities, where such person is not the issuer (reg. 13 (1)(e)). On the face of it, this would extend responsibility for misleading statements in a prospectus to, for example, employees or other individual shareholders offering for sale their shares as part of a public offer. However, reg. 13(2A) (inserted by the Public Offer of Securities (Amendment) Regulations 1999) states that a person shall not be responsible where:

'(a) the issuer is responsible for the prospectus . . . in accordance with this regulation; and

(b) the prospectus . . . was drawn up primarily by the issuer, or by one or more persons acting on behalf of the issuer; and

(c) the offeror is making the offer in association with the issuer.'

Therefore, in the example above, employees would not be held responsible unless they had somehow otherwise accepted responsibility for or authorised some part of the particulars. And it should be noted that reg. 13(4) protects a person from being held responsible for any prospectus or supplementary prospectus by reason only of giving advice as to its contents in a professional capacity.

Penalties for contravening the Regulations are a fine or imprisonment (see regs 16(1) and 16(2)), and the prospect of being sued by anyone who suffers loss as a result of the contravention (see reg. 16 (4)).

4.3.5 Aim rules

When an application is first made for a company's shares to be traded on the AIM, the AIM Rules require a document containing the information set out in sch. 2 to the AIM Rules, including, by virtue of para. (a) of that Schedule, information equivalent to the information set out in sch. 1 to the POS Regulations to be issued. This would be the case even if the admission to the AIM were by way of an introduction. In the context of the AIM Rules, the prospectus is known as an admission document (see AIM Rules 3 and 24).

4.3.5.1 Conditions for admission to AIM

The conditions for admission to AIM are:

(a) Having a nominated adviser (AIM Rules r. 1) and a nominated broker (AIM Rules r. 33). The nominated adviser is the substitute for the role of sponsor in an application for official listing. The adviser must be drawn from a register of approved advisers and could be a stockbroker, lawyer or accountant as well as an investment bank, and the nominated adviser must be retained at all times (AIM Rules r. 32). The nominated broker is a member of the LSE.

(b) The issuer must be a public company (CA s. 81(1)).

(c) The issuer's accounts must conform to UK or US accounting principles, or international accounting standards (AIM Rules r. 17).

(d) The securities to be traded must be freely transferable (AIM Rules r. 30).

(e) The issuer must have restrictions on directors' dealings (AIM Rules r. 19).

(f) If the company has been generating revenue for less than two years, the directors and all employees must agree not to sell their interests in the company's shares for at least one year from the date of joining the AIM (AIM Rules r. 7).

There are no requirements or limits regarding the company's level of capitalisation or trading history or the number of shares in public hands.

4.3.5.2   Continuing obligations

These relate principally to disclosure obligations (AIM Rules r. 9), particularly in relation to new developments or changes in the company's performance or financial condition (AIM Rules r. 10). There are no rules requiring the consent of shareholders to 'substantial' transactions (see AIM Rules r. 11) or 'related party' transactions (see AIM Rules r. 12), but r. 13 does require shareholder approval in the case of reverse take-overs.

4.3.6   Private companies

Section 81 CA is still in force. This makes it an offence for a private limited company to offer its shares or debentures to the public.

Therefore, when a private company is intending to make an offer to the public, its freedom to do so is governed by Part III CA. Bizarrely, the Public Offers of Securities Regulations 1995 will determine whether a prospectus is required in relation to the private company's offer, but Part III CA will determine whether or not there is an offer to the public which is prohibited. It is important, for private companies, to have regard to both provisions. It is not safe to rely on the exemptions to the Public Offers of Securities Regulations 1995. You must also be safe under the definition of an offer to the public in s. 81.

As regards listing, any application by a private company for its shares to be listed will not be entertained by UKLA. This is because a private company is a prescribed body for the purposes of s. 75(3) FSMA by way of reg. 3(a) of the Financial Services and Markets Act 2000 (Official Listing of Securities) Regulations 2001.

4.4   Proposed changes to the listing regime

4.4.1   FSA Discussion paper

In July 2002, the Financial Services Authority (the 'FSA') issued a review of the listing regime in Discussion Paper 14 ('DP14'), which sought to identify areas in the current listing regime that required review and reform. Following on from this, the FSA subsequently published Consultation Paper 203 in October 2003 ('CP203'), which is a policy consultation paper on which comments were invited by 31 January 2004.

4.4.2   Consultation Paper 203

In CP203, entitled 'Review of the Listing Regime', the FSA seeks to:

- highlight areas where the regime should be more rigorous:
- identify the outdated provisions of the Listing Rules which are no longer applicable; and
- make suggestions as to new rules which are required to bridge any gaps in the current regime.

The FSA published its proposals for detailed changes to the Listing Rules on 13 October 2004 (CP04/16: The Listing Review and implementation of the Prospectus Directive—Draft rules and feedback on CP203). At the time of writing, these detailed proposals have yet to be incorporated in this publication therefore, as a guide, the main proposals made by the FSA in CP203 are set out as follows:

(a) *Introduction of high-level principles*

It is proposed that the structure of the Listing Sourcebook (often referred to as the 'Purple Book'), which comprises the Listing Rules and the UKLA Guidance Manual, be changed by introducing a set of high-level principles to underpin the Listing Rules which would in turn be backed up by more detailed rules and guidance.

These principles would be enforceable as rules and would highlight the fundamental obligations of all listed companies such as the requirements that:

- directors should understand their responsibilities and obligations under the Listing Rules;

- adequate procedures and controls must be established to enable compliance with the Listing Rules;

- information must be communicated to shareholders in a clear and timely manner; and that

- companies must ensure that there is equality of treatment between holders of shares of the same class.

(b) *Restructuring of the Listing Sourcebook*

The FSA would like to restructure the Listing Sourcebook so that its format is in line with that of the FSA Handbook. The reorganisation would divide the Listing Rules into three sections, headed equity, debt and financial products.

(c) *Super-equivalence (requirements for eligibility)*

The EU Prospectus Directive, due to be implemented by Member States by 1 July 2005, prevents the FSA from imposing additional requirements in the Listing Rules in relation to the contents of a prospectus by virtue of the fact that it is a maximum harmonisation directive (**4.2.10.1**). However, the FSA is able to impose more stringent *eligibility* criteria on companies to be admitted to the Official List than those required by European legislation. This is known as 'super-equivalence'.

(d) *Overseas companies*

It is proposed that overseas companies with a primary listing in the UK should conform to the same standards as UK companies. There are currently certain exemptions which benefit overseas companies such as being able to submit accounts in local GAAP rather than US GAAP, UK GAAP or IAS (International Accounting Standards). CP203 also proposes that the Listing Rules be amended to extend compliance with the Combined Code to all overseas companies with a primary listing in the UK.

(e) *Conflicts of interest*

The FSA proposes introducing a subsidiary rule (in addition to the high-level principles referred to in (a) above) requiring a company to put in place procedures for dealing with conflicts. This additional rule would impose a continuing obligation on a company to ensure none of its directors have any conflicts between duties owed to the company and private interests or other duties, unless the company can demonstrate that arrangements are in place to avoid any detriment to its interests.

(f) *Power to disqualify directors*

The current powers of the FSA allow it to fine or publicly censure a director or former director of a listed company if such director was knowingly involved in a breach by that company of the Listing Rules. CP203 suggests that the FSA's powers be extended to include the ability to disqualify an individual from being a director of listed company where they have been involved in a serious breach of the Listing Rules.

(g) *Super-equivalence (requirements under continuing obligations)/Class Test*

Following the introduction of the Market Abuse Directive (**4.2.10.3**) and the Transparency Directive (**4.2.10.2**), there has been concern as to whether the UK will be able to enforce the requirements for all companies to comply with the current super-equivalent continuing obligations.

(h) *Delisting*

Delisting is currently a board decision rather than a shareholder decision. However, CP203 proposes that in order to delist, a company must obtain a majority approval of 75 per cent of the shareholders in general meeting, other than when the company moves to another quoted market when such shareholder approval is not required.

(i) *The Code of Market Conduct*

Once the UK legislation implementing the Market Abuse Directive has been finalised, the FSA proposal to streamline the FSA Handbook (as described in MAD JCD Chapter 4, including in particular, amendments to the Code of Market Conduct) are anticipated by March 2005.

(j) *Financial Information*

CP203 proposes a more flexible approach to the content of the financial information it must prepare including:

- allowing a company to include both audited and unaudited figures in any financial information it discloses as long as the source for such information is disclosed;

- removing the requirement to report on profit forecasts (unless where this is included in a prospectus);

- no longer requiring financial information to be presented in the form of a comparative table or accountant's report.

CP203 also consults on whether it is necessary to retain the requirement for a significant change statement which is required by Class 1 circulars under LR para. 12.11(a) given that financial reporting will be more frequent following the provisions of the Transparency Directive (**4.2.10.2**).

(k) *Sponsors*

CP203 consulted as to whether the UK listing regime should retain the mandatory requirement for a company to appoint a sponsor (**3.3.4**) for new issues and major transactions or whether to allow companies to chose for themselves whether or not to appoint such an advisor. The FSA has recently confirmed that it intends to retain the requirement for a company to appoint a sponsor in such circumstances but that it would also intend to introduce a Code of Practice for Sponsors to ensure they are fully aware of their responsibilities and a detailed knowledge of the listing regime which is expected of them.

4.5 Where to find........

The Model Code	Appendix to LR ch. 16.
The Combined Code	Appended to the Listing Sourcebook which contains the Listing Rules and UKLA Guidance Manual

The Purple book	The Listing Sourcebook containing the Listing Rules and the UKLA Guidance Manual.
The Code of Market Conduct	Chapter 1 of FSA Handbook
Price Sensitive Information Guide	Appendix 2 to the UKLA Guidance Manual
Continuing Obligations Guide	Appendix 3 to the UKLA Guidance Manual

Acquisitions

5.1 Introduction

The world of corporate finance uses the rather weighty term 'acquisitions' to describe anything from the humble sale of a small corner-shop business to the disposal of an international multimillion-pound supermarket chain. You will also come across the expression as a description of a takeover under the City Code (on which see **Chapter 8**)—hence the phrase 'mergers and acquisitions'. In this chapter, however, the term refers to sales and purchases of assets or businesses, or shares *outside* the City Code (essentially, private companies). The term is therefore quite distinct from the 'takeovers' covered in **Chapter 8**.

Acquiring things is the way of the capitalist world, and company strategy is no exception. Acquisition activity has been a feature of corporate finance work for many years. Why do acquisitions take place? There are some common factors which will help you to understand your client's particular motivation for making a specific acquisition or disposal. Without this understanding you cannot properly assess what is important to the client and what the client is seeking from the transaction.

When you look at these factors, do not assume that clients only fall into one of these categories: very often they fall into more than one at the same time or none at all. Nor should you assume that clients have always worked out what they are doing: often they are simply seizing an opportunity when it presents itself, whether or not it fits with whatever strategy they are developing.

We begin with the 'textbook' reasons for acquisition activity.

5.1.1 Diversification and conglomeration

This was particularly fashionable as an aspect of corporate strategy in the 1960s and 1970s. For listed companies in particular, the ethos was that it made better business sense to hold a portfolio of assets or companies in different sectors of the market. For example, a tobacco company might own an insurance company and a paper and packaging business. The thinking was that if one sector was depressed, another was just as likely to be booming, so as jack of all trades a diversified company could ensure an overall picture of steady performance and reduce the shareholder's investment risk. There might also be benefits from integrating certain common operations despite the diversity of business base—for instance, product distribution.

5.1.2 Consolidation

This is, as you might guess, the reverse of diversification, and is driven by the philosophy that a company does better when it concentrates on what it really knows. It is particularly the case in difficult economic times that companies feel safer when they only have to worry about what they identify to be their 'core businesses'. Obviously a strategy of consolidation could lead to a planned programme of disposals, and possibly one which needs to be carried out relatively speedily (which may affect your negotiation strength).

5.1.3   Vertical and horizontal integration

These are rather technical terms for simple concepts.

Vertical integration takes place when a paper manufacturer decides to buy a forestry business and a chain of stationery shops which sell the paper products it makes. In other words, it is the process of integrating into the company both suppliers and buyers of its goods or services as a way of producing those goods and services more cheaply—it reduces the transaction costs.

Horizontal integration is the process of buying a similar business to your own at the equivalent point in the production cycle: to take our example above, a paper manufacturer buying a packaging business or another paper manufacturer. Where the businesses are different, this may help to integrate expertise in certain common areas such as marketing. Where the businesses are the same, there may be a number of motivating factors. The businesses may be complementary in that they have different customer bases or geographical penetration. Possibly the objective is simply to achieve economies of scale, or to create a single organisation of sufficient size to compete with the rest of the opposition.

Both vertical and horizontal integration assume a strategy of acquisitions. Both may possibly give rise to questions of merger control.

5.1.4   International expansion

The rapid growth of international markets, particularly those throughout Europe, the former-Soviet Union and the Far East, creates possibilities for business expansion. One of the best methods of penetrating an entirely new geographical market is to acquire a business which already operates in it. International acquisitions can be some of the most difficult as cross-border difficulties are added to what is already a fairly thick stew.

5.1.5   Acquiring what you do not have or disposing of what you do not want

This sounds too simple to be a serious corporate strategy, but simple ideas are often the best. If a company is suffering from a long-term cash-flow problem, acquiring a cash-rich business with a strong and regular cash inflow might be an attractive solution to its dilemma.

By the same token, a company weighed down by liabilities in one or two of its business areas may feel that the best course is to ditch them at the best price possible so that it is free from such difficulties and can concentrate on its profit-making operations.

The following are some unstated factors for acquisition activity.

5.1.6   Rapid earnings growth

Institutions, other shareholders and analysts often place significant emphasis on the growth of a company's earnings per share as a sign of corporate success. One way of achieving rapid increases in earnings per share is to boost profits artificially year-on-year by fresh acquisitions of successful companies, as the profits of the acquired companies then 'top up' the buyer's existing results. This may often obscure underlying weaknesses in existing underperforming businesses (which may be the intention).

5.1.7 Asset-stripping

Some acquirers have developed notoriety for their fondness in buying businesses which they identify as undervalued, then selling off their assets individually to the highest bidder to make sizeable profits on the whole deal. Some typical aspects of acquisition work decline in significance if this is the client's motivation: the client is less likely to worry about working with existing management or retaining employee goodwill.

5.1.8 Management image

This is an intangible factor but is often present. A lacklustre performance by a company will often be blamed on a management with no sense of direction or ambition. An acquisition or disposal may be one way of correcting that image by showing that the management has focused clearly on what in business terms it wants or does not want and how it is dealing actively with that objective.

5.1.9 Falling in love

There are some acquisitions and disposals which are hard to understand at the time and later turn out to be dreadful mistakes. Often this is the consequence of the buyer falling in love with the prospect of a particular purchase, perhaps simply because of the target's reputation. In fact the acquirer is blinded by whichever feature it adores and later finds out that all is not what it seems: in these circumstances, advisers often despair, as it is very difficult to make the acquirer see reason.

All these factors are also relevant in the takeover context (see **Chapter 8**). Your first duty in these transactions is to take the trouble to find out what is really motivating your client.

5.2 Buying companies or businesses

In an acquisition, the buyer and seller have to agree on what is being transferred and, where there is a choice, to decide whether to transfer it as a company or a business. The choice may have quite different legal and tax effects for both buyer and seller, which it is the lawyer's job to understand and advise the client on. Let us look first, though, at what we mean by having a choice whether to transfer as a business or a company.

Assume P plc has several divisions, one of which is responsible for making televisions (others make radios, VCRs and stereo systems). P plc decides to sell off the TV side of its operation. It may do one of two things:

(a) Identify those assets which comprise the TV operation (for example, the factory, the employees, the machinery, the benefit of various supply contracts, the intellectual property, goodwill and debtors) and sell those off. This in turn could be done individually (for example, the factory could be sold off to a property investor while the intellectual property could be sold to an entrepreneur who wants to exploit a new invention). More usually it will be done on the basis of a going concern—in other words, the business is sold as a complete unit, lock, stock and barrel.

(b) Form a subsidiary company (M Ltd) which P wholly owns. P then makes M the owner of all the assets in the TV operation mentioned above. P retains control by means of the shares it holds in M, which it then sells, hence transferring control of M, and so the entire TV operation, to the buyer.

The asset or business sale involves selecting whatever is to be sold. The company or share sale involves a simple share transfer. There are a number of consequences of this difference. Let us look first at the legal or commercial reasons for picking one route rather than another.

5.2.1   Legal and commercial factors

(a) With the company sale, everything that is in the company goes across on transfer. The entity before is the entity after. In this way, the seller gets rid of everything, including all liabilities. Does the buyer want all those liabilities?

(b) With the asset or business sale, it is possible to 'cherrypick' whatever is to be transferred. The buyer may choose to buy only the assets and leave the seller with the liabilities (e.g., creditors, outstanding loans). Does the seller want this?

(c) As a company sale only requires a share transfer, it has the potential for being a speedy and simple way to do the transaction. In contrast the asset or business sale requires identification of the assets (and liabilities?) and the buyer's agreement to purchase every one of them. This needs documentation, a careful analysis of the state of all the assets and separate transfer arrangements where appropriate (for example, the owner of the factory in our TV operation will change, which will necessitate a conveyance, and so an extra document, negotiation and inevitably more time and cost).

The client's chief concern is the commercial result of effecting the transfer as a business or a company sale. In particular, the client will want to know whether it makes a difference in terms of speed and cost. Any financial difference in going one route or the other will be highly influential, and tax will play a central role in these calculations.

5.2.2   Tax factors

These are many and varied and only a brief mention of the salient factors is possible.

5.2.2.1   Asset or business sale

(a) *Capital gains tax*
CGT will be payable by the seller on the amount of any gain made on a disposal. The buyer will acquire the assets at a base cost equal to the price paid for them.

(b) *Capital allowances*
For the seller, there will be balancing adjustments on any outstanding capital allowances claimed for the assets sold. The buyer will be able to claim capital allowances for the assets bought.

(c) *VAT*
The assets need to be transferred as a going concern, otherwise VAT may be payable on the sale of assets as a supply of goods.

(d) *Stamp duty land tax*
Stamp duty land tax on 'land transactions' (in respect of non-residential property) is:

(i) 1 per cent of the consideration where the consideration is more than £150,000 but does not exceed £250,000:

(ii) 3 per cent where the consideration is more than £250,000 but does not exceed £500,000; and

(iii) 4 per cent where the consideration exceeds £500,000.

(e) *Losses*

If the seller has trading losses at the time of sale, these will be lost, as there is a cessation of trade.

(f) *Double charge*

Where the seller is a company, it may pay tax on the proceeds of sale of the assets (e.g., CGT). The shareholders may then pay tax again when they sell their shares in the company, which will have as part of their value the proceeds of the original assets sale—tax is effectively paid twice on this element. However, in practice the seller may be able to avoid this by stripping out the asset disposal proceeds from the company before the share sale, thereby reducing the value of the shares.

(g) *Hidden tax liabilities*

The buyer can 'pick and choose' whether to accept any of the tax liabilities held by the business.

5.2.2.2   Company or share sale

(a) *Capital gains tax*

CGT will be payable by the seller on the amount of any gain made on a disposal unless it qualifies as a disposal of a substantial shareholding or the gain can be rolled over into the buyer's securities as part of the consideration. The Finance Act 2002 introduced a new relief for trading companies providing an exemption from tax in respect of gains on the disposal of 10 per cent or more of the ordinary share capital provided that the shareholding has been held for a continuous period of twelve months during the two years prior to the disposal. In the case of a rollover, as the buyer acquires the shares at their base cost there is the risk of a very high gain on their subsequent disposal.

(b) *Capital allowances*

There will usually be no balancing adjustments on outstanding capital allowances claimed by the company which has been sold. The buyer will not be able to qualify for capital allowances on the sum it pays for the shares it has bought, but the target company itself should continue to claim capital allowances on its own assets.

(c) *VAT*

No VAT consequences.

(d) *Stamp duty*

Stamp duty on a sale of shares (to be paid by the buyer) is 0.5 per cent of the value transferred rounded up to the nearest £5 (and subject to a minimum £5 duty).

(e) *Losses*

Losses in the company when it is sold can be carried forward if the trade continues and there is no major change in its nature or conduct.

(f) *Double charge*

The selling shareholders sell their shares only once and are subject only to the one tax 'hit' at point of sale—unlike the situation where a company sells an asset and then the shareholders later sell the shares in the company.

(g) *Hidden tax liabilities*

The seller is able to get rid of all the company's tax liabilities when it transfers to the buyer. The buyer accordingly will ask for tax warranties and usually a deed of indemnity.

The consequence of this analysis, as you can probably see, is that from the tax point of view (in general terms) the buyer tends to prefer to acquire assets or a business and the seller to sell a company or shares.

5.2.2.3 Tax restructuring

Because of some of the tax implications mentioned in these two lists, there are some common methods used in the run-up to an acquisition to save tax.

(a) *Dividend strip*

The seller pays itself a dividend out of the target company prior to sale and then reduces the sale price of the company. The advantage of this is that the shareholder is likely to pay less tax on its dividend than on the capital gain on which tax might otherwise be payable when the shares are sold, and the buyer pays less stamp duty as the shares are worth less. This is likely to make a company sale even more attractive to the seller.

(b) *Creating a company*

As we saw in the example above, the seller can turn a business into a company and then sell the shares in the company and so get the benefits mentioned in **5.2.2.2**.

If you should be asked to advise your client on the tax factors to be considered when deciding how to go about buying and selling, detailed tax advice is likely to be appropriate.

5.2.2.4 Tax clearances

There are a host of clearances which you may need to seek from the Inland Revenue and HM Customs and Excise, for instance:

(a) that HM Customs and Excise will regard a transfer of a particular business as a going concern, and so not assessable for VAT purposes; and

(b) that the Inland Revenue will not treat as subject to CGT the disposal of shares in a company where the consideration is securities in the buyer (s. 135 Taxation of Chargeable Gains Act 1992).

The important thing always to recall in these transactions is that clients' preferences and circumstances do vary. It may for instance be vital to the buyer to inherit the target's trading losses (to set off against the client's own rocketing profits), in which case the attractions of buying a business (with the possible consequential disappearance of trading losses) will be significantly reduced.

Sometimes the question of whether it is to be a company or an asset or business sale has been decided before instructions reach the lawyers, frequently by the company in consultation with its accountants or other tax advisers—so your scope for advice in this area may already be curtailed.

5.3 The parties

The 'cast of thousands' is less likely to be in evidence for an acquisition than an issue of shares or a public takeover, though this does depend on the nature of the transaction. The reason is that acquisitions are more in the nature of 'private' transactions in character, between identified buyer and seller, rather than 'public' with the large volume of investors which this implies. The need for quite so many advisers is not felt to be so pressing. Acquisitions also tend to be transactions in which the lawyers play a larger role in directing events.

5.3.1   Buyer and seller

Buyer and seller will often both be companies but of course may be individuals, unincorporated associations, partnerships and so on. Care should always be taken to ensure that appropriate constitutional authority exists for both to enter into the transaction.

As we will see in **5.5.1.6**, warranties are normally demanded by the buyer from the seller. Sometimes, the buyer will insist that the target directors, or the seller's directors or one of its substantial shareholders (where it is a company selling) should be a party to all, or some of, the warranties. This is because they may have as much knowledge or information about the company being sold as does the selling shareholder.

Because of some of the tax problems which arise from intra-group activity, some of the tax warranties which the buyer will ask for in a share sale will have to be given not just by the selling company but also other companies in the seller's group.

Of course, in view of the tax issues mentioned in **5.2.2**, the seller may need to reorganise itself prior to effecting the sale. Even if the entity to be sold is a separate company, some work is likely to be needed to ensure that what belongs to it is distinct from the property the seller wishes to retain: this is even more acute a problem where it is a business which is being sold.

5.3.2   Target company or business

In a sense, the target is entirely at the mercy of its seller. Nevertheless, it does of course have employees (though care will have to be taken to see they are not in fact employees of the seller). The directors of both the selling company (if there is one) and (if it is a share sale) the company being sold have a duty to have regard to the interests of the company's employees under s. 309 Companies Act 1985. As for the buyer, although extensive consultation in advance of an announcement about a sale is often difficult because of the need to keep such information confidential, as a practical matter, the support or at least neutrality of the employees to the sale is vital. The last thing a buyer wants to inherit is a hostile workforce, so time will need to be spent explaining to the staff of the company or business what the sale will mean for them. Additionally, the Collective Redundancies and Transfer of Undertakings (Protection of Employment) Regulations 1995 (known as the Worker Representative Regulations) apply to any business transfer. This gives the employees affected by such a transfer the right (unless it already exists, for instance under trade union arrangements) to elect representatives to consult with the employer about his proposals. Failure to comply may give rise to financial penalties.

In addition, the buyer will probably seek to secure the continued loyalty of key employees of the target and may negotiate revised contractual terms with them to this end (particularly new service agreements with directors of a target company who are to stay on the board after the sale). The buyer may also wish to change the standard terms of employment of the target employees. The Transfer of Undertakings Regulations and the Acquired Rights Directive do not permit such a change, even if agreed between employees and buyer, if the reason for it is the transfer of the company or business itself. It is therefore advisable only to set about such changes some time after the transfer is completed.

The buyer may insist that the directors of the company being sold (where it is a share sale) or the key employees of the business (where it is a business sale), should also be a party to all, or some of, the warranties in the sale and purchase agreement. This is because they may have as much knowledge or information about the company being sold as does the selling shareholder.

When the sale negotiations get underway, there will be an enormous amount of information required on the target's business operations and administrative arrangements (see **5.4.1.2**), and both the seller and the target will need to spend considerable time making this ready for the buyer to review.

5.3.3 Investment bankers

Investment banks typically play a less prominent role in an acquisition than in issues and takeovers. The banker's task is usually to set the deal up. Often buyer and seller have already identified each other through ordinary commercial channels and settled the outline terms of their deal in direct negotiation. In these circumstances, the banker's presence is otiose.

There are three specific cases where the banker can be expected to play a part:

(a) Where the seller is having or anticipates difficulty in locating a potential buyer for its business: an investment banker will be able to use its existing contacts and clients to see whether it can solicit offers from any interested buyers.

(b) Where the seller wishes to sell its company or business off to the highest bidder, an investment bank is often appointed to produce an information memorandum on the operation to be sold and then set up the mechanism for conducting an auction or contract race. This will involve sending each potential bidder a copy of the memorandum and soliciting sealed bids from each before handling the negotiations with the successful bidder.

(c) Where part or the whole of the buyer's consideration is its own securities, the bank is appointed to conduct a vendor consideration placing (with or without clawback) on behalf of the buyer and also the seller (see **3.6.5**): this will also require the appointment of a broker to identify potential placees.

5.3.4 Accountants

The accountants for both the buyer and seller are certain to be involved in a number of aspects of the transaction:

(a) The buyer will frequently instruct accountants (usually its own auditors) to carry out a thorough investigation of the entity it wants to buy, and the buyer generally places considerable reliance on the report the accountants produce, as it will contain a detailed analysis of the entity's operational and financial performance, and its prospects. Crucial to these accountants' success is adequate access to the financial records and management papers of the company or business being sold— hence often there will already be a preliminary, though provisional, agreement for the sale of the entity between the buyer and seller before the accountants start work (see **5.4.1.1**).

(b) Accounts or financial statements will often need to be prepared up to the agreed date of completion (as buyers will insist on current financial data on the target), and in practice these generally need to be reviewed and approved by accountants for both buyer and seller. This is also true of any other figures which are the subject of agreement by the parties—for instance, it is as well to instruct accountants to check any earn-out formula appearing as part of the agreed consideration (see **5.5.1.2**).

(c) If the buyer or seller needs to produce a circular to shareholders as part of the acquisition (see **5.6.4**), the accountants will need to check any figures it contains.

5.3.5   Regulators

The role of the regulators will be discussed in more detail in **5.6**. Of course, both the Inland Revenue and HM Customs and Excise may be involved if clearances and/or consents from one or both are required.

A particular company or business transfer may require the consent of regulatory authorities relevant to the commercial sector in which that business or company operates. Financial services businesses or companies will be authorised by their self-regulatory organisation, which will have to approve the change in ownership of the operation. Broadcasting companies or businesses obtain their licences from the Independent Broadcasting Authority if they broadcast on television, and from the Radio Authority if on radio. Approval from these organisations for the transfer of the licence will be required. Of course these are only illustrations of what might be needed: the possibilities are legion.

5.3.6   Specialists

This heading does not assume that the other professionals referred to in this section are not specialists: the term covers those experts who are called in to advise in special circumstances, bringing with them a degree of know-how in their field of specialism which the other professionals involved do not have. The types of advisers required will vary, depending on the peculiar nature of the target's business or problems. Particular examples are:

(a) *Actuaries*

One of the most common areas of difficulty in these transactions is the value of any pension funds which may be transferred as part of the acquisition (see **5.4.1.2**). Valuations of the target's pension fund by both the buyer's and seller's actuaries to determine whether it has been properly funded are a normal feature of these transactions, simply because of the huge liabilities a buyer might otherwise incur if not and the huge windfall otherwise accruing to the buyer if the pension scheme has been over-funded. Since actuaries can rarely agree on a valuation, they need to be involved from the outset.

(b) *Surveyors*

The sale of a company or business with a number of properties to its name will inevitably require the appointment of surveyors not only to verify the condition of the properties but also to value them as part of the process of agreeing the consideration.

(c) *Environmental consultants*

The potentially extensive nature of environmental liabilities and the difficulty of establishing exactly what they are in a given case often leads to the involvement of environmental consultants. Their task is usually to conduct an environmental 'audit' of the company or business and report to the buyer on any identified liabilities and the approximate cost of putting them right, so that these can be considered when negotiating the price for the sale. Not all companies and businesses merit this kind of approach: high-risk businesses are those in manufacturing, the generation and supply of power, the supply of fuels and water and waste management, though for just about any kind of business some consideration should be given to the use of environmental experts.

5.3.7   Third parties

This refers to those parties with whom the target business or company has contracted for the supply or delivery of goods and services.

Where it is a company which is being sold, the company has entered into these contracts and the company will continue in existence after the sale as the same entity (only owned by different persons). Therefore these contractual relationships will continue automatically after the change in ownership. The only kind of contract which may be affected in these circumstances is one which can be terminated if there is a change of control of one of the parties to it. Joint venture agreements commonly have such provisions. The consent of the third party to the change of control in the company is then needed if the joint venture agreement is to stay in force.

With business sales, the contracts relevant to the business have been entered into by the legal entity which owns the business. In some cases, it will be open to the seller to assign its interest in the contract direct to the buyer (if, for example, there is an express contractual right to that effect). In others, the contract will not be assignable (if, for example, it is forbidden under the contract): this is something you will need to determine. In these cases, those contracts on which the business *depends* will need to be novated in favour of the buyer: but this cannot happen unless the third party agrees. The third party will therefore need to be cajoled into accepting the new owner of the business. Often business sales are made conditional on major contracts being novated, otherwise a buyer is at risk of inheriting valuable contracts which are unenforceable.

With less significant contracts, the objective is ultimately to substitute the seller for the buyer, though this will not be a condition of the agreement, simply an obligation the seller will continue to have after the sale completes. This is explained in more detail in **5.5.2.1**.

The point to remember is that third parties will play a role in the sale negotiations if their relationship with the entity being sold is important enough.

5.3.8 Solicitors

Last, but not least, are the legal advisers to the buyer and seller. As compared with equity offerings and public company takeovers, private company and business acquisitions offer greater opportunities to the solicitors to lead the transaction rather than playing second fiddle to others like the merchant bankers. In fact, it would be true to say that clients in this kind of work tend to rely on the lawyers, in conjunction with the accountants, to do the organising, thinking and negotiating for them. You are therefore much more likely to take on a management function in this kind of deal than in the others we have looked at. The solicitors' main tasks are these:

(a) Drafting: the agreement to buy the company or business (see **5.5.1** and **5.5.2**), the disclosure letter and all the other documents referred to below will be drafted by the solicitors.

(b) Negotiating these documents, particularly the agreement to buy and the disclosure letter, is largely the domain of the lawyer accompanied by the client.

(c) Due diligence: see **5.4.1.2**. Essentially this is a task for the buyer's solicitors and involves finding out as much information as possible about the target prior to signing the purchase agreement. The accountants' report is part of this process, though it tends to focus on the financial aspects of the target business or company. The lawyers are left with the task of unearthing and digesting all the documentary data which exists about the target so that the buyer gets as complete a picture as possible. The seller's solicitors will find a lot of their time is spent sorting out their client's documentary data for presentation to the buyer, and ensuring that the seller knows exactly what he is giving the buyer access to.

(d) Advising on the law: legal problems do arise on these transactions (it is not all practical issues!).

One thing that will characterise the approach of most firms to handling this kind of work is the team of specialists they are likely to draw on. It will already have become evident to you that these transactions throw up issues on tax, employment, pensions, property, the environment, and so on. Lawyers are rarely capable of a total command of all the relevant law in these areas, hence it is likely a number of solicitors will be involved in advising both clients on all the specialist aspects of the transaction. The skill for the solicitor is not only to keep the client happy but also to keep the rest of his team informed about what is going on and what problems the transaction has thrown up.

5.4 Timetable

It is difficult to provide an exact timetable for these transactions as so much depends on particular circumstances and what the parties agree between them. It is much easier to identify a standard series of events relevant to both company and business purchases. This is set out here. It should give you a reasonable idea of how these transactions proceed and who does what and when.

5.4.1 Pre-contract

This refers to the period leading up to signing of the purchase agreement.

5.4.1.1 Heads of agreement

The buyer and seller often agree to agree in the form of heads of agreement. These are usually denigrated by lawyers as worthless (as they have no legal effect), but they often help to focus the parties' commercial thinking much more effectively than any number of meetings.

They are usually expressed to be 'subject to contract' or 'not legally binding' to make it clear that they are a simple record of the main terms agreed between the parties in their preliminary commercial negotiations, rather than a formal and legally binding commitment. If you are advising on the drafting of the heads then you must ensure they are qualified in this way. If the parties want a legally binding contract then you may as well scrap the heads and move straight on to drafting and negotiating the sale agreement.

5.4.1.2 Due diligence

One of the most important activities in these transactions is the process of gathering as much information as possible about the target company or business. The buyer's warranties and indemnities offer it protection against the risk of unforeseen liabilities arising in the target after the sale is completed. However, it is not in the buyer's interest to have to take legal action to protect its investment. This uses up a lot of management time (it diverts attention from the real business of making money) and in any event may well take a lengthy period to resolve (leading to uncertainty).

Much the best solution is to take precautions to eliminate the risk of such liability arising or at least to identify and quantify it in advance. The due diligence process is designed to satisfy this demand. If the problems can be flushed out before they become the buyer's responsibility, then the buyer can use them as leverage in negotiations over the sale price rather than as the foundation of later, more expensive warranty claims.

Looking at this the other way around, it is in any event quite impossible for the buyer's solicitors to prepare appropriate warranties for the sale agreement until they understand better the protection the buyer will need. This in turn can only be discovered through the due diligence process.

What does due diligence actually involve? Usually, the parties will have agreed on the outline of the deal in their heads of agreement, and the seller will at the same time agree to the following:

(a) The buyer's accountants will be given access to the target's financial records to enable them to prepare a report on its financial history and performance and review its likely profitability in the future; this report will also require access to other information about the target, including material contracts, information about its existing assets (e.g., properties, investments) and liabilities (e.g., loans) and management history (including an appraisal of key staff). The buyer will rely on this report in making an informed assessment about whether to proceed with the purchase and, if so, at what price and on what terms. It is important to ensure that the accountants are clear about what exactly they are being asked to do, hence their instructions are often recorded in a letter.

(b) The buyer's solicitors will be given access to all the documentation relevant to an assessment of any legal difficulties which might be encountered in the transfer.

The buyer's solicitors will usually prepare a letter to the seller and/or its solicitors requesting the following information on the target:

(a) Material contracts: usually the seller or its solicitors will send copies of these to the buyer's solicitors to enable them to make a judgement about which contracts cannot be assigned to the buyer (if it is a business sale—see **5.3.7**), which contain 'change of control' provisions, and which of them contain terms which are unfavourable or onerous to the target and so might bring into question the value of that contract in the future.

(b) Licences and authorisations: the buyer will want to assess whether it can inherit the existing licence or should apply for a new one from the relevant authority, and to establish whether there have been any blemishes in the target's record of compliance with the terms of the licence.

(c) Pension scheme: there are two particular features in this area which need to be addressed early on:

(i) The adequacy of the funding of the target's pension scheme. If it has been inadequately funded, the buyer will look to the seller to make up the deficit prior to transfer, or to adjust the purchase price proportionately. Alternatively, the fund may have a surplus, which will enable the buyer to take a 'pensions holiday' and suspend contributions to the fund after completion—but it will have to pay for the surplus in the purchase price. To this end, the first priority is to obtain the relevant data and send it to the buyer's actuaries or pensions consultants for immediate review and advice.

(ii) Establishing whose pension scheme the target employees belong to. Is it the target's own or the seller's? If it is the target's own scheme, is it to be preserved as a separate scheme following completion, or integrated into the buyer's existing pensions scheme? If the latter, a transfer payment representing the accrued benefits under the scheme will need to be made by seller to buyer. If the employees belong to the seller's own scheme, will they be allowed to join an entirely new scheme replicating the seller's existing one, or will they be integrated into the buyer's existing scheme (which will also generally require a transfer payment)? These questions can only begin to be answered if the information about the existing pensions arrangements is obtained speedily.

(d) Standard terms of employment and service agreements: this is to help the buyer assess what obligations will be involved in taking on the target employees.

(e) Material litigation: this can seriously affect the value of the target's business operation, and it is probably only the lawyers who can make an informed assessment about its likely success.

(f) Property, real and intellectual: these constitute some of the most important assets a business is likely to have, so it is important to establish what their status is.

With real property, the first step will be to carry out the appropriate Land Registry and Land Charges Registry searches to disclose any interests registered against the title. Is the property freehold or leasehold? If leasehold, the landlord's consent to assignment will be required. Is the plan to:

  (i) get the seller to warrant good title to the property;

 (ii) get the seller's solicitors to certify that the seller has good marketable title (i.e., *they* do an investigation of title), or

(iii) have the buyer's solicitors carry out their own investigation of title into the property?

The last is the most secure method open to the buyer, but it is the most expensive and time-consuming as the buyer's solicitors will need access to all title documents.

With intellectual property, the aim is to establish the nature of the target's existing intellectual property rights (be they patents, trade marks, copyright, registered designs and so on) and the state of their protection.

(g) Any other information of relevance, including insurance policies for the premises and contents, share schemes available for members of the target's staff, financial and trading arrangements between the target and the seller's corporate group (if, for instance, there are inter-group loans involving the target, these will have to be re-arranged on an arm's-length basis or paid off), and the company books and records (where it is a share sale).

In a share sale, the buyer's solicitors will conduct a company search against the target as an additional precaution.

5.4.1.3   Confidentiality agreement

In exchange for all this information, any well-advised seller will require the buyer and its advisers to treat the acquired information as confidential and only to be used for the purposes of the acquisition or otherwise with the seller's consent. The tricky part is defining the information: does it, for instance, extend to all information received by the buyer in connection with the acquisition (which might catch the buyer's own market research), and what about oral statements? Usually some compromise is arrived at whereby the buyer cannot disclose or use for other purposes *written* information obtained from the seller or its advisers *in the course of the acquisition negotiations and due diligence process*.

5.4.1.4   Tax clearances

It would be usual to apply for any necessary tax clearances at this stage (see **5.2.2.4**), and obtain them prior to signing the contract.

5.4.2 Contract

This refers to the point at which the parties sign the sale agreement and so enter into a formal legal commitment to effect the acquisition. There are two documents you will always encounter at this stage, and one you may meet.

5.4.2.1 Share or business purchase agreement

This is discussed in detail in **5.5**. The agreement records all the principal elements of the acquisition and so is the key document in the transaction. Much of the lawyers' efforts will be devoted to drafting and negotiating this.

It is usual for the buyer to draft the agreement. Since the seller can hide behind the *caveat emptor* principle, the buyer has to make all the running in stating what he regards as appropriate protection in return for the price, so he will invariably draft his warranties and conditions first. The only circumstance where this is not the case is where the target is being sold in an auction. Here the seller does the initial drafting so as to use the competitive environment to obtain the most beneficial terms for the sale.

When the contract is signed and exchanged, the parties are committed to the acquisition. It is, however, quite typical for completion to be delayed following signing of the contracts, to allow time for any necessary consents and clearances (on which the contract will be conditional) to be obtained (see **5.5**). The signing will therefore be no more than that: no money will pass hands and, although in legal terms the beneficial ownership of the target will have passed to the buyer, the seller remains the legal owner until completion. Some transactions will be signed and completed on the same day if all conditions can be satisfied on signing the agreement.

If either or both the parties are corporate entities, it or they will need to produce evidence to the other party of due authorisation for the transaction in the form of board minutes and resolutions approving it. No party to a contract wants to take the risk that the company on the other side will later disown and seek to avoid the contract entered into by one of its directors on the grounds that he or she was acting without authority—hence this is simply prudent practice.

5.4.2.2 Disclosure letter

The disclosure letter is prepared by the sellers and their solicitors, and contains a list of all the facts already disclosed to the buyer which contravene the warranties contained in the agreement. The buyer agrees it cannot then sue for breach of the warranties caused by these disclosures, as they have already been notified before the contract is entered into. The buyer's remedy is, prior to signing, to negotiate a reduction in the price or to have the seller deal with and correct the disclosed problem. Since the disclosure letter limits the scope of the buyer's protection, it is the subject of fierce scrutiny and negotiation (as with the agreement itself). It will be signed by the seller at the same time as the contract is signed.

5.4.2.3 Vendor placing agreement

Where the buyer is using its own securities as consideration for the acquisition, it is usual for those securities to be placed with investors on behalf of the seller (and on the instructions of the buyer) to realise cash for the benefit of the seller. This arrangement is discussed in **3.6.5**. Particular care has to be taken to ensure that the conditions in the business or share purchase agreement and the vendor placing agreement do not result in circularity. The vendor placing agreement will be signed at the same time as the purchase agreement. If the securities are to be listed on the Stock Exchange, then listing particulars will be required (see **4.2**).

5.4.3   Pre-completion

This refers to the period between contract and completion. The parties will have stated a completion date in the contract, which they may agree to defer if further time is required to satisfy outstanding conditions. What needs to be done in this period is essentially the satisfaction of any conditions on which the contract depends. With the exception of tax clearances, which we have already seen should be sought as part of the pre-contract phase, pre-completion is the point at which all other necessary clearances should now be obtained.

Section **5.6** deals with the various regulatory regimes and licensing requirements likely to affect these transactions, and the pre-completion clearances needed are those which satisfy those regimes and requirements.

With business acquisitions, this is the point at which third parties who have contracted with the business will be asked to agree to the substitution of the buyer for the seller in those contracts. As discussed in **5.3.7**, the novation of major contracts will need to be a condition precedent. The treatment of a business's contractual obligations generally is discussed more fully in **5.5.2**.

5.4.4   Completion

This is the point at which the acquisition is finalised. Completion takes place on the date specified in the business or share purchase agreement. What actually happens at completion?

5.4.4.1   Buyer's obligations

(a) To provide the consideration: if by way of cash, a banker's draft will be required; if the finance is through a vendor placing, then the buyer will need to show that all the placing's conditions are satisfied and that the cash which it has realised is available.

(b) To provide copies of the new service agreements which the buyer wants the target's key employees to sign.

5.4.4.2   Seller's obligations

(a) To produce the share transfers, any resignations of directors and company secretary which are required, certificate of incorporation, company seal and so on (if it is a share sale).

(b) To produce board minutes of the target approving the transfer of the shares for registration and the appointment of new directors (if it is a share sale). The buyer's solicitors will in fact draft these.

(c) To provide the deed of indemnity for tax liabilities (if it is a share sale).

(d) To provide evidence that all the conditions which it was the seller's obligation to seek (for example, the consent of third parties to the substitution of buyer for seller in the business's contracts) have been performed.

(e) If it is a business sale, to provide evidence that the buyers will have vacant possession of any property agreed to be sold under the business purchase agreement.

In essence then, the target is transferred legally into the name of the buyer, the seller gets its money and the transaction is wrapped up.

5.4.5 Post-completion

There will be a few minor details to attend to following completion; for example, if it is a share sale, stamping the share transfers for stamp duty and submitting notices of changes of directors and company secretary to Companies House. There will of course be a significant number of commercial changes to be made to the target's operations, particularly if new managers or new service agreements have been introduced. For the buyer's solicitors, there may be a significant amount of ongoing work as the target operation is restructured or integrated into the buyer's corporate group.

5.5 Purchase agreement

The key document in any acquisition is the purchase agreement, whether it be a company or a business which is being bought. This will set out the agreed terms and conditions and apportion the risks as between the parties through the warranties. This section looks at the principal terms and warranties you can expect to find in any purchase agreement.

5.5.1 Share purchase agreement

We start by looking at the standard main clauses in the agreement for a share sale. The later section on business purchase agreements (see **5.5.2**) concentrates only on the principal differences between a share and business purchase agreement, so much of what is said here applies equally to business purchases.

5.5.1.1 Agreement to sell

This is easily forgotten amidst the panoply of other provisions! The shares are sold free of all charges and encumbrances, subject possibly to a dividend strip to be paid to the sellers (see **5.2.2.3**).

5.5.1.2 Consideration

Will the consideration be cash or securities? If securities, it may be that the seller wants cash but the buyer has to issue its own securities into the market first to obtain that cash—hence a vendor placing will result (see **3.6.5**). Securities will also enable the seller to shelter a capital gain for the time being through roll-over relief. Securities in this context means shares or loan stock.

How should the consideration be provided now or in stages? Deferred consideration is sometimes used where the sellers are also key personnel in the future management of the business, and so are to remain employees of the target after the acquisition; in order to provide them with an incentive to maintain the profit levels of the company after the sale, part of their consideration is paid in future years on the basis of a percentage of profit. This is known as an 'earn out'. It is likely to give rise in addition to detailed provisions in the agreement fettering the discretion of the buyer to do as it pleases with the company after the sale: otherwise there would be an obvious incentive for it to run the company in such a way that its profits declined significantly.

How is the value of the company to be determined? The buyer will want to rely on the most up-to-date accounts of the company and the picture they give of its net asset value and profits record in arriving at an assessment of the consideration to be paid. There is a risk otherwise that the buyer will pay consideration in ignorance of recent financial difficulties which current accounts would reveal. Hence completion accounts are often prepared which state the financial position of the company up to completion. They are usually audited. There will usually be a clause in the agreement providing for an adjustment to the consideration depending on what the completion accounts reveal.

5.5.1.3 Conditions

Typical conditions are described at **5.6.7**. If the conditions are not satisfied, the agreement may provide either that it lapses, or that the buyer has the option to terminate, or complete the acquisition in spite of the failure to satisfy the condition, or agree a new date for eventual completion which will allow enough time for the condition to be satisfied. Usually the parties will agree, whichever option is selected, not to bring claims against each other for an outstanding condition unless one of them is at fault for not bringing it about.

5.5.1.4 Completion

This records the events described at **5.4.4**: the primary purpose of this clause is to state when and where completion will take place and remind all parties that this is the point at which the money is paid over. The buyer will preserve a right to terminate under the contract if any of the completion requirements are not satisfied and a right to claim damages (though this will be subject to the point about damages for non-satisfaction of conditions mentioned above).

   One point covered later in the clause about warranties, but relevant to completion, is the restatement of the warranties at completion: in other words, the buyer will usually want the warranties repeated at completion (which will mean updating the disclosure letter accordingly). The buyer will insist on this because he is not taking over the running of the company until completion—and it is only when he is managing the operation that he can reasonably be expected to assume responsibility for its liabilities. If warranties are updated to completion, and between exchange and completion it then becomes apparent that a further disclosure against the warranties will need to be made, the buyer will usually insist on the right to terminate and claim damages if the identified problem is material.

5.5.1.5 Action pending completion

The purpose of this is to place restrictions on what the seller can and cannot do with the company between exchange and completion. The buyer's fear is always that the seller's incentive for running the operation in a business-like fashion will decline significantly following signing and exchange of contracts. Hence the agreement will usually constrain the seller between exchange and completion from entering into material contracts, or dismissing employees, or buying and selling material assets, or issuing further shares in the company (and a host of other things) without the buyer's consent.

5.5.1.6 Warranties

Put simply, these are promises made by the seller to the buyer regarding the state of all aspects of the company's operations. They are needed because, in these transactions, it is not even possible for the buyer to presume that the seller owns what it is proposing to sell, as would be the case with a sale of goods by virtue of the implied warranty as to title under the Sale of Goods Act 1979. As a result, warranties are the centrepiece of any negotiation on a share purchase agreement. The warranties will always vary, depending on the nature of the company's business, but there are some relatively standard provisions you would expect to see in all cases, of which these are the most important:

(a) Accounts: that the latest accounts have been prepared in a way which is consistent with the company's previous accounts (and so provide an accurate comparison), and that they give a true and fair view (as defined by the Companies Act 1985 (see **2.4.3**)) of the company's financial affairs at the time they were prepared.

(b) Title: that the sellers have full and unfettered title to sell the shares.

(c) Material contracts: that the sellers have not entered into any material or unusual contracts (for example, over a certain value, or of an unusually long term, or of a loss-making nature, or which contain particularly onerous obligations for the company to satisfy). This will usually give rise to an extensive set of disclosures in the disclosure letter, and in many ways the principal purpose of this warranty is to flush out copies of all the company's significant contracts as part of the due diligence exercise.

(d) Assets: that the company has full and unencumbered title to its assets.

(e) Litigation: that the company has no ongoing, threatened or pending litigation claims, and has conducted its operations in accordance with all legal requirements including relevant licences and consents.

(f) Borrowings: that the company has no undisclosed borrowings. Once again, this will inevitably force a series of disclosures.

(g) Information: that the information supplied by the sellers in the course of the due diligence exercise is true, complete and accurate in all material respects and no information has been omitted which might render the information given untrue, inaccurate or misleading in any material respect. Given the reliance which the buyer will place on the information which emerges from the due diligence process (see **5.4.1.2**), it is vital to have some protection against the risk of the seller concocting a tissue of lies—hence this warranty is of great importance.

(h) Disclosure letter: in connection with the information warranty, it will be of equal importance to ensure that the accuracy and completeness of the disclosure letter is warranted by the seller.

(i) Employees: that the company is not in breach of any of the contractual or statutory obligations it owes to its employees.

(j) Real property: the inclusion of this warranty assumes that the other possible methods of dealing with the company's real property interests in the acquisition (see **5.4.1.2**) are not being used. The seller will be warranting that the company has good marketable title to its real properties and they are not subject to any undisclosed mortgages or charges.

(k) Environment: that the company is in full compliance with all relevant environmental legislation. This often gives rise to difficult negotiations in view of the latent, long-term and very costly nature of many environmental liabilities, and the toughening legislative regime in the UK and EU.

(l) Taxation: that the company has complied with all relevant tax legislation. In addition to this, the seller will normally be asked to indemnify the buyer against any tax liabilities for the period up to completion. The indemnity will be a separate document attached to and to be read in conjunction with the agreement.

In addition to the warranties, the seller is likely to be asked to give indemnities to the buyer, particularly for tax liabilities and possibly for other liabilities such as those arising in connection with the company's environmental history. It is important to understand how the seller's liability under warranties and indemnities differs.

Where there is a breach of warranty, the seller is liable for any reduction in the value of the shares resulting from the breach (to put the buyer into the position the buyer would have been in had the warranty been true). Where there is an indemnity (or a similar so-called 'pound-for-pound' clause), the seller is liable for any increase in the company's liabilities or reduction in the value of the underlying assets, irrespective of the effect on the value of the shares. For example, the breach of a warranty about the value of book debts will only permit recovery if this affects the value of the shares; if the seller has indemnified the buyer against the risk of book debts becoming irrecoverable, and then one is indeed lost, all the buyer has to prove is the size of the lost book debt and the buyer can recover automatically—the effect the loss will have on the shares is quite irrelevant. Indemnities are therefore generally resisted by sellers except in the context of tax liabilities where they are standard.

The warranties will always be given by the seller. The buyer may also require directors of the company, or a parent company or directors or key shareholders of the seller, to join in the warranties where they have played a significant role in the management and direction of the target company. In this case, the buyer will usually make the warrantors jointly and severally liable for a breach of any of the warranties.

It is usual for warrantors to seek to qualify the warranties they give by reference to their knowledge at the time that they gave them: thus, wording is used such as 'to the best of the seller's knowledge, information and belief, there is no outstanding litigation' etc. Otherwise the seller will be concerned that the warranty is really a guarantee. Obviously the buyer will be keen to resist this kind of limitation to the scope of the warranties, which will depend largely on the comparative negotiating strength of the parties. A buyer who has to concede the qualification will usually insist that the phrase 'to the best of the seller's knowledge, information and belief' is itself qualified by the words 'having made all reasonable enquiries', so that at least the buyer is not relying on the seller's inadequately researched information.

5.5.1.7   Limitations on the warranties

The seller will only accept the raft of warranties and tax indemnity in return for some restrictions under the agreement as to the following:

(a) The maximum amount for which claims can be made (usually settled at the total consideration payable).

(b) The minimum monetary amount per claim (to deter frivolous claims).

(c) The time-limits within which claims must be brought: these will override the Limitation Act 1980, and usually parties settle on anything between 18 months and three years. This is on the basis that after this any undisclosed problems with the company will have become apparent and it is therefore pointless to keep the warranties open for longer. Sometimes an exception may be negotiated by the buyer for the environmental warranty. Six years for the tax deed of indemnity is common, because of the threat of Inland Revenue investigations into the tax affairs of a company that far back.

5.5.1.8   Pensions

Appropriate arrangements will need to be made for the continuing provision of a pension scheme to the company's employees following completion, and the various alternatives are described in **5.4.1.2**.

5.5.1.9 Restrictive covenants

The buyer will usually seek restrictive covenants from the seller to prevent the seller soliciting the company's customers or setting up an identical operation next door within a fortnight of completion. The covenants will need to be specific about the kind of business which is being restricted and reasonable in terms of geographical and temporal limitations.

5.5.1.10 Assignment

Unless the seller is happy to be sued by future buyers of the company, it will be necessary to prevent the buyer from assigning the benefit of the agreement, so there is usually a provision in the agreement requiring the seller's consent before this can be done.

5.5.1.11 Retention fund

The buyer may seek to have the seller's obligations under the agreement supported by a retention fund. Part of the buyer's consideration is paid into a retention fund until the claims period for the warranties (see **5.5.1.7**) is at an end. If the seller becomes liable under any of the warranties during that period, the buyer's claim (if proven) is paid out of the retention fund. Any outstanding amount in the fund is paid over to the seller when the claims period has concluded. This gives the buyer some assurance that his warranty claims will be met out of ready cash. Retention fund arrangements are usually resisted fiercely by sellers as they are kept out of a proportion of their consideration for some time.

5.5.1.12 Costs

Who will bear the legal and accountancy fees to which the transaction will give rise? Usually each party bears its own.

5.5.1.13 Interest

Any sum not paid over in accordance with the agreement will attract interest.

5.5.1.14 Arbitration

Do the parties want to refer disputes to arbitration rather than rely on the courts and normal litigation procedures? Arbitration may be costly, though it may also be quick and efficient. It may in fact be most appropriate to have an expert arbitrator appointed to resolve any differences arising on the more technical parts of the agreement, for instance, the drawing up of the completion accounts (see **5.5.1.2**), whilst relying on the courts to sort out differences arising elsewhere.

5.5.1.15 Governing law

If any of the parties to the agreement are foreign, it is prudent to state that English law is the governing law of the contract and require the foreign party to submit to English jurisdiction for legal proceedings: where there is no doubt that the *situs* of the contract is the UK, this clause is redundant.

5.5.2 Business purchase agreement

This section concentrates on the differences between share and business purchase agreements. Much of what was mentioned in **5.5.1** will be relevant for business purchase agreements as well. The following paragraphs discuss the clauses which will be different.

5.5.2.1 Agreement to sell

Obviously with the share purchase agreement, the agreement is to sell the shares. With the business purchase agreement, the agreement is to sell the business, which is in turn comprised of a collection of assets fused into a going concern. Hence the business purchase agreement will need to describe these assets and the fact that they are being sold as a going concern.

The assets to be sold obviously depend on the nature of the business which is being sold. Commonly, though, the following will figure in the list (and all of these will be listed individually in the agreement and defined):

(a) Property: freehold property will need to be sold free of encumbrances and mortgages. Leasehold property will need to be sold with the landlord's written consent. It is often not possible to obtain this in time for completion. Unless the property is absolutely fundamental to the business, it is not usual to make the landlord's consent a condition of the contract. More often, the seller agrees to use its best endeavours to obtain the consent within a reasonable period. Although there are risks associated with this (clearly the landlord may refuse consent and it may be reasonable for the landlord to do so), the agreement will often provide a fallback—namely that the buyer finds alternative premises and the seller funds the difference (or agrees to take less consideration).

(b) Stock: stock or work in progress of the business will need to have been recently valued. Since stamp duty is not payable on assets passing by delivery and stock is such an asset, it is helpful from the buyer's point of view to attach as high a value to stock as possible, as it saves stamp duty (which is imposed at rates of either 1, 3 or 4 per cent in business sales, rather than the effective $\frac{1}{2}$ per cent in share sales (see **5.2.2**));

(c) Chattels: this includes plant and machinery, cars, vans, fittings, office equipment and the like—it may be appropriate to draw up an inventory of everything included as a chattel and attach it as a schedule. As with stock, there is a considerable advantage to the buyer in having as much of the asset value being bought identified as chattels since that will save stamp duty.

(d) Intellectual property: this includes trade marks, copyright, registered designs, patents and know-how.

(e) Investments: for instance, shares held in other companies.

(f) Contracts: normally the parties will agree that the buyer takes over the business's ongoing contracts, whether they be for the supply of goods and services, joint ventures or other arrangements. Major contracts which the buyer regards as fundamental to the business will need to be novated prior to completion and so this will need to be a condition to the agreement. Less important contracts will need to be checked to ensure they can be assigned. If so, the seller will undertake to get this done. If contracts cannot be assigned, the parties will generally agree that the seller will hold the contracts for the benefit of the buyer and the buyer will function *de facto* as the contracting party. In this event, the seller will want to be indemnified against the risk of liability arising through the buyer's non-performance, and the buyer will seek an assurance that any money paid to the seller by the contracting third party are held by the seller for the buyer's benefit.

(g) Debtors: there are a number of options available.
    The first is to assign debts to the buyer: notice of assignment will then need to be issued to each debtor. There may be two reasons for avoiding this: first, the time it takes up, and second, if debts are excluded from the sale, no stamp duty is payable on them, which is tax-efficient from the buyer's point of view.

The parties may therefore agree instead that the seller legally retains title to the debts and the buyer collects them on the seller's behalf for a fee. The consideration payable is reduced accordingly. The buyer will want an assurance that the seller will not issue writs against outstanding debtors who continue to be customers of the business following completion. Alternatively, the seller retains and collects the debts itself and so any money it receives for them, and the buyer agrees to pay the seller any money it should accidentally receive in respect of them.

(h) Creditors: as far as creditors are concerned, there are also a number of options.

The buyer may agree to assume the obligation to pay the creditors. Legally, unless the third party agrees to the buyer replacing the seller, it is still the seller which is responsible for paying the outstanding debts of the business, hence the seller should obtain an indemnity from the buyer against any liability which the seller incurs because the buyer fails to pay up.

Alternatively, to save the buyer stamp duty (which is payable on the assumption of liabilities), the seller hangs on to the creditors and agrees with the buyer that it will pay its debts promptly, and indemnifies the buyer against any losses it may suffer if the seller does not.

A final option is for the buyer to agree to pay off the creditors as agent for the seller in return for a reduction in the consideration price. The seller will want the buyer to agree to do so promptly and to indemnify the seller if the creditors sue the seller for non-payment.

(i) Cash on deposit: this is often excluded from the sale as otherwise stamp duty is paid on it.

(j) Goodwill and transfer of the business as a going concern: goodwill covers the intangible benefits which the buyer will inherit with the business (for instance, reputation and the value which recognised brand names carry). The value of those benefits is represented by the amount which the buyer is willing to pay in addition to the net asset value of the business. If the goodwill is excluded from the assets to be transferred, this may cause difficulty in showing that the business is being transferred as a going concern. This would give difficulties with VAT and the transfer of employees.

VAT is payable on the sale of a business by the seller if the business is not sold as a going concern and the buyer is not registered for VAT. This means that the seller will have to pay VAT at 17.5 per cent out of the purchase price received, as the purchase price will be deemed to be VAT-inclusive. Obviously this reduces the net amount of consideration the seller expects to receive.

To counteract this, the transaction can be structured so that the business is sold as a going concern, and advance clearance obtained from HM Customs and Excise to confirm this.

If clearance is not forthcoming, the parties will generally agree (assuming the buyer is registered for VAT) that the buyer will pay the purchase price plus 17.5 per cent VAT, and the seller will give the buyer an invoice which will enable this output VAT to be set off against the buyer's input VAT—though sometimes, the parties may agree to split the cost of the extra VAT.

As for the employees, under the Transfer of Undertakings (Protection of Employment) Regulations 1981 (SI 1981/1794), employees working in the business immediately before the point at which the business is transferred (completion) will continue by automatic operation of law to be treated as employed by the business after transfer (and therefore as not dismissed), *provided* the business is transferred as a going concern. Despite the automatic application of the regulations, the agreement will usually identify the employees and state that they will be transferred as one of the business's assets.

In view of the importance of both these points, the agreement will usually state that the parties agree the business is sold as a going concern.

5.5.2.2 Warranties

Since the process of buying a business permits the buyer to select the assets it wants to buy and the liabilities it does not want to inherit (for example, creditors or outstanding tax liabilities), the warranties in a business purchase agreement are less wide-ranging and demanding than would be the case with a typical share purchase agreement. It is unlikely that the buyer will extract an indemnity from the seller for outstanding tax liabilities which the buyer chooses to take on, though there will probably be warranties that the liabilities do not exceed what has already been identified—hence there is usually no deed of indemnity in the purchase of a business. The warranties will cover similar ground to those sought in the purchase of a company. Their focus will be to seek assurance from the seller that the value of the individual assets is as stated and that there are no material undisclosed liabilities relevant to particular assets or in general which might affect the value of the business.

5.6 Regulation of acquisitions

5.6.1 The basic principle: freedom of contract

We start from the position that parties are free to buy and sell businesses, assets and companies under contract on terms they choose. The acquisition or disposal is governed by the private treaty which the parties freely enter into. This has a number of important consequences:

(a) The regulatory constraints considered in this section are very important. Your client, though, will not thank you for a masterful exposition of them if you cannot draft or negotiate a contract. It is in the contract that almost all of the issues arising in the acquisition will be settled or provided for. You have to know both the law of contract and be capable of drafting and negotiating a contract to advise properly in this area.

(b) Unlike a takeover, where regulation has defined quite closely the way in which the transaction may be conducted (see **Chapter 8**), acquisitions are inherently flexible transactions which can be moulded to suit the individual idiosyncrasies of clients. Regulation may interfere with this flexibility to some extent, but the starting-point is what the clients want rather than what the rule books say you can do. The lawyer needs therefore to be prepared to draft and negotiate creatively.

However, there are a number of rules which will contribute to the way the transaction is moulded. These regulations turn the transaction from one governed by purely private considerations to one with a public dimension.

5.6.2 City Code on Takeovers and Mergers

This is covered in detail in **Chapter 8**. Subject to some exceptions, the Code will apply if it is a *public company* which is being acquired. In these circumstances, an offer must be made to the target's shareholders to acquire their shares. The Code governs the nature, timing and content of that offer. You should refer to **Chapter 8** for detailed information.

5.6.3   Financial Services and Markets Act 2000

This bites on acquisitions in a number of ways.

5.6.3.1   Buying and selling businesses

Where there is a sale of a company's business, i.e., a sale of the company's assets, there should be no problems as regards FSMA, since a business is not an investment for the purpose of the Act. In comparison, where a company is bought through an acquisition of its shares, those shares are investments within the terms of FSMA. The actual purchase of shares by the principal to the transaction and any arrangements made or advice given regarding the purchase, are, on the face of it, regulated activities (within the meaning of FSMA s. 22) for which authorisation from the FSA is required (see **1.5.1**). However, there are a number of exclusions under the Financial Services and Markets Act 2000 (Regulated Activities) Order 2001 ('RAO'), which remove the need for authorisation. The most important of these is art. 70, which effectively excludes any purchase of shares the result of which gives the new owner 50 per cent or more of the voting shares in the target company. For the purpose of the exclusion, the new owner can be a group of connected individuals, as defined by the article. The exclusion means that both the acquisition and any arrangements made or advice given in connection with it are not regulated activities for the purposes of FSMA. Given the share ownership threshold, most company acquisitions will fall within this exclusion.

Another important exclusion for professional advisers is that any arrangements made or advice given in the course of a profession which does not otherwise consist of regulated activities are not regulated activities for the purposes of FSMA (see RAO art. 67). There is a requirement that the arrangements or advice must be reasonably regarded as a necessary part of other services provided in the course of the relevant profession.

5.6.3.2   Financial promotion

Section 21 of FSMA prohibits a person, in the course of their business, from communicating an invitation or inducement to engage in investment activity, unless they are an authorised person or the content of the communication has been approved by an authorised person. This section should not affect business sales (see **5.6.3.1** above) but there are situations in which a proposed share sale could involve parties in financial promotion. An example would be where a seller was carrying out an auction process and sending an information memorandum or draft acquisition agreement to a number of potential buyers. On the face of it, the content of these documents would have to be approved by an authorised person. However, art. 62 of the Financial Services and Markets Act 2000 (Financial Promotion) Order 2001 provides an exemption from the financial promotion regime where there is a sale of a body corporate. The terms on which the exemption is given are the same as those relating to regulated activities (see **5.6.3.1** above), i.e., where there is a purchase of over 50 per cent of the target company. There is also an exclusion in art. 55 for professional advisers.

5.6.3.3   Section 397

This has been discussed in **1.5.1.4**. Section 397 creates specific problems in the context of acquisitions which might not at first sight appear obvious.

(a) Investments for the purposes of FSMA include shares but *not* assets or a business—hence s. 397 is never of relevance to a business sale (unless the business owns investments such as shares), but does catch a company or share sale.

(b) One of the consequences of applying the basic principles of contract to acquisition work is the *'caveat emptor'* rule—let the buyer beware. At common law, the seller is under no duty to disclose information about the business or shares it is selling. Section 397(3) FSMA makes it an offence to do any act or engage in any *course of conduct* which creates, and is intended to create, a false or misleading impression as to the market, price or value in investments. Although at common law the seller is obliged to disclose nothing to the buyer, any failure to disclose a fact about the target company which might otherwise affect the price the buyer is prepared to pay will be creating a false impression and, if it is designed to have that effect, it will amount to a course of conduct caught by the section. If the facts are material and are concealed dishonestly, this will also be a breach of s. 397(1). To be safe, sellers of companies should disclose to buyers anything which might have an effect on the value of the target.

(c) Any representations expressly made to potential buyers of companies (whether orally or in writing) to encourage them to acquire will fall foul of s. 397(1) if they create a false or misleading impression and the makers of the representations know that or are reckless about it (see s. 397(2)).

5.6.3.4 Transfer of business carrying on regulated activities

FSMA regulates the conduct of a business which carries on regulated activities by requiring it to be authorised (see FSMA ss. 31 and 40). Authorisation is granted to the owners of that business. If those owners change because the business is being transferred, then the new owners may need to make an application of their own for authorisation, or approval for the transfer may be needed from the FSA (see FSMA s. 46). The background to the regulatory structure introduced by FSMA has been explained more fully in **1.5**.

5.6.4 Listing Rules regulation

This may have an impact on the acquisition of a private company or business in two ways: the definition of transactions and the issue of listing particulars.

5.6.4.1 Transactions

The Listing Rules oblige listed companies to observe certain requirements when involved in 'transactions'. The first general point to note is the breadth of the term 'transactions' (LR para. 10.1). It covers all transactions, exempting specifically only transactions in the ordinary course of business and issues of equity finance (provided they are not related to an acquisition). Nevertheless, what it will principally catch are acquisitions or disposals.

The purpose of these controls is to keep shareholders of these companies informed of purchases and sales their companies are making and to give them a veto over particularly large or sensitive transactions. The requirements which the companies must observe depend on how the relevant transaction is classified (see LR para. 10.4). They are set out in LR chs 10 and 11.

5.6.4.2 Classification of transactions

(a) *Class 1* transactions must be notified to a Regulatory Information Service and to the company's shareholders in a circular. They also require approval of the company's shareholders in general meeting (LR para. 10.37).

(b) *Class 2* transactions must be notified to a Regulatory Information Service. (LR para. 10.31).

(c) *Class 3* transactions only require notification if the consideration for the acquisition includes securities which are to be listed (LR para. 10.29) (or dealt with in the AIM if it is an AIM company), or if any details of the transaction have been released to the public (LR para. 10.30).

(d) *Transactions with related parties* may have to be notified to a Regulatory Information Service under LR ch. 10 and will generally require a circular and the approval of shareholders in general meeting (LR para. 11.4 and also paras 11.5 and 11.6).

Reverse takeovers require a Class 1 circular, must be approved by shareholders in general meeting and require listing particulars to be prepared if the company wishes to be listed following completion of the transaction (LR para. 10.39): they are dealt with in **8.10**.

What makes a transaction Class 1, Class 2 etc? This depends on the size of the transaction, which in turn is gauged by comparing the value of the company making the acquisition or disposal with the value of the company or business being acquired or disposed of. There are five methods by which value must be compared (LR para. 10.5):

(a) gross assets;

(b) profits;

(c) turnover;

(d) consideration paid compared with the market capitalisation of the buyer;

(e) gross capital.

If the comparison *in any one of the five categories* equals or exceeds the percentages set out in the table below (which is based on LR para. 10.4), then the transaction falls within the relevant classification and the appropriate requirements apply. The exception is Class 3: *all* the figures must be below 5 per cent for a transaction to be in Class 3. If one of those five methods of comparison produces an anomalous result, the UKLA may disregard the result it produces (LR para. 10.6). The UKLA may aggregate separate transactions for the purposes of these classifications if they are connected, or there have been multiple transactions in the last year.

Classification	Size of transaction
Class 1	25 per cent
Class 2	5 per cent
Class 3	less than 5 per cent
Related party transaction	see below
Reverse takeover	100 per cent or change of control in buyer

A related party transaction is one between the company and one or more of its directors or substantial shareholders, irrespective of the size of the transaction (LR para. 11.4). The UKLA is anxious to control these to prevent possible abuses by directors of their powers. The term 'transaction' is again very broadly construed, including not just sales and purchases. However, LR paras 11.7 and 11.8 exempt certain related party transactions which would otherwise be caught: for example, giving an indemnity to a director or granting options to directors under share schemes, or 'small transactions' (below 0.25 per cent in the table of comparisons above).

A reverse takeover is one where the target is at least as big as the buyer, with the possible result (where the buyer's securities are the whole or part of the consideration for the purchase) that the target shareholders end up controlling the buyer. The Listing Rules and AIM Rules require the consent of the buyer's shareholders to such a transaction (LR para. 10.39 and AIM Rules r. 33).

5.6.4.3 Examples

Let us look at some examples. Assume for these that Yellow plc (Y) is listed on the Official List. Y has gross assets of £100 million and profits of £10 million.

(a) *Y wants to buy G, an independent plc with profits of £3 million*
This is a public company takeover governed by the City Code on Takeovers and Mergers—refer to **Chapter 8** for further details. In addition, though, the transaction will be a Class 1 for Y on the profits comparison and so will require shareholder approval.

(b) *Y wants to buy B, a business with assets of £5 million and profits of £1.1 million*
The transaction is a Class 2 acquisition for Y on the profits and assets comparisons, requiring notification to a Regulatory Information Service and a press announcement.

(c) *Y wants to acquire 2 per cent of G's shares, and one of Y's directors already owns 0.1 per cent of the shares in G*
G is not a related party of Y, despite the director's shareholding. The director would need to control at least 30 per cent of G's votes or have a majority of votes on the board under his control for G to count as his 'associate' and so be caught by the terms of LR ch. 11, as a related party of Y.

5.6.4.4 Definitions of figures to be used

To assist in calculating the percentage ratios, The Listing Rules provide definitions of the figures to be used. These are set out in paras 10.7–10.19.

5.6.4.5 Notifications

Notification to the LSE must contain particulars of the transaction, details of whatever is being acquired or disposed of, the value of the consideration, other relevant financial information and the benefits resulting from the transaction (LR paras 10.29 to 10.37). What shareholders need to be told depends on the classification of the transaction. All circulars should comply with the general requirements of LR ch. 14 (including giving clear explanations).

(a) *Class 1 Circular*
The specific contents requirements for these are set out in LR ch. 10, app. (LR paras 10.38 and 10.40). They are more relaxed than the requirements we have seen for the contents of a prospectus or listing particulars (see **4.2.6.3**). They include the need for statements about working capital (LR paras 10.41(c) and 6.E.16) and changes in the financial position of the company since its last financial statement (LR paras 10.41(a) and 6.E.8). A Class 1 Circular needs to contain details of the company's litigation, (LR paras 10.41(a) and 6.D.8), material contracts, (LR paras 10.41(a) and 6.C.20), current indebtedness (Where a Class 1 circular relates to a takeover offer which is not recommended by the Board of the offeree at the time of publication of the circular: LR paras 10.45, 10.47(c) and 6.L.6) and trading prospects (LR para 10.41(c) and 6.G.1(b)). It also requires a directors' responsibility statement (LR para. 10.38(e)) and a recommendation paragraph stating that the proposed transaction is in the best interests of the shareholders as a whole (LR para. 14.1(d)). Like a prospectus or listing particulars, a Class 1 circular needs to be approved by the UKLA first before it can be distributed to shareholders (LR para. 10.38).

(b) *Related party transaction circular*
The contents requirements for listed companies sending out these circulars are set out in LR para. 11.10. The two most important requirements are for statements about material contracts (LR paras 11.10(a) and 6.C.20) and significant changes in

the financial position of the company since its last financial statement (LR paras 11.10(a) and 6.E.8). In addition, the circular must have a statement from an independent adviser describing why the transaction is reasonable and fair so far as the shareholders are concerned (LR para. 11.10(e)). The related party must not be allowed to vote on the transaction at the general meeting (LR para. 11.10(f)).

Consultation with the UKLA on a related party transaction and the contents of the relevant circular will be needed at an early stage.

5.6.4.6   Listing particulars and prospectuses

This is the second way in which the Listing Rules may affect an acquisition. If the consideration to be provided by the buyer consists (at least in part) of the issue of new securities, and the buyer is listed or dealt in on the AIM, then the issue will require listing particulars (LR para. 10.46) or a prospectus under the Public Offers of Securities Regulations 1995, with the possible additional requirement of a further admission document under. 24 of the AIM Rules (as appropriate). You should refer to **Chapter 4** for further details about these documents.

If the transaction requires listing particulars or a prospectus, the company is likely to combine such a document with any circular it needs to send shareholders to satisfy the requirements of the Listing Rules (LR para. 10.43).

5.6.5   Merger control

The statutory and regulatory provisions intended to prevent undue restrictions in the competitive environment in the UK and EC are considered in detail in the context of public company takeovers in **8.16**, though they are of equal relevance to private acquisitions or disposals. A decision by the Office of Fair Trading not to refer a merger for consideration by the Competition Commission (see **8.16**) will usually be a condition of the acquisition. Any reference will therefore lapse the purchase agreement.

5.6.6   Other regulatory restrictions

The range of other possible regulatory constraints which may catch a specific acquisition is limitless, and the lists above and below contain only the most obvious and routine snags you are likely to encounter. You must never disregard any licensing requirements particular to the industries in which the acquired entity operates. We have already mentioned FSMA, but in addition other financial concerns will be subject to regulatory controls. The transfer of a banking business will need the approval of the Bank of England; the transfer of an insurance business that of the Department of Trade and Industry. There are a number of other industry-specific restrictions which are of special importance:

5.6.6.1   Industry Act 1975

The President of the Board of Trade may prevent the transfer to a non-UK resident of 30 per cent or more of a manufacturing business if he considers it to be specially important. Exercise of this discretion is rare.

5.6.6.2   Inland Revenue

Tax consents, rulings or clearances are often needed, as we have seen (see **5.2.2.4**).

5.6.6.3   Companies Act 1985

In all the excitement of assorted regulations, it is easy to forget the standard Companies Act 1985 requirements which need to be observed.

If the consideration for the acquisition includes the issue of the company's own securities, do bear in mind the possible need for a s. 80 authority to allot or a s. 89 disapplication.

The LSE may require related party transactions to be approved by the shareholders in general meeting but, in the event that it does not, is the transaction caught by s. 320 (substantial property transaction involving directors)? If so, it will in any event need approval from the shareholders in general meeting.

5.6.6.4   Corporate regulation

Any acquisition or disposal by a company must comply with a company's memorandum and articles of association. The transaction must fall within its objects, and special requirements in the articles regarding shareholder approvals need to be observed (as do borrowing restrictions if the buying company is borrowing to fund an acquisition).

5.6.7   Conditions

Most of these regulatory controls will not inhibit a transaction proceeding (the merger control provisions are the most obvious exception). It is essential though to ensure they are complied with in case sanctions should follow: failure to observe the Yellow Book requirements could lead to de-listing. Hence it will always be a condition of the acquisition proceeding that relevant regulatory requirements are observed and fulfilled. You need to ensure therefore not only that your client is properly advised about the application and effect of any relevant regulations but also that the contract has been adequately drafted to deal with their impact on the transaction.

5.7   Checklists

The following checklists summarise the issues which you will need to address in structuring an acquisition, advising your client on the due diligence exercise on the target, drafting the agreement and ensuring you have all the documents the transaction requires.

5.7.1   Structuring the transaction

(a) What is the business or commercial background to the transaction?

(b) Has any decision been made as to whether this is to be a company or business sale? If not, see **5.2**.

(c) Are either of the entities listed on the Official List or dealt in on the AIM? This will help determine whether there are any UKLA and LSE requirements to observe regarding notification of the transaction.

(d) Is there any overseas element involved in the transaction? Consider the impact of overseas regulators and the need for overseas advice.

(e) What is the expected value of the transaction? This will determine whether:

    (i)   the class requirements of the Listing Rules come into play, possibly requiring shareholder's approval—see **5.6.4**;

    (ii)   there are any merger control implications—see **8.16**.

(f) What is the nature of the business to be acquired? This will help determine whether there are likely to be any special approvals or consents needed for the transaction—see **5.6.6**.

(g) What form will the consideration take? Securities may also require a vendor placing. Will it be deferred? Will there be an earn-out element? (See **5.5.1.2**.)

(h) What tax clearances will be required? (See **5.2.2.4**.)

5.7.2 Getting to grips with the target

Information and documents are needed on the following:

(a) the memorandum and articles of association of the target if it is a share sale, and the seller if it is a business sale;

(b) accounts relevant to the company or the business (and accountants' report);

(c) material contracts;

(d) employment contracts, and any materials relevant to the benefits enjoyed by those working for the target, e.g., pension rights, share schemes etc.;

(e) loan documents, mortgages, charges, debentures relevant to the company or the business;

(f) title deeds relevant to the property belonging to the company or business;

(g) the target's intellectual property rights.

5.7.3 Drafting the agreement

You should expect your agreement to cover the following points:

(a) agreement to sell;

(b) consideration;

(c) conditions;

(d) completion and action up to completion;

(e) assignment;

(f) costs and interest;

(g) restrictive covenants regarding non-solicitation of customers or non-competition;

(h) warranties and limitations thereto. Warranties should cover:

    (i)   capacity and title of the sellers;

    (ii)   information supplied;

    (iii) accounts;

    (iv)   borrowings and liabilities;

    (v)   material contracts;

    (vi)   compliance with laws and litigation;

    (vii) employees and pensions;

    (viii) assets;

    (ix)   real and intellectual property (if relevant);

    (x)   environment.

Do not forget the tax deed of indemnity!

5.7.4 Additional considerations for purchases of businesses

These are the assets the agreement and its warranties will need to deal with:

(a) property (freehold and leasehold);

(b) stock;

(c) intellectual property;

(d) contracts;

(e) investments;

(f) chattels, plant, machinery;

(g) cash;

(h) goodwill;

(i) possibly debts;

(j) possibly liabilities.

5.7.5 Documents list

This is a summary of the key documents you are likely to require in a typical acquisition:

(a) heads of agreement;

(b) confidentiality agreement;

(c) instructions to accountants;

(d) request for information from the seller;

(e) due diligence documents;

(f) share or business purchase agreement and deed of indemnity;

(g) disclosure letter;

(h) vendor placing agreement;

(i) completion documents (share transfers, conveyances, satisfaction of conditions, shareholder and board resolutions to show corporate approval for the transaction);

(j) circular to shareholders and, if necessary, listing particulars or prospectus.

Joint ventures

So far we have concentrated on the acquisitive side of corporate finance activity. There is of course a cooperative side as well, and this is epitomised by the joint venture.

6.1 What is a joint venture?

The idea is simple, though the number of forms it may take are legion (see **6.3**). In essence, a joint venture is a cooperative enterprise between two or more persons pursuing an agreed commercial goal or set of goals and in which the joint venturers share in agreed proportions the financing and control of the enterprise and the profits and losses it makes. The parties to such a venture can just as easily be individuals as companies.

It is perhaps easier to define a joint venture by reference to what it is not:

(a) *A franchise arrangement*
The nature of a franchise is that the franchisee is much more free than under a joint venture to pursue a personal business aim and the franchisor does not share in the profits in a true sense as usually only a premium or fixed fee is taken.

(b) *A collaboration agreement*
This will usually involve an agreement to share information and work on a specific area, often intellectual property, but not to form a joint enterprise in the process.

(c) *A service contract*
This term is not used in its more normal context of a director's employment contract. An example is a management services agreement in which one party agrees to provide the management services for a project or manufacturing facility owned by the other in return for a fee. Other examples are marketing or distributorship arrangements. There is no sharing of profits or risks (as there would be in a joint venture), simply a contractual deal in which one party supplies its expertise to the other at a price.

6.2 Why a joint venture?

It may seem perplexing that two parties would agree to establish a joint venture as opposed to pursuing a business goal for their own individual benefit. Are the commercial rewards forsaken not greater than those gained? This of course is always a difficult matter of judgment, and the parties to a joint venture clearly judge not. There are a number of reasons why a joint venture may suggest itself as the natural vehicle for a business venture:

(a) In a new venture, particularly one where the initial investment required is very large, or the potential losses very substantial, sharing the costs and liabilities with someone else may be the only viable way to launch the operation. In a sense, the joint venture here is a way of spreading cost and risk where both are difficult to quantify: no one wants too much of either.

(b) A joint venture may be a genuine sharing of different capacities and expertise. One party may have an outstanding business idea and the expertise to make it work, but no resources. Whilst a loan may be one solution, another is to find someone who has resources and is looking for a good idea to fund on the basis of taking a slice of the profits if the idea comes to fruition. A joint venture has been formed.

(c) Sometimes joint ventures are designed to create a virtual monopoly in a market. Life becomes much more comfortable for two competitors, each holding 40 per cent of a particular market and therefore close rivals, if they agree to pool resources and efforts: then they hold a combined market share, are not undercutting each other's margins and can cooperate gradually to squeeze out their smaller competitors. Of course this sort of conduct is anticompetitive and subject to regulatory restraint (see **8.16**), but it may still be a strong driving force behind a joint venture.

(d) We look at public company takeovers in **Chapter 8**. One of the longer term defensive strategies for a company which fears it may be the target of a takeover bid is to lock some of its assets or resources away in a joint venture. The joint venture will usually provide that if either party to it experiences a change of control (such as would obviously be induced by a successful takeover offer for one of them) then the other party has a pre-emptive right to take over the entire joint venture. This is likely to be a significant deterrent to a would-be predator as the predator may forfeit the most coveted assets in the target.

Joint ventures therefore present a number of attractions. Of course, they are only one possible solution to the sort of problems described above. Certain business cultures have arguably proved more fertile for the sort of cooperative exercise which the joint venture entails than others (such as the US and the UK) which put a premium on acquisitions as the preferred business development method. Certain business areas, such as property investment and development and technology, attract a significant number of joint ventures, primarily because of the investment needed.

6.3 What is needed for a joint venture?

One commodity which is absolutely essential at the start and indeed all the way through, and over which the lawyer can have a significant influence, is goodwill. The joint venture is a cooperative enterprise. It depends on a spirit of mutual trust. This is not to say that the parties to it will not disagree or negotiate fiercely for what they want. But without some mutuality of understanding the venture will not get started. The lawyer can do great damage to perfectly amicable relationships by approaching the transaction in a confrontational style. This will not enhance your client's prospects nor endear you to the client in the long run.

Let us look at the sort of questions you will need to ask:

(a) How will the joint venture be constituted? The assumption here is that the enterprise is to be conducted through a body or entity jointly owned—so a new body of some sort will need to be created. What alternatives exist?

(i) Company. The parties can become shareholders in a company. This is likely to be private and limited. Will it become a subsidiary of either or both of the parties (see **9.2**)? The articles of association will regulate the parties' management and shareholding rights, though they will enter into a shareholders' agreement as well to govern other aspects such as the funding of the venture (see **6.4.1**).

(ii) Partnership. A partnership may arise if the conditions of the Partnership Act 1890 are satisfied. If the parties choose a partnership as their preferred vehicle, they will want to draft a partnership agreement rather than rely on the Act.

A looser arrangement such as an unincorporated association is not appropriate given the doubt in law about the use of such a structure for business purposes; in any event, your clients would be well-advised that this kind of informal approach is not ideal in offering suitable legal safeguards.

If the joint venture is to operate overseas, or the parties are prepared or want (perhaps for tax reasons) to site the joint venture offshore, some jurisdictions offer the potential for a limited partnership which combines the benefits of the more flexible and less regulated partnership with limited liability status.

The principal attraction of selecting a corporate entity is limited liability status, and this is the more typical route for joint venturers to choose. The rest of this chapter will assume this is the entity preferred.

(b) Have the parties agreed in principle on the structure and operation of the joint venture in heads of agreement? If not, do they wish to sign these to form the basis for further discussion? Heads of agreement in this context need to be treated with the same sort of care as for those signed in business and company acquisitions (see **5.4.1.1**).

(c) Joint ventures often involve the parties sharing, or giving access to, information about each other which is confidential. Have the parties considered the need for a confidentiality agreement to deal with this?

(d) What is the joint venture's business aim? Apart from anything else, some objects for the memorandum of association will need to be drafted.

(e) How will the parties set the joint venture in motion? Will they provide premises, staff and equipment, or will the joint venture arrange this from the funds it inherits?

(f) How is the venture to be financed? Simply through the money put in when the shareholders subscribe for their shares? If so, will they contribute in equal measure? Will there be any debt financing? If so, from whom and how will it be secured? Who will provide future financing? If from the shareholders, will it be in equal shares?

(g) Will the joint venturers take equal profit shares? If it is a company, will the profits be paid by way of dividend?

(h) How will the management of the venture be organised? Will it be 50–50? What if there is a deadlock? Will the managers have the right to decide everything in relation to the venture's affairs or will some of the more important decisions be referred to the venturers themselves?

(i) How is termination of the venture to be governed? Will breach of the shareholders' agreement be a termination event? If one party wants to get out of the joint venture, will the other party or parties have the right to buy the departing party's interest?

There will always be a host of other issues to address: this list is only of the most obvious and important. The rest of the chapter is devoted to a closer look at the physical and documentary structure you would seek to give a corporate joint venture.

6.4   Joint venture companies: the lawyer's role

You will need to begin with the questions above and refine them further (see below). What you are aiming to do is to gather the necessary information to prepare the two crucial governing documents for the joint venture, the shareholders' agreement and the articles of association.

6.4.1   The shareholders' agreement

Why are the articles of association not sufficient to bind the joint venturers together? The articles in a joint venture company regulate the affairs of the joint venturers as shareholders and managers. Some other document will have to record the arrangements regarding provision of staff, premises and facilities for the venture, the provision of finance, and termination, amongst other things. This is the role of the shareholders' agreement. The shareholders' agreement, as a private contract, is not subject to the disclosure requirement of the articles, and so is a perfect vehicle for any confidential or sensitive material.

However, the normal procedure is for the parties to agree on their respective shareholding interests and structure, and the powers of the managers, in the shareholders' agreement and make it one of the terms of the agreement that the articles will be drafted (they are usually attached to the shareholders' agreement as an appendix) in accordance with its provisions. Since it is easier to amend articles (by 75 per cent of the shareholders) than the shareholders' agreement (all parties will need to consent), usually the shareholders' agreement will state that it will be a breach of the shareholders' agreement for the articles to be amended without the consent of all the joint venture parties. The shareholders' agreement will invariably state that it takes precedence over the articles if there is any conflict between them: obviously the technique is to ensure this does not arise in the first place.

So, what does the shareholders' agreement consist of? The answer is that it depends entirely on the nature of the particular joint venture in question. The following are the most important of the subjects you would expect the agreement to tackle, and some have already been raised in the checklist of questions above:

(a) *Termination*

Usually mutual consent, a material breach of the agreement or insolvency, administration or receivership procedures against any of the parties will be a termination event, but there will generally be others, including possibly force majeure.

The agreement will need to address what happens to the venture on termination. Does it dissolve, with the assets returning to the contributing venturers? It will depend on the event of termination. If the event is a breach of the agreement, the transfer provisions described below in (b) are likely to be invoked. If the parties have agreed to terminate, dissolution would be the normal procedure.

(b) *Transfer of an interest*

If one of the venturers would like to pull out, what will happen to that party's interest? Will it be an event of termination in itself? More usual would be a pre-emptive right for the other joint venturer(s) to buy that interest out. Often this will be on the basis that the transferor's shares in the venture will be offered to the other parties at a price per share which they can accept or reject. If they reject, then, under the terms of the agreement, the party who intended to depart must buy the other shares in the venture at the same price. This is known as the 'Russian roulette' procedure, for obvious reasons. It concentrates the mind on calculating a fair value for the shares. The articles will need to reflect this pre-emption arrangement. These provisions will often apply both to voluntary transfers and forced transfers (for example if there is deadlock or an event of termination—see (a) and (c)).

(c) *Deadlock*

If the management of the venture is unable to decide an issue, it is wise for the parties to consider in advance how this will be dealt with. If the agreement simply says the parties will talk about it, this does not take you very far. Consider the following solutions:

(i) Referring the issue to an independent third party or an arbitrator.

(ii) Giving a casting vote to the chairman of the venture, whichever of the two parties he or she happens to represent.

(iii) Deadlock is an event of termination (see (a)).

(iv) Deadlock forces the pre-emption procedure into play (see (b)).

(d) *Management of the company*

How will the board of directors be constituted (i.e., how many directors will be appointed by each of the venturers)? What is the quorum for their meetings (one director from each of the venturers would be normal)? Can the venturers appoint whoever they choose to the board or is there a process of mutual consultation or consent? Will the directors have unreserved managerial powers or will certain decisions be reserved to the shareholders? Often the shareholders reserve to themselves decisions requiring expenditure over a certain value, or relating to activities such as further issues of shares, indebtedness, acquisitions and disposals and so on. Once again, the articles will need to reflect the terms of the agreement on these points.

(e) *Financing, both initial and subsequent investment*

Is all the initial investment to be by way of cash? Will payments in kind, for example, assets or know-how, be acceptable in lieu? If the parties are to match each other's initial contributions, is this to be repeated for future contributions? What happens if one of the parties cannot find the money for subsequent investment—is this a breach which forces a transfer of that party's shares or an event of termination leading to dissolution? Is any of the financing by way of debt? Will there be any security arrangements, for example, charges over the venture's assets?

(f) *Restrictive covenants*

It will be in the interests of each of the parties to ensure that the other joint venturers cannot compete with the joint venture or solicit any of its customers for their own business. Such activities will undermine the viability of the venture. There may also sometimes be an obligation on the joint venture parties to refer business relating to the venture's own activities (for example, new customers) to the venture on a pre-emptive basis.

These provisions are at the core of the agreement.

6.4.2 The articles of association

Some of the provisions of the shareholders' agreement described above will find their way into the articles, in particular the terms about management, share transfers and pre-emption, and voting deadlock. In addition, there are a number of other elements which you would not normally expect to find in standard articles:

(a) *Share capital*

Will there be different classes of share capital for different parties to the joint venture? Sometimes this is done so that a shareholders' meeting is only quorate if holders of each class of share are present, and to confer the right to appoint a certain number of directors on the holders of each class (so that each venturer has its own director(s) on the board).

(b) *Members' meetings*

What will the quorum be? A representative from each class of shareholder would be normal. Will there be a chairman and, if so, will he or she have a casting vote? Often the role of chairman alternates between the parties and no casting vote is allowed (see also **6.4.1**). Will it be possible to pass resolutions in writing?

(c) *Managers or directors*

The articles will need to deal with the quorum, appointment and their powers. How are they to be removed? Only with the consent of the shareholders who appointed them? Normally this would be the case, subject to automatic vacation of a position on the board for failure to attend board meetings and so on. Will the directors be allowed to appoint alternates?

(d) *Dividends*

The shareholders will receive their profits on their investment in the joint venture company largely by way of dividend. The articles will need to specify what the policy on dividend payments is and how often dividends will be paid out.

6.5   Other issues

Some of the issues mentioned so far, for instance, the issue of classes of shares, have company law implications which need to be thought through carefully. Any joint venture will have to consider a number of other issues, most of which we have come across before:

(a) The potentially anticompetitive effect of joint ventures was noted earlier. Advice will be needed on the application of the following to the joint venture: the Fair Trading Act 1973, the EC Merger Regulation and arts 81 and 82 of the Treaty of Rome (see **8.16**). Clearance from the Office of Fair Trading may be required as a condition of the shareholders' agreement. Depending on the nature of the business the venture will be entering into and which its joint venturarties are involved in, consider also the need for regulatory approvals from other sources.

(b) If any of the joint venturers are listed companies, their participation in the joint venture may amount to a transaction for the purposes of the LR ch. 10, in which case, depending on the size of the transaction in comparison with the company's own assets, the company may need approval from its own shareholders (see **5.6.4** for a more detailed analysis of the application and operation of these provisions). This will also need to be a condition to the shareholders' agreement.

(c) There is likely to be some need for agreements accompanying the other documents described so far. In particular, the joint venture may well be dependent on information, know-how or technology developed to date by the joint venturers, who will want to ensure that their rights over such property are protected. Thus there would usually be a licence from the joint venturers to the joint venture company to use such property only for the venture's purposes and, if the venture terminates, it reverts to the licensor.

(d) It will be important for corporate joint venture parties to decide whether the joint venture company of which it is a member is a subsidiary undertaking under the Companies Act 1985. If so, it will qualify as a subsidiary for accounting purposes and so will require disclosure in the parent's annual accounts, a result the parent may find undesirable (see **9.2**).

(e) As with other corporate finance transactions, joint ventures have tax implications. These will depend largely on whether it is an incorporated or unincorporated structure which is used. It is advisable to bring the tax experts into the planning for the transaction at an early stage.

This is only a very broad overview of this type of transaction and the typical areas in which the lawyers are called upon to advise. Each joint venture is different and different issues will inevitably arise.

7

Management buy-outs

Management buy-outs ('MBOs') are acquisitions and disposals by another name. Often the most appropriate buyer of a company or a business will be its existing management, who understand the business better than anyone else and are likely to be ready buyers—after all, they have a vested interest in securing its future. The MBO is nothing more nor less than an acquisition of assets, a business or shares by the incumbent management from the existing owners of the relevant enterprise. This type of transaction does, though, have a number of distinct features.

7.1 Typical structure

7.1.1 Who is the buyer?

The directors and/or managers (supported by their financing arrangement—see below) will usually become shareholders in a company as the vehicle with which to acquire the target enterprise.

7.1.2 What is being sold?

The same issues arise in this context as with ordinary acquisitions. The managers are likely to prefer an asset purchase as they can select what to buy and leave the liabilities with the seller. Furthermore, problems with s. 151 Companies Act 1985 are often encountered in MBOs (see **7.2.4**), and these can be avoided entirely with an asset purchase as there is no acquisition of shares involved. It would, though, be normal for the purchase to be of an existing company, or of a new company set up by the seller as a sale vehicle, and to which the assets or business to be sold are transferred prior to the disposal (this is sometimes known as a 'hive-down'). The rest of this chapter assumes this structure.

7.1.3 Financing

The single biggest practical problem the managers will have is financing the acquisition. After all, it is very unlikely that they will personally have the resources to fund a multi-million pound acquisition. Normally, they will therefore need external investment from venture capitalists and lending institutions.

The arrangement is usually that the corporate vehicle set up by the managers to make the acquisition buys the whole of the target's issued share capital: this will be the only asset held by the acquiring company which is purely a holding company. The managers subscribe a significant proportion of the shares in the acquiring company out of their own resources, and this money goes towards the acquisition price. The majority of the finance for the acquisition, though, comes from borrowings from investing institutions. The lenders will secure this debt on the assets and shares of the target company. They may also purchase a slice of the equity in the acquiring company in their own names so they can benefit from any improved performance which the managers are able to reap from the target.

There may be separate institutions prepared to buy up some of the shares in the acquiring company to help the managers out, without providing any debt financing. These are the venture capitalists. Sometimes they may prefer the securities they buy to be preference shares, convertible loan stock or some sort of debt instrument which carries either a guaranteed entitlement to a dividend or interest: this sort of finance is known as 'mezzanine finance', as it is somewhere between secured debt and pure equity or risk capital. It offers them more protection for their investment than ordinary shares.

The extent of borrowing which is normally needed in this sort of transaction means they are often said to be highly 'leveraged'—in other words, the proportion of debt to equity is very high. This also creates possible problems for the managers after they have completed the purchase. All available cash generated by the company is likely to be needed to pay off the interest and principal on the debt, which makes it difficult for the management to generate adequate amounts of working capital for ordinary business needs. The consequence has been that the MBO company often finds it very difficult to survive: this has been true of a number of MBOs in recession-hit industries such as retailing. It is usually only 'mature' businesses, where there is a reliable profits stream founded on a well-established customer base, which can produce the cash supply needed to pay off the heavy debt financing in these transactions.

7.1.4 Agreements

There will of course be the sale agreement between the acquiring company on the one hand and the selling shareholders on the other. This will generally follow the familiar form already seen (see **5.5.1**). There will be a number of differences from the typical sale agreement, though:

(a) The acquiring company will not secure the standard warranties a purchaser would seek—after all, the management team will know the business better than the selling shareholders.

(b) The sellers will often wish to be paid part of their consideration on a deferred basis related to future profits of the target: they are keen to ensure they do not lose out completely if the company makes good in the future.

In addition, there will be a subscription or shareholders' agreement between the directors/managers and their backers who are taking shares in the acquiring company. This will govern the management of the company and the board, future financing of the company and other issues such as the company's dividend policy. A much more detailed picture of what you can expect to see in this kind of document will be found in **6.4.1**. Accompanying the shareholders' agreement there will of course also need to be articles of association for the acquiring company, which will reflect the provisions of the shareholders' agreement (see also **6.4.2**).

The last of the most important documents will be the loan agreement between the lenders and the acquiring company. The terms will include restrictions on disposals of the target's assets (in addition to security in the form of a charge), restrictions on any change in the nature of the acquiring or target company's business, warranties by the managers and events of default under which the lenders may terminate the loan agreement.

7.2 Issues to watch

There are a number of areas to be particularly cautious of with MBOs.

7.2.1 Tax

As with other acquisitions, tax considerations can be critical, and the issues addressed in **5.2.2.2** are equally relevant here. Additional factors to be conscious of are:

(a) If the sellers need to create a new company first as a target vehicle for the sale (the process referred to earlier as a 'hive-down'), it is vital for the seller to ensure that the creation of this new company and the transfer of assets to it do not discontinue the trade, otherwise there will be a danger of the loss of capital allowances and tax losses. The managers will be particularly keen to retain these as they will help significantly to reduce the size of the target company's tax bill following completion of the acquisition, provided its trade is not subject to a major change in the period after the sale.

(b) One of the disadvantages of the hive-down is that, at the point when the new target company leaves the seller's group (when sold to the managers), the target company is subject to CGT on the gain in value of the assets transferred to it while a member of the seller's group. The managers usually seek an indemnity from the seller against the costs of such a tax charge.

(c) The sale of the target is a disposal by the seller which is subject to CGT. One way of minimising any chargeable gain is, where possible, for the seller to ensure that the gain arises in a vehicle (say, another group company) where there are tax losses against which the gain can be offset.

(d) As far as the managers are concerned, it will be vital to ensure that the interest costs on the loan financing after the sale can be set off against taxable profits.

7.2.2 Directors' responsibilities

The usual problem with MBOs is that some members of the board of the selling company are also involved in the MBO team. Special care should be taken to minimise the resulting problems arising from this potential conflict of interest.

As a practical matter, and also in conformity with Investment Committee guidelines, it is therefore normal for a committee of independent, non-executive directors on the selling company's board to be established to consider the commercial merits of the MBO offer for the target in comparison with other possible offers. Should they choose not to recommend the MBO offer, institutional shareholders will almost certainly not back it and it is therefore unlikely to get off the ground.

Another issue is the advisers used by the MBO team. These must clearly be different from those used by the selling company.

If the seller is a company which is disposing of net assets worth more than £100,000 or more than 10 per cent of its net assets, and one of its directors is involved in the buy-out team, s. 320 CA needs to be watched carefully and may require shareholder approval for the transaction (see *LPC Guide: Business Law*).

If the seller is a listed company, and one of its directors is involved in the buy-out team, this will be classified as a related party transaction under LR ch. 10 (see **5.6.4**), which may require a circular to shareholders and their approval.

7.2.3 Takeover

The City Code will apply as much to an MBO as any other transaction. If the MBO team is acquiring a UK public company, the provisions of the City Code on Takeovers and Mergers and the jurisdiction of the Takeover Panel will be relevant (see **Chapter 8**).

7.2.4 Financial assistance

Section 151 CA (see **8.12** for more details) will effectively prevent the target company from contributing to the MBO team's costs, or providing guarantees, security (including a charge over its shares or assets) or indemnities to the lenders or equity investors unless:

(a) the buyers acquire assets rather than shares; or

(b) you use the s. 153 exemption, that the principal purpose of the assistance is not to acquire shares but as an incidental part of some larger purpose of the target company (such as facilitating the MBO); or

(c) you use the so-called 'whitewash' procedure under ss. 155 to 158 CA (see **8.12**), which is only available for private companies and so would only apply if the target company were a private company.

Takeovers

8.1 What is a takeover?

You have now encountered 'acquisitions', and have probably heard of 'mergers' as well as 'takeovers'. So what is the difference?

There is no simple definition of these terms by which everyone abides. They are often used interchangeably: the same transaction may be referred to as a merger, a takeover and an acquisition.

An acquisition is in fact *any* transaction in which something is acquired. Since a takeover involves the acquisition of shares, takeovers are also acquisitions, though for the purposes of this book 'acquisition' means sales and purchases of assets or businesses *or* shares falling *outside* the City Code on Takeovers and Mergers ('City Code') (essentially, those involving, private companies). A takeover implies the acquisition of control over assets, a business or a company. We use the term 'takeover' in this chapter in the sense of a purchase of *shares* falling *inside* the City Code. These transactions are also often referred to as public company takeovers. In short, a person (an individual or a company) takes over a public company by writing to its shareholders and offering to buy their shares in return for cash or, in many cases, securities such as shares or debt instruments.

The term 'merger' has no precise definition, but is often used in preference to 'takeover' where the takeover is intended as a fusion of two companies and not a submergence of one within another. Some takeovers are what is known as 'recommended', which is explained in **8.5.3.1**. Recommended takeovers are often characterised as mergers as they usually imply a meeting of minds between the company taking over and the one being taken over.

Before we take this chapter any further, there are two other terms you need to understand. Any takeover, as with the acquisitions we saw in **Chapter 5**, will involve a buyer and a seller. However, the terms used when referring to buyers and sellers in the takeover context are slightly different. The buyer will offer to acquire the shares it wants, hence it is referred to as the 'offeror' or the 'bidder'. The company whose shares the offeror wants to buy, as it is on the receiving end of the offer, is referred to as the 'offeree' or the 'target'. In a sense, this is slightly misleading. Those who sell their shares to the bidder are in fact the target company's *shareholders*, so the proper legal analysis is that they are the offerees: but the term 'offeree' in this chapter conforms with its practical use and means the target.

8.2 Why launch a takeover?

We saw in **5.1** some of the main reasons for acquisitions taking place. Exactly the same factors are relevant in takeover activity.

One additional factor in takeovers is opportunism. Takeovers are public transactions, and the City Code sets out certain unassailable limitations on the timetable which applies to them. Unlike an acquisition by private treaty or contract, this means it is not possible simply to announce to the world that a takeover has taken place. Under the rules, as we will see, it has to happen under the full gaze of the world at large, and any takeover offer made has to be held open for a fixed period of time. Consequently, there is every opportunity for a potential rival offeror to hear of the bid, and to have time to prepare and ultimately make an alternative offer to the target shareholders, even though no such thought was in its mind before the first bid was announced. In other words, once a target is put 'in play' by an offer, there is nothing to prevent the quick and the wily from joining the game—and they often do, recognising it may be their best chance to snap up a good buy. There have been numerous examples of this in practice. The infamous takeover of Distillers by Guinness in 1986 (which led to a series of criminal prosecutions in the late 1980s and early 1990s) was just such a piece of opportunism, since it was preceded by an initial bid from Argyll which eventually failed.

8.3 The takeover 'market'

Much as there is an equity market which companies tap when seeking capital investment (see **Chapters 3** and **4**), so there is a distinct market in the UK for takeovers.

Since the Takeover Panel began work in 1968, there has been on average 225 announced takeover proposals in the UK every year. Approximately three-quarters of all public takeover offers in the EU occur in the UK. Takeover activity is therefore, in absolute and relative terms, an important 'industry' in this country.

There is a well-established body of precedent and rules governing the form and conduct of takeover offers in the UK. In large part, this is because of the work of the Takeover Panel (see **8.8.5**) and the corpus of regulation in the City Code for which it is responsible.

There has developed, on the back of the emergence of takeovers as a significant feature of City life from the 1950s onwards, considerable expertise among City professionals and business people in advising on and handling takeover transactions. This expertise has grown to a point where a company interested in expanding its operations through an acquisition, but without a clear idea as to whom, what or where to acquire, can approach an investment bank in the City and obtain advice on potential suitable targets and an appropriate takeover and marketing strategy. By the same token, a company which fears a potential bid can approach an investment bank for advice and assistance in preparing a pre-emptive defence strategy for use in the event that the company's fears are realised: many UK companies hold so-called 'defence manuals' at the ready for precisely such an eventuality (see **8.6.7**). Investment banks can and do make substantial profits out of their takeover advice. Another feature of this expertise is the assortment of professional so-called asset-stripping individuals and companies who have built their reputations and their wealth entirely through acquiring companies and then making them profitable or selling them off at a profit. For these, takeovers is their trade.

8.4 Parties to a takeover

A first step in understanding the structure and mechanics of a takeover is clarifying who is involved and their contribution to the transaction.

8.4.1 Bidder

Typically the offer is made by a single bidder but occasionally an offer is made by a consortium of individuals or companies, sometimes to spread the cost. The separate members of the consortium will almost certainly be treated for the purposes of the Code as if they were one bidder (see **8.5.3.2**).

Where listing particulars are required in connection with a takeover offer, the bidder will be a person responsible for those particulars under s. 150 Financial Services Act 1986 (see **4.2.5.7**).

The bidder's shareholders may have to approve or be informed of the takeover under LR ch.10 (see **5.6.4**), or consent to the issue of new shares under ss. 80 and 89 Companies Act 1985 (see **3.3.1.3**) or for other Companies Act 1985 purposes such as an increase in authorised capital. Target companies may also on occasion write to the bidder's shareholders and try to persuade them that the bid is not in *their* best interests: this is quite permissible though usually ineffective.

8.4.2 Target

The target shareholders are the recipients of the offer and its success lies in their hands. If those holding a majority of the shares choose to accept the bidder's offer, control of the target will pass to the bidder.

One exception to this is that a very few UK companies have provisions in their articles of association which effectively prevent a change of control without the consent of the UK government. These are usually companies which have been privatised—particularly utilities such as water and electricity companies. Articles may provide for the government to have a so-called 'golden share' giving it special voting rights or veto powers. Alternatively or additionally, there may be restrictions on shareholders holding more than a 15 per cent interest in the company. The restrictions generally have a limited life: the 'golden shares' in the electricity industry expired in March 1995.

The target board of directors may often prefer, for whatever reason (and this is considered in more detail in **8.5.3.1**), to recommend the bidder's offer to the target shareholders. In these circumstances, the offer document from the bidder will contain the target board's recommendation and some information about the target for which the target will be a person responsible if the offer requires listing particulars (see LR para. 5.3(b)).

8.4.3 Directors

Rule 19.2(a) of the City Code makes the respective directors of the offeror and offeree companies responsible for the documents issued by their companies in the course of the takeover and requires them all, individually, to take responsibility expressly for all such documents save for some advertisements. If listing particulars are required by the transaction, the bidder's directors will be persons responsible under s. 150 Financial Services Act 1986, and if the takeover is recommended, the target board will be persons responsible for those parts of the particulars describing the target.

Therefore, whether advising the bidder or the target, ensure early on in a transaction that all the members of the board will be available to approve documents to be issued during the takeover or that they have appointed an attorney (preferably another member of the board) to do so on their behalf. Standard practice is for the main board to convene at the very early stages of the bid to appoint a committee of directors to take all decisions on behalf of the main board in relation to the takeover, including the approval of documents.

Many decisions in takeovers have to be taken at short notice when it is often difficult to pull together the entire board.

Directors will of course also need to be advised of their responsibilities and the potential liabilities which may result.

The target board is obliged to obtain and communicate to its shareholders competent independent advice by r. 3 of the City Code. The offeror board must also do this where the directors have a conflict of interest, the most obvious example of which is where a target director is also a director of the bidder.

8.4.4   Investment bankers

Both bidder and target will appoint their own investment banks (in some cases, joint banks may be appointed). Much as we saw for equity offerings, the investment bank takes on the role of 'manager' of the transaction, in the sense that it coordinates the activities of the other parties and is the client's main sounding-board when devising and planning strategy and tactics in the course of the bid. In connection with this, the investment bankers are chiefly responsible for communicating with the Takeover Panel on issues of interpretation of the City Code and obtaining guidance or rulings where necessary, with the lawyers assisting when needed (see **8.8.5**).

The investment bank to the bidder issues the offer document on behalf of the bidder, for purely traditional rather than legal reasons. This means it is a person responsible under s. 90 FSMA if listing particulars are also required for the transaction (as it will have authorised the issue of the document). The bank will also have to approve any documents which as a financial promotion require an authorised person's imprimatur under s. 21 FSMA.

One other aspect of the bidder's investment bank's role will be to arrange and underwrite a cash-underwritten alternative where this is to take place (see **8.6.3.1**): it will negotiate and agree the form of the underwriting agreement with the offeror and appoint a broker to arrange the sub-underwriting on its behalf.

For its services, the investment bank will usually negotiate a fee structure which will be substantially success-related but guarantees it something in the event of failure. These fees are in addition to anything received by way of commission for any underwriting which takes place.

8.4.5   Brokers

The bidder and the target will each have a firm of brokers to their names who will be responsible for observing and reporting back on movements in and the inclination of the market towards the takeover offer. This is vital for the offeror properly to gauge whether the value and nature of its existing offer are satisfactory, and for the target to determine its strategy. For example, if the market is generally perceived to favour the offer, will the issue of an optimistic profit forecast by the target be enough to mollify investors?

It is also important for both sides to track significant share purchases: once a target is 'in play', there is the danger to the offeror of a rival bidder emerging. The tell-tale signs of this will be significant levels of share purchases by an unknown buyer. Obviously the target needs at all times to know how many shares a bidder holds to ascertain whether it is winning or losing the battle.

The bidder's brokers will also handle any purchases of the target's shares which the bidder makes and will arrange the sub-underwriting for any cash-underwritten alternative (see **8.6.3.1**). Where the offer includes securities to be listed, the brokers will, as with ordinary listing arrangements (see **3.3.4**), liaise with the UKLA and the LSE, prepare a derogation letter and ensure that the UKLA is satisfied that its requirements for the contents of offer documents (see **8.5.5.1**) have been met.

8.4.6 Accountants

Both sides to the bid will appoint accountants. The bidder's accountants will need to consider (where the offer includes securities to be listed) the requirements in LR ch. 6 and ch. 12 (see **4.2.6.3**). However, r. 24 of the City Code requires the offer document to contain a significant amount of financial information on the offeror and the offeree company. This needs to be extracted from the relevant company's most recent financial statements. As a matter of practice, the bidder's accountants will be asked to confirm, in the form of a comfort letter, that they are satisfied that the information produced is correct and accurately set out. They will also need to report to the directors that any profit forecast for the bidder has been compiled with the care and objectivity which r. 28 demands. This rule also imposes a duty on the accountants to discuss the assumptions underlying any profit forecast with their client. They must also satisfy themselves that the forecast has been properly made and is based on the stated assumptions.

The same requirement regarding profit forecasts will extend to the target's accountants.

Accountants to the bidder and target are in practice also asked to review the figures and statistics produced by their opposite numbers to help in constructing their respective clients' arguments in the bid.

8.4.7 Public relations consultants and parliamentary lobbyists

Public relations consultants are frequently hired to improve the presentation of the case of both sides to the bid, both in the formal documents and through advertising campaigns. Parliamentary lobbyists assist in the process of influencing the Office of Fair Trading's decision as to whether to refer a merger to the Competition Commission (see **8.16**); they will do the same should the European Commission be involved or the consent of any other regulatory bodies to the merger be required.

8.4.8 Solicitors

Both parties to the bid will appoint solicitors and it is possible that other advisers will appoint their own legal advisers (often a merchant bank will seek advice independent from that taken by the company it represents, particularly in hostile offers). What do the solicitors do?

Much of their work is concerned with checking the accuracy of documents produced in the course of the bid, which will generally demand a verification exercise akin to that for equity offerings (see **3.3.7**).

Of course they also spend much of their time advising on the legalities of a transaction, which requires consideration of all the legal and regulatory issues, partly to ensure that any action proposed is legal, decent, honest and truthful and partly to help in the formulation of the most effective strategy for their client.

The role of proffering legal advice extends to the City Code, though the Introduction to the City Code makes it absolutely clear that 'to take legal, or other professional, advice on the interpretation or application of the Code is not an appropriate alternative to obtaining a view or ruling from the [Panel] Executive' (see **8.8.5** for further analysis of this). This is not to say that the lawyers have *no* role in relation to interpretation of the Code, simply that their view is not of itself sufficient.

There is to some extent a tension between the merchant bankers and the lawyers. The merchant bankers often see it as their role to deal with the Takeover Panel, and the lawyers, quite legitimately, feel that they are probably better placed to offer an informed view on what the City Code means, given it is now a detailed set of rules which runs in totality to just over 150 pages. Lawyers accordingly need to be sensitive to other advisers and particularly the role of the Takeover Panel when they set about advising on the City Code.

8.5   Outline of a takeover

The easiest way to understand how a takeover fits together is to look at a skeleton timetable and examine each phase of the transaction.

In the timing of a takeover, there are certain things which are laid down by the City Code and immutable (or pretty much so, unless the Panel otherwise decides). There are also certain things which are optional. This timetable indicates the points in the timetable fixed by the rules of the City Code.

As every takeover is unique, this timetable only sketches what you are likely to find in a typical or ordinary transaction: more complex deals, involving, for instance, the intervention of overseas regulatory bodies (such as the US Securities and Exchange Commission) will alter the timetable in some respects.

The timetable here assumes the bid is contested: where a bid is recommended, only those references marked * are relevant. The rest can be discounted. The rules cited are those in the City Code, of which more later.

Some of the terms mentioned here may be unfamiliar: they are explained in **8.5.2**.

8.5.1   Timetable of a takeover

Day	Activity
Before announcement	In the period leading up to the announcement, the bidder prepares its strategy (see **8.6.6**): this may take days, weeks or months; * for a recommended bid, this is the period in which negotiations between bidder and target boards will take place.
1	Target board informed of bid (r. 2.5). Bid announced publicly.* Offer period begins.*
3	Target posts announcement of bid to its shareholders (r. 2.6).*
28	Last day to post offer document (r. 30.1), though this is often in practice done earlier. *The rest of the timetable takes its lead from the day the offer document is posted (whenever that actually happens). This day is referred to from now on as day 0.**
0 + 14	Target posts first defence circular to its shareholders (r. 30.2).
0 + 21	First closing date for offer (r. 31.1).*
0 + 39	Last date target can announce profit forecast or other significant financial information (r. 31.9).
0 + 46	Last date for bidder to revise its offer (r. 32.1).
0 + 60	Last date on which offer can be declared unconditional as to acceptances (r. 31.6).*
0 + 81	Last date to declare offer wholly unconditional (r. 31.7).
0 + 95	Last date for money or other consideration to be provided to target shareholders (r. 31.8).*
Thereafter	Section 429 CA notices dispatched (see **8.13**).*

Before we move on, let us pause to understand what some of these terms mean.

8.5.2 Definitions

8.5.2.1 'Closing date'

This is the date on which the offer will lapse unless the bidder extends it. The first closing date cannot be less than 21 days after the posting of the offer document (r. 31.1). At that point, the bidder can choose to call the whole offer off. Alternatively, the bidder can announce that the offer has gone unconditional as to acceptances (see below). In practice, this only happens with a recommended offer (see **8.5.3.1**), so the bidder normally announces it will extend the offer. The extension cannot last beyond 0 + 60, which is the final date by which the offer must either have succeeded or lapsed.

8.5.2.2 'Unconditional as to acceptances'

The bidder must obtain at least 50 per cent of the target's shares and have that as a condition to the offer (r. 10). An offer is unconditional as to acceptances where the bidder has got the 50 per cent. The bidder may declare the bid unconditional as to acceptances whenever the 50 per cent target is reached. If the bidder does not get the 50 per cent by the final closing date (0+60), the offer must lapse.

8.5.2.3 'Wholly unconditional'

This means that all the conditions of the offer have been satisfied, including the condition about 50 per cent acceptances, the condition that the offer not be referred to the Competition Commission and any others set out in the offer document.

Do bear in mind that some of the dates here are dependent on the occurrence of earlier events in the timetable, which may in fact happen earlier than the date required by the rules. Therefore treat these dates in practice with care.

Let us look now in more detail at the activity taking place around this timetable.

8.5.3 Before the announcement

This is the stage at which the bidder prepares strategy, and decides how to finance the bid and what sort of a bid to make (see **8.6.2**). A lot of analysis will be needed to assess the strengths and weaknesses of the target for the forthcoming battle.

8.5.3.1 Recommended offers

Of course, it may be that the target board is interested in the idea of a takeover, so an initial approach to its directors may prove fruitful and lead to a negotiated merger which the target board is prepared to recommend to its shareholders. Although it seems perverse for directors effectively to sign away their company, there may be all sorts of reasons for them taking this action: they may feel their company has no real prospect of survival as an independent entity, or they may feel it is simply in their shareholders' and employees' best interests.

Target boards should, however, be cautious about the information they give away to a potential bidder. Rule 20.2 of the Code requires the target to give equality of information to any other genuine potential bidder, even if the other bidder is not to the target board's taste. In a 1992 bid, Midland Bank (the target) sought to resist giving Lloyds Bank, a competitor bidder, the same information as Midland had given Hongkong and Shanghai Bank, but the Takeover Panel required it to do so.

Should the bidder attempt to persuade the target directors of the value of a merger only for them to turn the idea down, there is nothing then to prevent the bidder from launching a hostile bid for the target, though on average some 30–40 per cent of hostile offers do fail. If the bidder has any inside information about the target as a result of the discussions which have taken place, the Criminal Justice Act 1993 may prevent the bidder from making market purchases of the target's shares (see **8.14**).

8.5.3.2 Share purchases

If the bid is to be contested, the bidder may build up a stake in the target to facilitate reaching the ultimate target of 50 per cent of the target's shares. When doing this the bidder needs to take account of the consequences of buying stakes of a certain size.

Stake	Result
3 per cent	Notification of bidder's interest to the company under CA Part VI (see **8.11**).
10 per cent	If 10 per cent of the target shares are acquired in the year leading up to the offer or during the offer period, the bidder must offer all the target shareholders *cash* at the highest price the bidder has paid for those shares in that time (r. 11).
15 per cent	The Substantial Acquisitions Rules (SARs—see **8.9**) prevent the bidder (or indeed, anyone) from acquiring 10 per cent or more of the target's shares in any seven-day period if that gives the bidder between 15 per cent and 30 per cent of the target in total. Either the bidder buys less than 15 per cent in total, or spreads the 10 per cent acquisition out over more than a week.
30 per cent	Rule 5 of the Code places a prohibition on the bidder acquiring 30 per cent or more of the target. The prohibition does not apply in certain circumstances, including where the offer is recommended by the target. Acceptances of the offer are not counted in determining whether 30 per cent of the target has been acquired, only purchases in the market. As soon as the bidder does go through the 30 per cent limit (pursuant to one of the exceptions to the prohibition in r. 5), it must make a takeover offer for all the target's shares in accordance with r. 9 (unless the bidder intends to make a partial offer—see **8.6.2.4**). This is the case *even if it* has already made an offer. The real problem about a mandatory offer under r. 9 is that it must be in cash at a price equal to the highest price paid by the bidder for target shares in the past year. Therefore, if the bidder has already made an offer, it may at this stage have to increase it. Furthermore, apart from the 50 per cent acceptance condition, virtually no other conditions are permitted, which may not suit the bidder.

In addition to these restrictions, the bidder should also consider, when making share purchases:

(a) The Criminal Justice Act 1993 on insider dealing (see **8.14**), which may prevent any purchases if the bidder has acquired price-sensitive information about the target, perhaps through discussions with the target itself.

(b) The market abuse provisions of FSMA s. 118 (see **1.5.1.3** and **8.15.2**) may also have an impact, although the FSA Code of Market Conduct suggests at MAR 1.2.8G that, in considering whether behaviour amounts to market abuse, it will take into account whether a person is complying with other rules, such as the City Code. The conclusion which may be drawn from this is that compliance with the City Code is likely to lessen (but certainly not exclude) the probability of behaviour amounting to market abuse.

(c) Rule 6, which obliges the bidder to pitch its offer at a *price* at least equal to the highest price it has paid for the shares in the past three months (r. 9 applies to mandatory offers only).

(d) The restrictions mentioned above apply to the bidder acting alone or in concert with others, so there is no point in believing that the bidder can appoint several friends to buy shares on its behalf and thus escape the trap set by the various percentages mentioned above. In fact, the City Code presumes the bidder's subsidiaries, directors and professional advisers amongst others to be acting in concert with the bidder, though these presumptions are rebuttable. This is covered in detail in the Definitions Section of the City Code and further guidance with regard to behaviour which constitutes acting in concert is given in the Notes on r. 9.1. The target, unless an offer takes it completely by surprise, will have gleaned from purchases of its shares or rumours on the stock market that a bid is in the offing and so will have begun to plan its defence. This involves instructing its advisers and discussing with them strategic alternatives (for example, what submissions to make to the Office of Fair Trading to have any proposed merger referred, whether the company's performance can in any way be improved before a bid emerges, launching an advertising campaign, and so on—see **8.6.7** for a discussion of the target's strategic alternatives). Most listed companies have so-called 'defence manuals' on the shelf with a ready-made 'action list' to put into effect in the event of a sudden bid announcement: the list will detail the sort of activities mentioned above.

8.5.4 The announcement and after

In a hostile bid, the target board is informed of the bid and the bidder immediately circulates a press announcement describing the terms of its offer. The target will need to communicate this to its own shareholders as soon as possible. A fairly hectic process of campaigning by the opposite sides begins almost immediately through the financial pages of the newspapers. Both sides will also prepare their submissions to the Office of Fair Trading as quickly as they can and start to use the lobbyists to influence the decisions of any of the regulators involved.

The bidder's main focus at this stage will be to prepare its offer document within 28 days of the announcement (r. 30.1). Usually the bidder will seek to move much faster than this to keep the pressure on the target.

8.5.4.1 Rule 6

The bidder will continue to buy shares in the market but must beware of all the issues raised above. In addition, if the bidder or anyone acting in concert with it buys shares at a price above the current value of the offer, then r. 6.2 requires the bidder to raise the value of its offer to match that price—so bidders need to take precautions not to buy shares if the market price is currently above the offer price.

8.5.4.2 Irrevocable undertakings

To assist the bidder in obtaining the 50 per cent acceptance needed, it may also approach certain institutional shareholders in the target to see if they will be prepared to oblige themselves irrevocably to accept the offer (r. 24.3(3)(iv)). In a recommended offer, the target directors generally sign themselves up to such an undertaking. Usually the party giving the undertaking agrees to accept the offer and agrees not to do anything which might prejudice it. This is perfectly proper practice. Care has to be taken with the law regarding unsolicited calls (see **1.5.1.4**) and insider dealing (see **8.14**) in this context. These 'irrevocable undertakings' also count when counting up the shares which the bidder holds for the purposes of the r. 5 restrictions mentioned above in **8.5.3.2** (including the SARs), but they do not count for the purposes of the r. 9 mandatory offer.

With a recommended bid, the same process of announcement and preparation of the offer document is required, though here of course the bidder will receive the target's cooperation.

8.5.5   Posting of the offer document and after

The bidder's offer document will need to be posted within 28 days of the announcement of the bid (r. 30.1). This is a time-limit the Panel rarely relaxes.

8.5.5.1   The offer document

For a start, though the offer is made by the bidder, the offer document is usually issued on behalf of the bidder by its merchant bank, for reasons of convention only.

The document is a contractual offer and so will need to set out the terms on which the offer is made, provide an acceptance form and stipulate how the contract between the bidder and target shareholder is effected.

The document must 'sell' the bidder to the target shareholders, so it will contain a fair amount of 'marketing copy' on the qualities of the bidder and what it can offer the shareholders. It is also likely to detail the existing weaknesses of the target's management or its strategy. Aside from the legal risks associated with this (see **8.17.4**), the Takeover Panel has made it clear (in a statement regarding the Enterprise bid for Lasmo) that 'tendentious and excessive claims and allegations should be avoided'.

The document must comply with the City Code's own requirements (which incorporate requirements of the UKLA in relation to takeovers) and are set out in r. 24. These are very detailed. In essence, it should contain:

(a) A responsibility statement from the bidder's directors in which they say they take responsibility for it and reasonably believe it to be accurate and not misleading (r. 19.2(a)). All the directors need to be a party to this. In a recommended offer, parts of the offer document will describe the target and the directors of the target will take responsibility for those parts of the document which relate to it.

(b) What the bidder intends to do about the target and its employees (r. 24.1(d))—this is usually confined to something reasonably positive about its and their future but nothing expansive or which might tie the bidder's hands in future.

(c) Financial information about the bidder (r. 24.2 (a), (b) or (c) as appropriate) and the target (r. 24.2 (e)), including the figures for the two companies' net profits and dividends for the past three financial years and a statement of the assets and liabilities of the bidder in its last accounts (r. 24.2(a)(ii) or (b)(ii) as appropriate).

(d) Disclosures as to shareholdings of the bidder (r. 24.3(a)(i)) and persons acting in concert with it (r. 24.3(a)(iii)) in the target.

(e) Directors' pay and benefits (r. 24.4).

(f) Where the bidder is using cash as consideration for the offer, the merchant bankers or accountants must confirm that the resources to finance the cash element of the offer are available (r. 24.7).

(g) Sufficient information to enable the shareholders to reach a properly informed decision about the merits of the offer (r. 23).

(h) The terms of the offer, including the consideration offered (r. 24.2(d)(iv)), how it will be paid (r.24(f)) and the method of acceptance of the offer.

(i) The nature of the offeror's business, its financial and trading prospects and borrowings (r. 24.2(a)(x)).

(j) References to both bidder's material contracts (r. 24.2 (a)(xi), (c))and target's material contracts, which include constitutional documents (r. 26(a)), two years of audited accounts (r. 26(b)) and directors' service agreements (r. 26(c)), as well as all contracts outside the ordinary course of business entered into in the past two years (r. 26(f)).

In a recommended offer, the offer document will set out how the merger will work (for example, how the two businesses will be fused; whether all the target directors will remain on the board), its commercial rationale and a description of the two businesses (r. 24.1).

8.5.5.2 Layout of a typical offer document

You have seen what an offer document should contain to comply with the City Code's requirements. How will it actually be set out?

There are no formal obligations regarding this, nor does the Takeover Panel pre-vet documents in any way. Offer documents, therefore, do not need to follow a set pattern, though in practice (often through the influence of precedent) they do. This is broadly what you could expect to find.

Front page

- Advice to shareholders to obtain independent financial advice (which r. 24.2(d)(i) requires as a 'heading').

- If the bidder is offering its own securities as consideration, the offer document may also constitute listing particulars (see LR ch.6) and so the points mentioned in **4.2.6.3** should be included.

- A statement that the offer is being made by the merchant bank on behalf of the bidder (the usual arrangement) (r. 24.2(d)(ii)).

- Any provisions to deal with US securities regulations.

Following pages

- Letter from bidder's chairman describing the rationale of the bid (r. 24.1(c)), the bidder's intentions (r. 24.1(a), (b) and (d)), information regarding the bid (for instance, the consideration offered) (r. 24.2(d)(iv)) and how the offer is to be financed (r. 24.2(f)).

- Business statistics illustrating the comparative performance of bidder and target, and showing what the bidder will do for target performance and strategy (r. 24.1(c)).

- Offer letter from merchant bank to target shareholders setting out the terms of the offer, its value, financial information relating to bidder and target (r. 24.2), statement regarding bidder's intentions towards target employees (r. 24.1(d)), any offers for other classes of target securities (r. 14.1 and r. 14.2), and the procedure for acceptance (r. 24.2(d)(v)).

- Conditions to the offers (for example, obtaining 50 per cent acceptances (r. 9.3(a))) and further terms of the offers (much of this is required by r. 24), including rights of target shareholders to withdraw their acceptances (r. 34), and whether the bidder leaves open the possibility of a revised offer (r. 32.2).

- Rights of overseas shareholders.

Forms of acceptance

There may be two separate forms of acceptance (r. 24(d)(v), and see also Appendix 4 to the City Code), one for CREST members (see **1.6.2**) and one for non-CREST members. Alternatively, there may be one acceptance form which combines to serve both types of shareholder.

Additional information

This will include the directors' responsibility statement pursuant to r. 19.2, disclosures of bidder's interests in target shares (r. 24.3(a)(i)), and documents available for inspection (as required by r. 26).

Definitions

These usually conclude the document.

8.5.5.3   The defence document

Once the document has been posted to the target shareholders, the target board gets to work preparing its first response. Needless to say, this is not the case with a recommended offer.

The defence document must be ready within 14 days of the offer document being posted (r. 30.2), though the Panel will sometimes be prepared to grant a limited extension to this where the offeror has attempted to spring a surprise and left the target very little time to prepare.

The defence document, like the offer document, is also a selling document and so needs to contain all the arguments which refute the bidder's assertions and persuade shareholders to hold on to their shares.

It also is subject to detailed requirements from the City Code, and, in particular, r. 25. In outline, the defence document should contain:

(a) A responsibility statement from the directors of the offeree (r. 19.2(a)). Only in rare cases where, for instance, a director suffers a conflict of interest, will he be relieved of the need to take responsibility (r. 19.2(b)).

(b) Sufficient information to enable the shareholders to reach a properly informed decision about the merits of the offer (r. 23).

(c) The views of the board on the offer, and the views of its merchant bankers (r. 25.1(a)). The verbal formula typically used is something like, 'The board, which has been so advised by [its investment bank], considers the offer to be inadequate, etc.'. The idea is that the shareholders receive a considered and objective view and not one which just represents the potentially prejudiced judgement of the directors.

(d) A reaction to the bidder's plans for the target and its employees (r. 25.2).

(e) Shares in the bidder held by the target (r. 25.3(a)(i)), shares in both held by the target's directors and associates (r. 25.3(a)(ii)), and whether the target directors will be accepting or rejecting the offer in respect of their own holdings in the target (r. 25.3(a)(iv)).

(f) Details of target directors' service contracts (r. 25.4).

In addition to all this work on the preparation and dispatch of documents, both sides will continue with their campaigning and lobbying, and the bidder will progress (subject to the restrictions mentioned earlier) any share-buying programme it has initiated.

8.5.6   The first closing date and after

Rule 31.1 dictates that the first closing date of the offer can be no earlier than 21 days after the offer document has been posted. At this point, if the bidder has not yet received

50 per cent acceptances, it must decide whether to allow the offer to lapse or extend it. The bidder must also announce the level of acceptances from target shareholders immediately after the closing date.

In a recommended offer, normally a bidder can announce it has 50 per cent acceptances by this time, because target shareholders tend to follow their board's recommendation and accept quite quickly. In a contested offer, however, very few shareholders will have accepted by the first closing date. They tend to wait as long as possible in case a revised offer emerges, another bidder appears, or the target announces better than expected prospects. As a result, the bidder in this kind of offer does not expect to win by 0 + 21 and will therefore usually anticipate extending the offer. This extension cannot be beyond 0 + 60, what you might call the final closing date for the offer (r. 31.6).

The other thing for the bidder to watch is r. 31.5 which prevents a bidder from going back on its word. If, at some stage during the offer, the bidder tells the world that it is not prepared to extend its offer beyond a certain time, then it will be held to that even if it later changes its mind—so make sure there is no implication in press announcements or offer documents or television interviews to this effect.

Assuming it is a contested bid and the offer has been extended, the target will prepare further arguments in its defence. It must release any new information (such as profit forecasts, announcements about restructuring its operations, asset revaluations and so on) by 0 + 39 (r. 31.9). This is usually treated fairly inflexibly by the Panel. In normal practice, therefore, the target makes every effort to release a circular to its shareholders just before 0 + 39 containing encouraging news which will entice them to hold on to their shares. Any profit forecasts must comply with the standards of care stipulated in r. 28 and have a series of assumptions stated and effectively reported on by the accountants. One word of warning: it is very easy to make statements about future prospects which are not intended to be profit forecasts, but which do in fact amount to the same thing. They will need to comply in exactly the same way as an express profit forecast with r. 28.

Meanwhile, in the contested bid, both sides will continue with their campaigning and the bidder with its share-buying. The restrictions under r. 5 (the cap at buying more than 30 per cent of the target) disappear after the first closing date provided there is to be no reference to the Competition Commission or the European Commission and the bidder does not mind complying with the requirements for a r. 9 bid (see **8.5.3.2**).

When the bidder sees the target's new information, it has seven days (up to 0 + 46) within which to decide whether to revise the offer. Much as with extensions to the offer, r. 32.2 prevents a bidder increasing the value of its offer if such a move has already been ruled out in a statement, even if there is a later change of mind.

Whether or not the bidder chooses to revise the offer (if that option is open), it is likely to issue a further document in reply to the target's new information.

8.5.7 Methods of acceptance

Those members of the target who hold share certificates will be required to send in the form of acceptance and share certificate. Those who hold their shares in uncertificated, dematerialised form (see **1.6.3**) will be required to complete a form of acceptance and to arrange for the input of instructions to CREST to transfer their shares to an 'escrow account', under the control of the bidder's receiving agent. The latter (a member of CREST (see **1.6.3**)) will transfer the shares from this account to the bidder on the offer becoming unconditional. Should the offer lapse or the shareholder withdraw acceptance, then the receiving agent will be required to transfer the shares back into the shareholder's main CREST account.

For the purpose of declaring an offer unconditional as to acceptances (see **8.5.2.2**) before the final closing date, the bidder's receiving agent can take into account shares standing in the escrow account.

8.5.8   The conclusion of the offer

The offer will conclude in one of the following ways:

(a) The bidder will have obtained its 50 per cent acceptances by 0 + 60 and can declare the offer unconditional as to acceptances. The offer must go wholly unconditional (that is, satisfying all other outstanding conditions) within 21 days of the offer being declared unconditional as to acceptances (r. 31.7). Sometimes this is difficult to fulfil because of the delay in obtaining a definitive ruling from the OFT as to whether the merger is to be referred. The Takeover Panel is usually prepared to oblige with a relaxation.

The Takeover Panel is very unlikely to relax the final date in the offer timetable—14 days after the offer is declared unconditional in all respects (r. 31.8)—because this is the point by which the target shareholders must be paid their money.

There is likely to be a minority left in place and so the bidder will activate the s. 429 Companies Act 1985 procedure if it holds over 90 per cent of the target shares (see **8.13**).

What if the bidder does not have the requisite 90 per cent? This is rarely a problem. Once the offer has gone wholly unconditional, the target board will usually recommend its shareholders to accept the offer (if it is still open) or sell their shares in the market as there is little to be gained from holding on. If it is a problem, then the bidder is simply left with a minority shareholding which it will hope to be able to buy out at a later date by negotiation.

(b) The bidder does not attain 50 per cent by 0 + 60 and so its offer must lapse. The bidder now has, perhaps, a sizeable stake in the target. Why does it not use this as a platform for an immediate fresh bid? The Code restricts this under r. 35 by preventing the bidder from making a new offer for a year and from buying any shares in the target in that time if that would take the bidder over 30 per cent.

Both of these possibilities apply equally to a recommended offer.

Let us look now at some of the strategic decisions which will figure in the planning of both bidder and target in the bid.

8.6   Strategic planning in takeovers

Both the bidder and the target need to undertake a significant amount of planning to ensure they decide on the most appropriate strategies, and to avoid potential pitfalls. This section will look at some of the most prominent issues you will need to think about to advise properly on strategy, or, at least, to make an informed contribution to the debate.

8.6.1   Tax issues

Before we look at the alternatives open to the bidder, we need briefly to address the most important of the tax questions and the effect they will have on the nature of the takeover offer.

(a) Will the offer give rise to a tax charge for the target shareholders? If so, what can be done to minimise this? This is considered in **8.6.3.9**.

(b) If the acquisition is to be financed by debt, the bidder will want to deduct its interest costs from its taxable profits to reduce the size of its tax bill. How can this be achieved?

The simplest method is for the bidder to make its offer through a vehicle resident for tax purposes in the UK. Then, once the bid is complete and the UK target is merged with the offering vehicle, the offering vehicle's financing costs can be set off against the target's profits. Given the UK is a relatively high-tax jurisdiction, this is a tax-efficient way of keeping the new merged company's tax bill low. Where the bidder is an overseas company, this may suggest the need for a UK-resident subsidiary to be established through which to make the bid.

(c) If the bid is unsuccessful, and the bidder has acquired some target shares, what is its exposure to tax if it chooses to sell those shares?

This is a real issue because (i) there is always a chance the bid will fail, (ii) the value of the stake acquired could be very high and the capital gains charge for an immediate disposal could be substantial, given that target shares usually appreciate in value significantly during the course of a bid, and (iii) if the offering vehicle is in the UK, the shares will be held in the UK and so will be subject to tax in a high-tax jurisdiction if sold.

One way around this is to establish the offering vehicle initially in a non-tax-paying jurisdiction. If the bid fails and the offeror has to sell the target shares it has acquired, it keeps its tax charge to zero on that disposal. If the bid is successful, the offering vehicle can later migrate to a jurisdiction where the bidder has a high tax bill, for example, the UK. The offering vehicle will generally have incurred significant costs (including possible ongoing financing costs), which can be set off against profits elsewhere in the bidder's group.

There are of course a host of other tax issues which will need to be addressed. It is vital to involve tax specialists to deal with these from the earliest point.

8.6.2   The nature of the offer

What sort of offer should the bidder seek to make? A number of possibilities are canvassed below.

8.6.2.1   General offer

This is the sort of takeover offer this chapter has hitherto been concerned with, namely an offer to acquire all the securities of a company which falls within the City Code's jurisdiction. We have seen that with this type of offer, either the target directors will recommend it to their shareholders, or else the bidder will have to make a hostile offer leading to a contested bid.

Some of the factors behind the target board's decision to recommend a bid have already been discussed (see **8.5.3.1**). The reason the bidder may particularly want to explore the possibility of a recommended bid is that it will generally be a quicker route than a hostile bid.

As we saw when looking at the timetable earlier (see **8.5.6**), you can generally assume that target shareholders will respond quickly to a recommendation from their board that they should accept an offer. There is usually every chance that such an offer can be declared unconditional as to acceptances by $0 + 21$, whereas most contested bids will not be settled until the eve of $0 + 60$.

In terms of cost, any cash underwriting required goes unconditional much sooner if the timetable is shorter, hence working out cheaper for the bidder on a recommended offer (see **8.6.3.1**). Furthermore, the expense of lobbying and advertising campaigns will be substantially reduced.

There is also an argument that a bidder will have a better chance of making a takeover work if it has secured the cooperation and goodwill of the incumbent management before the offer. A hostile bid is likely to create significant tensions and frictions for the bidder's management when it comes in to assume the reins of power, both from existing managers and employees. It may therefore be significantly to the bidder's advantage to exploit any opportunity that exists to persuade the target's board to contemplate a recommended bid.

8.6.2.2   Schemes of arrangement

A scheme of arrangement is a statutory procedure whereby a compromise or arrangement is proposed between a company and its creditors (or any class of them) or between the company and its members (or any class of them). This method of corporate restructuring is not confined to takeover activity but it is quite often used in this context. A scheme of arrangement is a scheme proposed by the target company to its members and/or creditors and, as such, differs to a takeover offer under which the bidder makes an offer to the target shareholders not involving the target as such. Accordingly, the scheme requires the target and the target's board of directors to be 'on side' and to cooperate in terms of driving the transaction forward. Therefore schemes are rarely an option for structuring hostile takeover bids. They are much more common and appropriate in the context of a 'merger of equals' (see **8.19**).

Put very simply, a scheme enables a company to restructure itself provided that its members approve the scheme at a special meeting convened by the court. Once approved by the shareholders, the scheme must be sanctioned by the court; the scheme then becomes effective and is binding on all shareholders. The detailed statutory requirements are considered in detail at **8.19**.

Typical schemes in the context of a takeover follow one of two paths:

(a) *Reduction scheme*

Due to the stamp duty saving involved, this is the more common type of scheme for takeover situations. Typically the shares in the target which are not already owned by the bidder are cancelled by the target reducing its share capital. The cancellation creates a reserve in the target which is capitalised and used by the target to issue new target shares to the bidder (so the target becomes wholly owned by the bidder). In consideration of the target shareholders cancelling their shares, the bidder pays the target shareholders (usually either in shares or in cash). So if the bidder issues shares to the target shareholders, they no longer hold shares in the target (as they have been cancelled), they are now shareholders in the bidder (the bridder shares being the purchase price) and the target is a wholly owned subsidiary of the bidder (the target using the reserve to issue new target shares to the bidder). This route involves a reduction of capital so the target has to comply with the provisions set out in s. 135 CA. This means that, in addition to the court meeting (see **8.19**), the target also has to hold an EGM to approve the reduction of its capital. The benefit of this path is that as there is no *transfer* of shares, no stamp duty is payable by the bidder.

(b) *Transfer scheme:*

This type of scheme involves a third party being appointed to execute, on behalf of the target shareholders, the transfers necessary to transfer all the shares in the target not already owned by the bidder, to the bidder. In consideration of this, the bidder pays the target shareholders. This is quicker than a reduction scheme but stamp duty is payable due to transfer of shares to the bidder.

8.6.2.3   New holding company

A third option is to set up a new company ('Newco') which is to acquire the shares of both bidder and target, so the two existing companies disappear into a new entity. Two routes for the acquisition of the shares of bidder and target exist: either Newco makes a general offer for all the securities in both bidder and target, or both companies enter into a scheme of arrangement under which their shareholders agree either to transfer their existing shares to Newco or to have their shares cancelled, and take Newco shares or cash instead.

Why do this rather than pursue one of the other options? The likeliest reason is the desire to effect a genuine merger of two equals.

There are some disadvantages. To use a general offer to acquire both bidder and target requires the appropriate percentage of acceptances from each of the companies, so there is twice the risk of failure. Stamp duty is payable on two lots of shares to be transferred (unless the scheme of arrangement is used which enables the shares to be cancelled). It is nevertheless a route which the parties sometimes find it to their advantage to utilise.

8.6.2.4 Partial or tender offer

These are both methods for securing less than 100 per cent control of the target.

(a) *Partial offer*

A partial offer is like a general offer save that the bidder is bidding only for a proportion of the voting share capital of the target. Each target shareholder may accept the offer in respect of an equivalent proportion of his shareholding. Thus if a bidder wants to acquire 25 per cent of a target, a shareholder with 100 shares may accept in respect of 25 of his 100 shares.

The main benefit to the bidder is the prospect of acquiring either significant influence or negative control (i.e., the ability to vote down anything requiring a special resolution) over the company for much less than it would cost to make an outright bid.

If the bidder wishes to acquire more than 30 per cent of the target, this requires the preliminary approval of shareholders with more than 50 per cent of the voting rights (excluding the bidder and those acting in concert with it) (r. 36.5). This is a material disincentive.

Partial offers are in practice therefore rare in the UK as they present significant practical problems. Rule 36 governs them and it requires the Takeover Panel's consent in advance of any such offer.

(b) *Tender offer*

A tender offer is governed by r. 4 of the Substantial Acquisition Rules ('SARs'). It is specifically the procedure whereby a bidder seeks to acquire less than 30 per cent of the target (a partial offer may be made for larger stakes).

The offer must be made by means of an advertisement placed in two national newspapers (SAR r. 4.2(a)) which should state the terms of the offer (SAR r. 4.1(a)). The offer must be open for at least seven days (SAR r. 4.1(a)). The bidder cannot send the equivalent of an offer document to target shareholders persuading them to take up the offer, but the target is entitled to circulate a document detailing why they should reject the offer. The offer must also be made for a specified proportion of the target shares and only cash is permitted by way of consideration.

Mechanically, the bidder may fix the price at which it is bidding for target shares, or it may set up an auction in reverse, so that it states the maximum price it is prepared to pay (SAR r. 4.2(a)(vii)) and shareholders state the minimum price they will accept and the bidder then sets a striking price once all the tenders are in from shareholders. All bids at or below that price will qualify under the tender.

Once again, given the strictness of the rules, tender offers are not popular mechanisms in UK takeover practice.

8.6.2.5   Reverse takeover

A reverse takeover is simply a takeover by a smaller company of a larger company, the effect of which is that the target company's shareholders become the majority shareholders in the bidder. Usually the target company board also becomes the controlling interest on the bidder's board. This type of bid is treated exactly like an ordinary general offer. The LSE requires the bidder in such a bid (obviously if listed) to obtain its shareholders' approval in general meeting, as the effect of the transaction will be loss of control over their company.

8.6.3   The nature of the consideration

The consideration for the offer is essentially a matter of commercial judgment of what looks most attractive from both the bidder's and target shareholders' points of view. In very general commercial terms, the kind of consideration most likely to appeal to target shareholders is cash. If there are competing bids, one cash and one not, and the value of the two bids is equivalent, the cash offer is likely to be the most attractive. It is for that reason that many non-cash bids offer a cash alternative (see below).

We will look at various types of consideration in turn and consider their respective advantages and disadvantages.

8.6.3.1   Cash

As we have seen already, the bidder may in fact have no choice about offering cash. The City Code requires it in two circumstances:

(a) Rule 11, which requires a cash alternative where the bidder has bought at least 10 per cent of the target's shares in the year leading up to the offer or during the offer period. The value must be the equivalent of the highest price paid for the shares bought in that time. The basic thinking behind this is to ensure that, if the bidder has paid a significant number of shareholders (which the Takeover Panel deems to be 10 per cent) cash for their shares, then all the shareholders should be entitled to participate in this.

(b) A mandatory bid under r. 9 (where the bidder acquires more than 30 per cent of the target's shares) must have a cash alternative at the same price as the highest the bidder has paid for the target's shares in the past year (r. 9.5(a)).

The principal difficulty for the bidder, even if it wants voluntarily to offer cash, is that cash may be in short supply. How can this be resolved?

The common method is through a cash-underwritten alternative. This is very much like a vendor placing (see 3.6.5) and exists to solve the same basic commercial problem, namely the mismatch between the need for cash and the availability of non-cash assets in the form of securities. The bidder offers target shareholders its securities with an express cash alternative. In respect of any securities for which the cash alternative is chosen, the bidder's investment bank is instructed to procure subscribers for those securities by placing them in the market. The cash paid by the placees in consideration for the securities is then passed on to the target shareholders. As with a vendor placing, the investment bank agrees to underwrite the placing if it does not attract investors, and it will also instruct the brokers to arrange a subunderwriting on its behalf. The terms of the underwriting agreement are similar to the agreement we saw in 3.5.4.1.

The other way of obtaining cash is through a loan. The main technical issue this raises for the company is whether it is able under its articles of association to borrow at the required levels. Commercially, of course, borrowing always brings with it an interest cost, and the real issue here is whether that can be set off against profits to reduce tax (see 8.6.1).

8.6.3.2   The bidder's own securities

The bidder will think about using its own securities as consideration for any number of reasons. It may have no or insufficient cash resources available and be close to the limits on the borrowing restrictions in its articles of association. It may simply be that it regards its gearing ratio as too high.

8.6.3.3   What type of securities?

The securities can, in commercial terms, cover the whole spectrum of financial instruments from ordinary shares to bonds. There is no restriction in the City Code on what can be offered, which allows for maximum flexibility.

Commercial considerations usually play the critical role in determining the nature of the securities to be issued. One such is that the cost of debt to the company is generally cheaper than that of equity, provided the interest payable on the debt instruments can be set off against tax. Another key factor in this choice is the effect it has on the bidder's accounts.

8.6.3.4   Accounting treatment

There is no getting away from the fact that this is a complex subject! Although the accountants will of course have prime responsibility for dealing with this question, the lawyers involved also need to grasp the issues as they will have a significant impact on the structure of the offer. A takeover brings two entities and hence two sets of accounts together. The question arises how the merger of those accounts is to be achieved. The methods are described below, together with their relative attractions and limitations.

8.6.3.5   Merger accounting

The target's assets and liabilities are merged into the bidder's at the value stated in the target's accounts, and the appearance is as if the two entities have always been one.

Merger accounting can only be used in rare cases. The requirements are currently set out in CA Sch. 4A, para. 10 and FRS 6. Essentially, the bidder must acquire 90 per cent of the target's equity securities (shares with unrestricted rights to income and capital) with its own equivalent securities. Other criteria set by FRS 6 relevant in determining whether the transaction is a merger or an acquisition include the management of the combined entity (is it truly merged?) and the parties' relative sizes (if the acquirer is much larger, this makes it less likely to be a genuine merger).

Thus, if the bidder wants to be able to use the merger accounting method, it will need to issue equity securities or, at least, securities which carry such rights. This will restrict the nature of the securities it can offer.

8.6.3.6   Acquisition accounting

The target's assets and liabilities are accounted for in the merged accounts at a 'fair value' (not necessarily the same as the value stated in the target's accounts but the price at which the asset or liability could be exchanged in an arm's length transaction). In addition, the profits and losses of the target can only start to appear in the merged accounts as from the date of the acquisition, and not as if the two entities have always been one and the same. Any excess of the price paid by the bidder over the total fair value of the assets and liabilities is treated as 'goodwill'.

This method of accounting has to be used where merger accounting is not available (CA Sch. 4A, para. 8), though it may also be used instead of merger accounting. It is subject to the requirements set out in FRS 7: the underlying thrust of this is that the target should be accounted for as it actually stands at the time of the acquisition, not as the acquirer intends to organise it. Post-acquisition reorganisation costs are not therefore part of the cost of the acquisition. It is an attractive method from one point of view, in that the addition of the target's profits from the date of acquisition can give the impression of a sudden increase in the merged entity's earnings. With merger accounting, profits are restated as if the two entities have always been together and so the rate of profits increase will seem flatter.

Its disadvantage is the creation of goodwill. Goodwill may be treated in two ways. The first is as an asset, and the Companies Act 1985 requires that it be written off over a number of years (Sch. 4, para. 21). This will have an adverse impact on the merged entity's reported profits as an element of these is being accounted for in writing off the goodwill.

The alternative (in fact preferred by SSAP 22) is to write goodwill off straight away against reserves. Obviously this may have a significant impact on the available distributable reserves of the merged entity. There are two ways around this:

(a) The first is a reduction of capital (CA s. 135), either of the company's share capital or share premium account (see **9.7**). This creates a reserve against which goodwill can be written off.

(b) The second is to create a merger reserve as a result of obtaining merger relief (CA s. 131) (see **8.6.3.7**). Goodwill can then be written off against this.

The accountancy profession is currently debating the best approach to dealing with goodwill when the acquisition accounting method is used, as the technique of immediately writing goodwill off against reserves tends to emasculate balance sheets and has resulted in other 'creative' accounting measures to restore their appearance.

8.6.3.7   Merger relief

As mentioned above, the availability of merger relief may facilitate the use of the acquisition accounting method. When a company issues shares, the difference between the nominal value of the shares and the value of the target shares acquired (the premium) must be paid into the share premium account. This is then treated as capital and is subject to the restrictions in CA s. 130.

Under CA s. 131, if the bidder obtains a 90 per cent holding of the equity securities of the target in exchange for equity securities of its own, merger relief is available. This allows the bidder to create a merger reserve with the premium which would otherwise have been transferred to the share premium account. As discussed above, goodwill can then be written off against that reserve.

8.6.3.8   Summary of accounting treatments

(a) Both merger relief and merger accounting depend crucially on structuring the bidder's consideration as equity securities (that is, shares with unrestricted rights to income and capital) and planning to do what will effectively be a straight share-for-share exchange with the target shareholders.

(b) The requirements for using the merger accounting method are stricter than those for obtaining merger relief.

(c) If the issue of equity securities is either not possible or not desired, the bidder will have to acquisition account, and then some careful thought will need to be given to the appropriate method for writing off the arising goodwill.

(d) Of course, it is possible for the bid to be structured in such a way that the bidder obtains merger relief and still chooses the acquisition accounting method.

The lesson is: consult the accountants early on and consider carefully the impact on the accounting position of the use of certain types of securities as consideration.

8.6.3.9   Tax treatment

The securities offered to the target shareholders are largely chosen for the commercial or accounting reasons already considered. Another factor in the choice is tax.

A target shareholder resident in the UK who accepts an offer of cash for his shares will be treated as having disposed of those shares and so will be subject to capital gains tax ('CGT') on the gain arising. The charge to CGT can be deferred if the shareholder accepts securities as consideration. The advantage of deferral to the shareholder is that he can then choose to realise the gain (i.e., sell the securities he has accepted) at a time when available reliefs can help significantly to reduce the extent of the chargeable gain. This is therefore one more favourable factor suggesting the use of securities as consideration, and it is also why, even with an all-cash offer, bidders will usually offer a 'loan note alternative'. Those shareholders with a particular CGT problem can then consider taking up the loan note option. A loan note in these circumstances is usually denominated in sterling, carries interest at a rate slightly below LIBOR, is unsecured, unlisted and repayable at the option of the holder every six months or so over something like a five-year term.

8.6.4   What is being bid for?

This may seem a strange question, but remember that the City Code itself states that it does not apply to offers for non-voting, non-equity capital (see r. 14.1 and also rr. 9.1 and 15). The exception to this is mentioned later. Where there is more than one class of equity share capital, r. 14 requires that a comparable offer be made for each class whether such capital carries voting rights or not.

A comparable offer is one that compares in terms of value (though it need not be identical) and is made simultaneously with the 'main' offer. It does not have to be the same type of consideration: it may be possible to offer one type of security to one class and another type to a different class.

The exception to the principle that offers for non-voting and non-equity capital are irrelevant under the City Code is r. 15. If a target's equity share capital is the subject of a bid, any securities with conversion rights, subscription rights or options over that equity share capital must be the subject of an 'appropriate offer' (r. 15(a)). This should be appropriate in terms of value and type of consideration. As far as timing is concerned, it is quite normal to await the outcome of the 'main' offer before implementing a r. 15 offer: then if the 'main' offer fails, the r. 15 offer need never arise.

8.6.5   Deals with third parties

The bidder may identify before it announces its offer that it will have difficulties satisfying the requirements of the Office of Fair Trading and Competition Commission because of the potential anticompetitive effects of its bid. A preventive measure to ease the path of the bid is to agree a sale of part of the target's operations to a third party before the bid begins. There are, though, a number of issues to watch here:

(a) There is always the risk that this will amount to the giving of unlawful financial assistance by the target for the acquisition of its own shares (remember s. 151 Companies Act 1985 catches indirect financial assistance as well).

(b) If the third party is already a shareholder in the target, this sort of deal will probably fall foul of r. 16 of the City Code as it is an arrangement with a shareholder with favourable conditions attached which are not being extended to all shareholders: this is a rule which will strike at other possible bid tactics which may suggest themselves.

8.6.6 Bidder's tactics

All the issues set out so far in **8.6** are of course strategic questions for the bidder to decide. There are also tactical questions to consider about the conduct of the bid. Some of these have already been discussed. The list below is no more than a summary of some of the key tactics which may be considered and some of the limitations on them which will need to be observed.

(a) The bidder may attempt to build up a stake in the target through share purchases in the market to help it towards its goal of acquiring 50 per cent: we have already looked at some of the restrictions to be considered when doing this (see **8.5.3.2**).

(b) The bidder will also attempt to secure support from existing shareholders in the target by getting them to pledge their shares irrevocably to the offer (r. 24.3 (a)(iv)): we have looked at irrevocable undertakings and some of the issues to think about when seeking them (see **8.5.4.2**).

(c) The other crucial issue for the bidder to focus on is price. Remember that 0 ± 46 is the last date on which the bidder can revise its offer. Most institutional and other shareholders will be swayed ultimately by an attractive price for their shares. If the first offer was not compelling, a revised offer may be a 'knock-out' blow.

8.6.7 Defence strategy and tactics

To a great extent this is necessarily reactive—it depends on the nature and circumstances of the offer. All that this section therefore does is offer some general guidance on ideas for defence which the target will usually want at least to consider.

As a prelude to this, it is important to dwell for a moment on the legal responsibilities of the target board, who, after all, will be in charge of the direction of the target's response. Some case law exists (*Dawson International plc* v. *Coats Patons plc* [1989] BCLC 233 and *Heron International Ltd* v. *Lord Grade* [1983] BCLC 244) which indicates that where the target directors are faced with two competing bids and certain defeat, their duty is to act in the best interests of the existing shareholders. This may not be simply to recommend the higher bid. The lower bid may be in the best interests of the company where, as happened recently, the target board judged it was less likely to be the subject of a Competition Commission reference and so more likely to proceed successfully (the target was UAPT–Infolink). Where the future of the company is open to doubt, the target directors will need to judge what is in the company's longer term commercial interests as well as in the immediate interests of current shareholders, and justify their conduct by reference to that standard. It is also important always to recall that the directors can exercise their powers of management only for proper corporate purposes and not simply to protect their own positions as either directors or shareholders (*Hogg* v. *Cramphorn Ltd* [1967] Ch 254). Nor should the managers forget their responsibility to have regard to the interests of employees under CA s. 309.

The City Code (r. 3) stipulates that the board should obtain competent independent advice on any offer and communicate the substance of that advice to its shareholders.

Now to turn to some of the possible strategies available.

(a) The temptation for a target under threat is to secure its position by making a takeover bid effectively impossible or practically unwinnable. One method which suggests itself is to increase the shareholding interest of 'friendly' shareholders by issuing further shares to them so that majority control cannot be obtained without acquiring these shares. In the United States, some companies have provisions in their articles of association which are automatically activated in the event of a takeover offer being made and which bring about circumstances which block any chance of such an offer succeeding, such as enhanced voting rights for certain shares. This is a strategy known as the 'poison pill' because of its effect on those who swallow it!

These strategies may not work in the United Kingdom. The City Code states in General Principle 7 that:

'At no time after a bona fide offer has been communicated to the board of the offeree company, or after the board of the offeree company has reason to believe that a bona fide offer might be imminent, may any action be taken by the board of the offeree company in relation to the affairs of the company, without the approval of the shareholders in general meeting, which could effectively result in any bona fide offer being frustrated or in the shareholders being denied an opportunity to decide on its merits.'

Rule 21 develops this by stipulating certain types of prohibited frustrating action, including issuing further shares (r. 21.1(a)) and selling or agreeing to sell assets of a material amount (r. 21.1(d)). Remember, though, these are all subject to shareholder approval. Furthermore, defensive measures can be built in, provided this is done well in advance of any possible offer: of course, any listed company will have difficulties in amending its articles of association in the ways described given The Listing Rules' provisions.

(b) One thing which neither General Principle 7 nor r. 21 prevents, and which is a defensive strategy regularly employed by targets, is the lobbying of public authorities such as the Office of Fair Trading and the Competition Commission in an effort to persuade them to prevent the bid proceeding. In many cases, this is the method most likely to succeed in thwarting a bid. References to the Competition Commission are the commonest form of regulatory intervention sought by targets.

Related to this is the use of tactical litigation to hold up a bid. This is very uncommon and difficult to mount in the UK following the Court of Appeal's ruling in *R v Panel on Takeovers and Mergers, ex parte Datafin plc* [1987] QB 815 regarding the justiciability of the Takeover Panel's decisions (see **8.8.7**). Such litigation is much more widespread in the USA. In the UK, it will be subject to r. 21.

(c) A target may recognise that the game is up, that it cannot survive as an independent entity and that its only strategy is to find the best way to lose which is in the interests of the target shareholders. The target board may therefore recommend the bid to its shareholders. Alternatively, it may not trust the bidder or feel that its plans for the target are unsuitable or that the price it is offering is inadequate. One solution would be to seek an alternative bidder prepared to offer more money and with plans more in keeping with the existing management's own ideas—a so-called 'white knight'.

A competing offer may be announced at any time in the course of an existing bid. If this happens, the timetable for the first bid is adjusted so that it corresponds exactly with that for the second (i.e., giving the first bidder time to react to the 'white knight').

(d) Of course the only way the target will lose the takeover battle is if its shareholders sell out to the bidder. This they will only do if either the price they are given is one they believe they cannot refuse or if they believe the bidder can offer a better future in terms of direction for the company and quality of management. The target's best form of defence therefore must be to show its shareholders that (i) the price offered undervalues the worth of the company, and (ii) the target management and its strategy are clearly better. This is of course what the defence documents will seek to do. The target needs, however, to ensure that its case is presented well in the press and is understood by investors. Someone will therefore need to work hard on the company's public relations image and its communications with shareholders.

By the same token, effort expended in producing an encouraging profit forecast for the target (if that is possible) is likely to be well rewarded with loyal support, as this is tangible evidence of a future pay-off for shareholders.

As well as working on the profit forecast, a target may try to show that the offer undervalues the company's worth because it attaches too low a figure to the company's assets: a revaluation reported to the shareholders will strengthen the target's case. It will be subject to the same timing restrictions as for a profit forecast: the last date on which either could be announced is 0 + 39.

(e) Particularly where the substance of the bidder's case is that the target needs to restructure its business, the target's best response may be to adopt the bidder's idea and to effect a reconstruction of its operations. Once the bid is announced or in the offing, this will fall foul of r. 21 unless the shareholders approve. If a bid is likely but not imminent, this may be a useful pre-emptive strike.

In some cases, companies on the receiving end of a bid are far-sighted enough to have produced a 'defence manual', an internal and obviously highly confidential document, which will describe its proposed defence strategies, contain draft documents such as the outline of relevant press announcements and set out how the defence of the bid will be managed (for example, who from the target will work on the defence team and what support and information they will require). This is then kept in readiness (and updated as appropriate) for any possible bid—otherwise, a bid will catch the target completely napping and give the bidder a significant head start.

Let us now return to look in detail at the legal and regulatory provisions relevant to takeover practice.

8.7 Law and regulation in takeovers

There are a number of areas of law and regulation relevant in takeover work:

(a) the City Code and the jurisdiction of the Takeover Panel (see **8.8**);

(b) the SAR (see **8.9**);

(c) the UKLA and its requirements under the Listing Rules (see **8.10**);

(d) the continuing requirements under the LSE's Admission and Disclosure Standards;

(e) the Companies Act 1985, and in particular those sections dealing with:

    (i)   notification of interests in shares (Part VI of the Act, ss. 198–220, see **8.11**);

    (ii) financial assistance for the acquisition of shares (ss. 151–158, see **8.12**);

    (iii) acquisition of minority interests under ss. 428–430 (see **8.13**);

(f) the Criminal Justice Act 1993 on insider dealing (see **8.14**);

(g) the FSMA, particularly ss. 21, 118 and 397 (see **8.15**);

(h) the merger control regime in the UK and the EC (see **8.16**);

(i) the application of the common law and, in particular, the law of defamation, which rears its head quite frequently in takeovers (see **8.17**).

Of these areas, the City Code is clearly the most important. It is the foundation of takeover regulation.

8.8 The City Code on Takeovers and Mergers and the Takeover Panel

We have already heard much of the rules of the City Code. When do we have to worry about them? How does the Panel work?

8.8.1 When does the City Code apply?

The answer to this is set out in para. 4 of the Introduction to the City Code (sometimes referred to as the 'Blue Book' by practitioners, to distinguish it from the LSE's Purple Book). Basically, you need to look at two things, the nature of the target company and the nature of the transaction.

8.8.1.1 The nature of the target company

If the target company is a UK incorporated *public* company, and is resident in the UK, the Isle of Man or the Channel Islands, the City Code applies to the takeover offer made for it (para. 4(a)). The company does *not* have to be listed. A private company which has been listed in the past 10 years but is no longer listed will also be caught, as are some statutory companies (like water companies), and Isle of Man and Channel Islands listed companies. It makes no difference in determining whether the City Code applies where the offeror comes from. It may be a company registered in the Cayman Islands and conducting most of its business in the USA, but if it is acquiring a UK public company resident in the UK, the City Code bites.

8.8.1.2 The nature of the transaction

The City Code catches a takeover transaction however it arises (para. 4(b)), whether via the normal route of a takeover offer made to all target shareholders, or through some other route such as a scheme of arrangement (see **8.6.2.2**). Basically, the Takeover Panel will look through the substance of a transaction and, if it looks like a takeover, it will regard the City Code as applying (provided the target company is covered by the City Code).

8.8.2 What is the City Code?

This was explained in **1.6.4**. Essentially it is a set of principles of best practice in these transactions, now regularly updated and refined by the Takeover Panel as the organ designated for this purpose by an assortment of City bodies. Though the system of regulation can best be described as voluntary, because there is no formal legal sanction for ignoring the City Code, this is fundamentally to misconstrue how it works.

8.8.3 What happens if the City Code is ignored or breached?

There are a series of sanctions, described in more detail below, which may be visited on a party in breach of the City Code.

The point of most of these sanctions, and what has made them so effective in practice, is the risk they carry that a party on the receiving end (or associated with that party, including advisers) will have its reputation tarnished or, worse, be shunned or excluded from the takeovers market or the securities market as a whole. All parties therefore take the risk of any of these sanctions being applied very seriously indeed: they may have highly damaging commercial consequences (see Introduction, para. 1(c)).

(a) The Takeover Panel may make a public announcement to the effect that a party has failed to comply with the City Code's provisions. This would be highly damaging to the chances of a takeover's success.

(b) The Takeover Panel may issue a censure or reprimand (see Introduction, para. 1(d)(ii)). Companies and advisers fight very hard to avoid this due to the potential detrimental effect on their businesses.

(c) The Takeover Panel will bring pressure to bear on investment banks to bring the companies they are advising into line, and may, simply through the threat of censure or worse, force the investment bank to take drastic action and resign from acting for the company in question. In terms of strategic direction for the takeover and public relations, this would be disastrous for the company.

(d) The Takeover Panel may ask City institutions not to act for a particular individual or company in any takeover or similar transaction, so that he or it is unable to carry on that sort of business in the City. This is known as 'cold-shouldering' and has only happened once in the Panel's history. Once again, the self-regulatory organisations support the Panel in this by including in their rules a requirement that member firms will not act for a party which has been 'cold-shouldered' in this way.

It is true to say, though, that it is unusual for these sanctions to be invoked. The reason is not so much that everyone lives in dread of a thunderbolt from the Takeover Panel, but that the Takeover Panel itself prefers to seek a remedy for a breach of the City Code than to punish the offending party. The following are illustrations of what in practice the Takeover Panel may require where the City Code has been breached. The basic philosophy under which the Takeover Panel operates is not to be hidebound by fixed rules about available remedies, but rather to identify and apply a remedy appropriate to the circumstances.

(e) The Takeover Panel may require a company to amend a document issued in the course of the takeover, for instance, the offer document. This will be to correct a misleading statement. It would be easy for the Takeover Panel publicly to castigate the party for getting the document wrong, but its preferred approach is to ensure that everyone knows what the document should have said.

(f) The Takeover Panel may require that a party which has bought shares in the market in the course of a takeover has to sell them. This would be the case where the purchase was in breach of the City Code.

There are other remedies which the Takeover Panel has used in particular cases, for example, preventing a potential bidder from launching a bid at all because of its conduct leading up to that point. The point is that the Takeover Panel has the flexibility to devise solutions to fit the bill.

Let us look now at the way in which the City Code is interpreted, as this is central to the entire regulatory system for takeovers.

8.8.4   The nature and interpretation of the City Code

To understand the methodology of interpreting the City Code, we need to see first how it is set out. It comes in two parts, the general principles and the rules. We will focus for now on the general principles, as this is where the City Code starts and it is from them that the rules themselves are derived.

8.8.4.1   The general principles: what are they?

There are ten general principles and they are, to quote the City Code, 'essentially statements of good standards of commercial behaviour'. This may sound pretty meaningless, but in fact, they play an integral part in defining the nature and interpretation of the City Code. They play two principal roles:

(a) The first has already been mentioned: they form the basis of the more specific rules, and are an aid to their interpretation. If, for example, a question arises as to the specific application of one of the rules to a particular takeover, the first question the Takeover Panel will ask itself will be, does this case come within the principle underlying the rule? If so, the Takeover Panel is very unlikely to entertain any arguments that the rule be disregarded.

(b) They are binding on the parties to a takeover offer, and so may prevent conduct which might otherwise appear, from an analysis of the rules, to be permissible.

8.8.4.2   The general principles: the basic themes

The general principles have five basic themes:

(a) *Equality of treatment and opportunity for shareholders*
Any aspect of an offer which treats target shareholders of the same class differently is unacceptable (GP 1).
    All shareholders should receive the same information and get new information at the same time. (GP 2) The appropriate method of releasing information is either through a general press announcement or a circular to all shareholders.

(b) *Adequacy of information and advice*
The highest standards of care and accuracy should be applied in the preparation of documents or advertisements during an offer (GP 5).
    Directors, in advising their shareholders, should act independently and therefore without reference to any conflicting or personal interests (GP 9). The principle extends to the directors' own advisers, namely, the merchant bank and other advisers like accountants and solicitors. The Takeover Panel will prevent an adviser from acting if its independence is in any way in doubt.

(c) *Prohibition on frustrating action*
We have already seen in **8.6.7(a)** that general principle 7 prevents the target from doing anything (after it becomes aware that a bid is looming) which frustrates an offer or denies the shareholders the opportunity to decide it on its merits, unless the shareholders have consented to this in general meeting. The principle is that the shareholders, as owners of the target, should be free to make up their own minds on what they want. Rule 21 expands on this by stipulating some situations which are considered frustrating action.

(d) *Maintenance of an orderly market*
An offer should be announced only after careful and responsible consideration (GP 3). This is designed to prevent a 'stop-go' policy on the part of a potential offeror which creates a highly volatile market in the target's shares, which is not in its or its shareholders' interests.

(e) *The 'siege' principle*
Although this is not embodied as such in a general principle, the Takeover Panel takes into account a fifth general theme in practice, which is that the target company should not be laid siege to from an unwanted offeror beyond a reasonable length of time. This explains the timing restrictions placed on a bid (see **8.5.1**), and r. 35, which prevents a failed bidder from trying again for another year.

8.8.4.3   The general principles: limitations

The general principles are not to be taken as the last word on what is or is not acceptable. There are a series of unwritten limitations which apply. It is not possible in the space here to be comprehensive about the extent of these, but a number of examples will illustrate that exceptions to the application of these principles do exist, and that they should not therefore necessarily be taken as gospel.

First, the principle of equality of treatment ought to mean that the same offer and information are made available to all shareholders, *wherever they live*. In general terms, that is true. Regulatory complications in the United States and Canada mean, however, that it is often not possible to extend offers to those jurisdictions, because compliance with the relevant regulations is wholly impracticable. The Takeover Panel understands and accepts this and so some offers are simply not made available to North Americans.

Secondly, as we have seen (**8.6.7**), the principle prohibiting frustrating action does not prevent the target from seeking to persuade the Office of Fair Trading that the bid should be referred to the Competition Commission, even though such a referral would effectively kill the bid.

8.8.4.4   The general principles: how are they interpreted?

The general principles are not like statutory provisions: there is a woolliness about them which makes a lawyer feel uncomfortable. However, this is central to the interpretation of the general principles and the entire City Code. The thinking behind them is set out in para. 3(a) of the Introduction to the City Code. This is fundamental to a proper understanding of the City Code and so to any advice to be given in relation to it:

'These general principles . . . are . . . expressed in broad general terms and the Code does not define the precise extent of, or the limitations on, their application. They are applied by the Panel *in accordance with their spirit to achieve their underlying purpose*; the Panel may modify or relax the effect of their precise wording accordingly.' [Emphasis added.]

There are two things to note about this:

(a) The general principles are not capable of strict legalistic analysis: this approach will get you nowhere. Normal principles of interpretation must give way to what might be called a purposive approach—what is the spirit of the provision? This will govern the Takeover Panel's view. Lawyers must therefore not treat the principles or, indeed, the rest of the City Code as if they were a statute.

(b) The Takeover Panel is the arbiter of the application and operation of the general principles, hence an understanding of how it works is vital to an adequate appreciation of the Code. Moreover, a point in the general principles which is unclear cannot be resolved by the lawyers giving an opinion—the Panel has to be consulted (Introduction para. 3(b)) (see below and **8.4.8**).

In conclusion on the general subject of the interpretation of the City Code, the general principles can in general terms be regarded as a distillation of basic principles of commercial morality and fairness as applied to takeovers. It is in this spirit that the Takeover Panel adjudges conduct in the course of a bid, whatever the specific wording of the City Code, and the advice of the lawyers must be tailored accordingly.

We have already seen what the Takeover Panel is (see **1.6.4**); what is its role?

8.8.5   What is the Takeover Panel's job?

When referring to the Takeover Panel in this section, you should take this to mean not just the full Panel but the Panel Executive too. The Takeover Panel's job is the regulation of the takeovers market. It does this in a number of ways.

(a) It updates and revises the City Code through its Code Committee.

(b) It responds to enquiries from parties to a takeover (or, more likely, their financial and legal advisers) about the interpretation and application of the City Code. The Panel Executive never gives advice in writing and confines itself to oral statements over the telephone or in meetings. The full Panel will issue written decisions. It is possible to obtain guidance from the Panel Executive on a 'no-names' basis, though this can never be categorical. Firm rulings are only possible when the Panel Executive knows who the parties involved actually are.

(c) It monitors developments in the takeovers market through regular checking of share price movements and reports in newspapers and journals. The object of this is to ensure that the Takeover Panel is fully apprised of all information of significance in relation to current or potential takeovers.

The Takeover Panel sees its primary and overall objective as being the protection of equity shareholders and what might be called the maintenance of an orderly takeovers market. Its concern is, put very simply, that the holder of equity, and particularly the individual shareholders as opposed to the institutions, does not have legal or economic rights prejudiced or oppressed in the course of a takeover.

We have already seen what the general principles have to say, and you will have begun to appreciate that underlying much of the Takeover Panel's *raison d'être* is a desire to ensure that takeovers are governed by basic principles of commercial morality and fairness.

There are two common misconceptions about the Takeover Panel's role.

The first is that the Takeover Panel's approval for documents issued in the course of takeover offers is required as a precondition of their issue: this is not the case. In other words, the Takeover Panel does not operate like a clearing house for these documents in the way in which the LSE does for listing particulars. If documents are incorrect when issued in the course of a bid then, as we have seen in **8.8.3**, the Panel will take steps to ensure errors are subsequently remedied.

The second is that the Takeover Panel considers the commercial benefits or viability of a proposed offer: once again, this is not the case. It is concerned solely to ensure that the correct procedures are complied with. It simply ignores the question of whether an offer is a good thing or not, though this does not of course prevent it from ruling on whether the offeror has been behaving badly in the course of its bid.

8.8.6   How does the Takeover Panel function?

The first point of contact with the Takeover Panel on a particular takeover is likely to be a telephone call to the Panel Executive from one of the advisers involved, either checking on a point of interpretation or informing the Takeover Panel that a bid is on its way. Thereafter, the Takeover Panel acts primarily as a reactive body, responding to requests for guidance on interpretation of the City Code or what the parties should do as the bid proceeds. On a day-to-day basis, it will act through a case officer appointed to oversee a particular bid.

In the event that the parties or advisers to a takeover are unhappy with the ruling they have received from the Panel Executive, they may appeal to the full Takeover Panel (Introduction para. 3(c)). This means that the full committee is summoned to hear the particular point, and usually in very short order in view of the fact that speed is of the essence in takeovers. The hearing is not like a court of law and there is no formal process laid down. The full Takeover Panel gives its decision in writing soon after the hearing. It is possible to appeal against that decision to the Appeal Committee, either where the full Takeover Panel permits it or there is an allegation that it has exceeded its jurisdiction

(Introduction para. 3(f)). The Appeal Committee consists of two senior judges and two Panel members not otherwise involved in whichever case is being appealed, although the quorum for the Appeal Committee is three people. It is technically the final port of call, subject to what is said about judicial review below.

More generally, it is important to be clear about the way in which the Takeover Panel handles the interpretation of the City Code. This is covered in **8.8.4**.

8.8.7   Is the Takeover Panel the final arbiter?

Is there, in other words, any appeal from the decisions of the Takeover Panel after its own appeals process has run its course?

The Takeover Panel's decisions are open to judicial review (*R v. Panel on Takeovers and Mergers, ex parte Datafin plc* [1987] QB 815), but only on a historical rather than a contemporaneous basis. What this means is that the Takeover Panel's decisions cannot be interfered with in the course of a takeover, only after the event as a way of ensuring that the Takeover Panel does not make the same mistake twice. The case has since been supported by a decision in the House of Lords and another one in the Court of Appeal. The basic thinking behind it is that, if parties could obtain judicial review through the courts in the course of a takeover battle, it would give enormous scope for tactical litigation, undermine the authority of the Takeover Panel, slow the whole timetable for a takeover down and make the transaction a great deal more expensive for the parties involved. The flexible and informal procedure which the Takeover Panel operates would be wholly overturned if takeovers began to end up in the courts. As it is, the effect of the *Datafin* case is to kill off judicial review in the context of takeovers: it is difficult to summon up the motivation (and hard to justify the cost) to resurrect points from a takeover when it is dead and buried, simply for the benefit of the next generation of takeover practitioners.

8.9   The Substantial Acquisitions Rules (the 'SARs')

Though not part of the City Code, these are issued and administered by the Takeover Panel. Their purpose is to 'restrict the speed with which a person may increase his holding of shares and rights over shares to an aggregate of between 15 per cent and 30 per cent of the voting rights of the company'. The SARs achieve this under r. 1 by preventing a person from acquiring 10 per cent or more of a company's voting rights over a seven-day period if that would give the buyer more than 15 per cent (but less than 30 per cent) of those voting rights. This explains why buyers of shares frequently stop at the 14.99 per cent threshold. It also gives them the best possible position from which to initiate further share-buying—given the restrictions of the SARs.

The intention is not to prevent buyers from making substantial acquisitions of shares, simply to slow them down. This is in response to the old practice of the 'dawn raid', in which a buyer would 'swoop' on a target's shares when the stock market opened. Before the target had time to draw breath, substantial amounts of its equity would be in unwelcome hands. The SARs therefore give targets time to think and respond.

SAR 1 is supported by SAR 3, which obliges any buyer to disclose to the LSE when it goes through the 15 per cent threshold, and any further 1 per cent increases beyond that.

Sanctions are applied by the Takeover Panel in the same way as for breaches of the City Code (see **8.8.3**).

The SARs will not apply where purchases go through the 30 per cent barrier—this is governed by r. 5 (and r. 9) of the Code. More important still, the SARs do not apply where a takeover offer has been made under the City Code. Hence, they are only relevant in the build-up to the announcement of the offer.

8.10 The Listing Rules

The Listing Rules are relevant in a number of ways in takeover work.

8.10.1 Reverse takeovers

The Listing Rules require a company effecting a reverse takeover (and which is already listed) to publish a circular and obtain approval from its shareholders in general meeting for the transaction to proceed (LR para. 10.39—see also **8.6.2.5**).

8.10.2 Transactions

We saw in the context of acquisitions the impact of the Class requirements on companies making disposals or acquisitions of companies, assets or businesses. The requirements apply equally to public company takeovers, and will catch a listed company making an offer to acquire all the shares in a public company: if the transaction is of a sufficient size by comparison with the value of the bidder, it may be a Class 1 transaction. Shareholder approval and a shareholder circular are then necessary. Section **5.6.4** contains further details on the Class requirements. Some of these, including the requirement to describe material contracts and litigation in the circular, require information to be included about the target as well as the bidder. This applies even to a hostile bid since the bidder is expected to make reasonable enquiry of the target's published sources of information.

8.10.3 Listing particulars

In relation to some takeovers, listing particulars may be required. This is where all or part of the consideration being offered by the bidder consists of securities for which listing on the Official List will be sought. The listing particulars contents requirements (see **4.2.6.3**) will apply equally to a takeover as to an ordinary equity offering, and so these will need to be added to the list alongside the requirements stated in r. 24 of the City Code (see **8.5.5.1**).

It is not necessary to issue the offer document and the listing particulars separately—the one may be incorporated in the other. If printed separately, listing particulars will generally need to be published at the same time as the offer document, and so it is important to ensure that the takeover announcement is not made until the listing process is well advanced (see **4.2.6.4**).

If the offer is recommended, and listing particulars are required, the target and its directors will have to accept responsibility in the listing particulars as well as the offer document for information about the target (LR para. 5.3(b)).

The final point to be made about the role of the UKLA in takeovers is that it is there to be consulted by companies and advisers alike if there are any doubts about the application of the Listing Rules to the transaction.

8.11 Companies Act 1985: notification of interests in shares

These are provisions which apply in contexts other than takeovers but it is here that they are most frequently encountered.

The basic principle behind Part VI of the Companies Act 1985 is that public companies (the only ones to which the sections apply) have an interest in identifying substantial shareholders on their register of members and in monitoring the sizes of their shareholdings. They are at least then put on notice if a potential predator should emerge.

The method for achieving this is to require a shareholder who acquires a 3 per cent interest (CA s. 199(2)) in a public company's relevant share capital (essentially issued shares carrying a right to vote at general meetings (s. 198(2))) to notify (s. 198(1)) the company within two working days (s. 202(1)). Failure to do so is an offence under s. 210. If the percentage of the shareholder's interest increases to a new whole number (for example, from 3.9 per cent to 4.1 per cent), that too requires disclosure (s. 200). Disposal of an interest previously notified, or reduction of that interest from, say, 4.1 per cent to 3.9 per cent, must be similarly disclosed.

An interest in shares is very widely defined by s. 208 as 'an interest of any kind whatsoever in the shares'. It includes a beneficial interest under a trust or a right under an option. Some interests are exempt by s. 209, including that of a bare trustee or a market maker properly holding shares for the purposes of his market-making business. Some interests are defined as not 'material', for example, holdings by investment managers and unit trust managers, and they need to be disclosed only when they amount to 10 per cent or more of the relevant share capital: even if these interests are more than 3 per cent, no obligation of disclosure arises.

It would be tempting to circumvent these provisions by dividing an interest between a number of associates or subsidiaries, giving each less than 3 per cent. The legislation deals with this by requiring so-called 'concert parties' to amalgamate their interests for the purposes of disclosure. A concert party exists if two or more persons agree to buy and hold shares in a public company (whether in writing or not) and actually go ahead and make the purchase (s. 204). Each member of the concert party is taken to be interested in the interests of other members of the party. The consequence is that they all need to notify the company if the accumulated total is over 3 per cent.

As for the use of subsidiaries, if a company controls one-third of the voting power of another company, by s. 203 it is taken to be interested in the interests which that other company holds in a public company: hence parent companies are interested in the holdings of their subsidiaries.

The provisions also give a public company the power to investigate the identity of any shareholder on its register of members. Section 212 enables a company to require anyone whom it *reasonably believes* either holds, or in the past three years has held, shares in the company to disclose whether he is interested in the company's shares (s. 212(1)). This may also be useful where an interest is held by a nominee company and the identity of the underlying beneficiary is unknown—the beneficiary only needs to make a disclosure where the interest is 3 per cent.

The use of s. 212 notices is likely to have become more widespread following the introduction of CREST (see **1.6.3**) since many shareholders now hold shares through nominee accounts on CREST.

The recipient of a s. 212 notice must reply within a reasonable time—taken to be two days in an urgent situation such as the middle of a takeover and five days at other times.

Failure to do so may result in a court order under s. 216 forbidding the shareholder from selling his shares, voting on them or receiving a dividend. Some companies have automatic powers under their articles of association to impose such sanctions in the event of no reply (though the LSE has time limits which listed companies wishing to exercise these powers should observe). If a shareholder has an exempt interest under s. 209, he must still disclose his interest if he receives a s. 212 notice—effectively it overrides the exemption.

The effect of these provisions is that a target facing a perceived takeover threat will dispatch a flurry of s. 212 notices to establish precisely who is the enemy and how many shares it already has. During the course of a bid, the target will continue to send out notices to monitor the bidder's performance. The bidder must be careful to comply with these and particularly careful where it is acting in association with others (including advisers buying shares on its behalf) to stay within the concert party provisions.

8.12   Companies Act 1985: financial assistance for the acquisition of shares

You will already be familiar with CA s. 151. Like Part VI of the Act, it is not just in the context of takeovers that this becomes an issue (see also **7.2.4** on management buy-outs), but it is one of the more important areas where it becomes relevant in corporate finance work.

In essence, s. 151 prevents a company from giving financial assistance for the acquisition of its own shares. The policy reason is to help maintain the company's share capital for the benefit of creditors and shareholders alike. The financial assistance can take the form of a gift, a guarantee, indemnity or anything else which materially reduces the net assets of the company (anything over about 1 per cent is likely to be material).

Exceptions exist if the assistance is only an incidental part of a larger purpose of the company and given in good faith, or the assistance is for an employees' share scheme or by way of a dividend (for example). Private companies may take advantage of the 'whitewash' procedure under s. 155 provided the directors sign a statutory declaration that the company is still solvent, the company's auditors report to the same effect and the shareholders approve by special resolution.

In the context of takeovers, many s. 151 questions arise because it is a regular part of practice in these transactions for the bidder to instruct its investment bank to acquire the target's shares in the market. The investment bank will usually only be prepared to do this if the bidder indemnifies it against any possible losses it may suffer as a consequence. If the bid is a share-for-share exchange, there is the prospect that the investment bank, having acquired target shares for the bidder, will accept the bidder's offer in respect of those shares, and so acquire the bidder's shares. Will the indemnity in these circumstances amount to financial assistance?

It seems bizarre that this was ever intended to be caught by the legislation; however, the words of the Act technically trap this sort of arrangement and it is important for the lawyers to be alive to it. In fact in this situation, the s. 153 'larger purpose' exception is almost always available as the assistance is given to facilitate the takeover (the larger purpose) and not to enable the investment bank to acquire the bidder's shares.

There may be other circumstances in which these sections become relevant in the course of a takeover and it is important always to consider their application.

8.13 Companies Act 1985: acquisition of minority interests

Where a bidder acquires 90 per cent of the target shares through *acceptances* of its offer (not including shares held when the offer was made), it can compulsorily purchase the remaining 10 per cent under CA ss. 428–430. This will enable it to remove the potentially troublesome 'rump' of shareholders left who, for whatever reason, have chosen not to accept the offer.

The bidder's right to acquire arises only if it obtains its 90 per cent within four months of making the original offer. Once the 90 per cent has been obtained, the right to acquire the rest must be exercised within two months (s. 429(3)).

The bidder must send a notice to the outstanding minority offering to acquire their shares on the same terms as the original offer (s. 429). Shareholders can object to the court and the court may prevent the acquisition or vary its terms. In practice this is extremely rare. Occasionally it is difficult (if not impossible) to offer shareholders precisely the same terms as in the original offer: for example, as regards consideration, the bidder may not be able to offer the choice of a loan note alternative any longer. In this case, a cash sum equivalent to the value of a loan note alternative (if selected by the shareholder being bought out) is acceptable.

Should a bidder choose not to acquire the outstanding minority shares, the shareholders themselves (despite having declined the offer originally) may force the bidder to acquire their interests under s. 430A. They can do this only if the bidder has acquired 90 per cent of the shares *in total*, whether through acceptances or purchases. The buy-out must be on the same terms as the original offer. Section 430A sets out the timetable to be followed in these circumstances.

8.14 Insider dealing

Insider dealing is now notoriously associated with takeover activity, but it may occur with any of the other transactions dealt with in this book.

It is now defined by Part V of the Criminal Justice Act 1993 ('CJA'). The main offence is to deal as an insider in securities on a regulated market (essentially the LSE or the AIM but extending also to other EC-regulated markets (see the Insider Dealing (Securities and Regulated Markets) Order 1994 (SI 1994/187)) while in possession of inside information, though off-market deals by or through professional intermediaries are also caught by the CJA. An insider is a director or employee of the company or someone who has a professional or business relationship with it or someone whose direct or indirect source of the information is one of these CJA s. 57)). Inside information is basically any specific information not made public relating to particular securities or companies which is likely to have a significant effect on the price of any securities if known to the market (CJA s. 56(1)). Securities are defined quite broadly and include equities, gilts, debt securities, options, futures, warrants and the like (CJA s. 54(1) and Sch. 2). It is also an offence to encourage someone else to deal in securities on the basis of inside information (CJA s. 52(2)(a)) or for an insider to disclose inside information otherwise than in the proper performance of his job (CJA s. 52(2)(b)), unless he did not expect anyone to deal as a result (CJA s. 53(3)).

There are exceptions where the insider did not expect to make a profit or avoid a loss through dealing (CJA s. 53(1)(a), (2)(a), (6)), or where he reasonably believed the information was widely known (CJA s. 53(1)(b), (2)(b)), or where an insider who has inside information would have done what he did (either dealt or encouraged) even without the information in his possession (CJA s. 53(1)(c), (2)(c)). Nor will it be an offence for the insider to disclose information in the proper performance of his job (CJA s. 53(4) and Sch. 1).

The offences under the CJA are triable either way. If a defendant is convicted in the magistrates' court, the maximum sentence per offence is a fine of £5,000 or imprisonment for up to six months, or both. For more than one offence, the aggregate maximum imprisonment is 12 months. If a defendant is convicted in the Crown Court on indictment, the maximum offence is imprisonment for up to seven years and/or an unlimited fine (CJA s. 61(1)). It would be open to the court to seek to confiscate the benefits of insider dealing under the Criminal Justice Act 1988 and to disqualify a director for an insider dealing offence.

As far as civil liability is concerned, there may well be liability for directors who use confidential information: they might be held liable to account to a company for any profits made as a result of using price-sensitive information for their own advantage.

Any information about a target acquired through discussions with the target (perhaps with a view to a recommended offer which in fact never materialises) will be inside information. This will effectively prevent the bidder or anyone associated with it from buying shares in the target before the bid is announced: it could therefore be a useful defence tactic for the target to release such information selectively to potential bidders.

Care should be taken when seeking to obtain irrevocable undertakings from target shareholders as part of a bid. If there is any inside information of which the target shareholder is unaware, he should be told, so that the insider has the benefit of the s. 53(1)(b) CJA defence (a reasonable belief that the information has already been disclosed widely enough).

It is as well for the lawyers to ensure that everyone involved in the takeover is made aware of the restrictions imposed by the CJA. The LSE monitors untoward share price movements and investigates any suspicious evidence of insider trading. Apart from the obvious risk of prosecutions and the fall-out which may result, it is highly embarrassing for all concerned to be subject to damaging investigations of possible infringements of the CJA.

8.15 Financial Services and Markets Act 2000

Three sections of FSMA should be considered within the context of takeovers: ss. 21, 118 and 397. These were introduced in **1.5.1**.

8.15.1 Section 21

Section 21 FSMA places restrictions on financial promotions. A financial promotion is a communication, in the course of business, which invites or induces a person to engage in investment activity. The basic rule is that, unless a specific exemption applies, a financial promotion must be made by an authorised person or have its content approved by a person authorised by the FSA (FSMA s. 21(1), (2)). An offer document is within the definition of a financial promotion and therefore should either be made or approved by an authorised person. As noted in **8.5.5.1**, offer documents are usually issued by a merchant bank, which will almost certainly be an authorised person. It should be noted that a defence document will not be a financial promotion as it does not seek to invite or induce a person to engage in investment activity: it specifically encourages target shareholders *not* to engage in investment activity by retaining their shares.

A bidder may wish to make calls on shareholders to persuade them to give irrevocable undertakings (see **8.5.4.2**) or to persuade them to accept the offer through a telephone campaign. Under s. 21 and the Financial Services and Markets Act 2000 (Financial Promotions) Order 2001, such calls are 'real-time' communications which constitute financial promotions (see reg. 7(1)). They should therefore be made by an authorised person. Regulation 19.5 of the City Code regulates such telephone campaigns and requires them to be conducted only by staff of the relevant financial adviser to the bidder or, if this is not possible, by others under the supervision of the financial adviser. The callers should use an approved script for each call. If the City Code guidelines are followed, then they should be permissible under s. 21.

8.15.2   Section 118

Section 118 FSMA deals with the issue of market abuse. If a person misuses information not generally available (s. 118(2)(a)), gives a misleading impression as to the supply of, demand for or value of investments (s. 118(2)(b)), or distorts the market in investments (s. 118(2)(c)), the FSA may impose a penalty (s. 123(1)). In the context of a takeover, a bidder may obtain confidential information about a target (often from the target itself in the case of a recommended bid). Given that the City Code contains provisions relating to confidentiality and equality of information, how do these provisions sit alongside the FSMA provisions on market abuse? The FSA Code of Market Conduct provides for a number of 'safe harbours': types of behaviour which will not amount to market abuse (see MAR 1.1.10G, and also MAR 1.4.20C, MAR 1.4.21C, MAR 1.4.24C, MAR 1.4.26C, MAR 1.4.28C, MAR 1.5.24C, MAR 1.5.25C, MAR 1.5.27C, MAR 1.5.28C and MAR 1.6.19C). Safe harbour status is given to those rules of the City Code which deal with (a) the timing and content of disclosures, and (b) restrictions on dealings by offerors and concert parties, provided that the relevant behaviour is not in breach in any of the City Code's General Principles. This safe harbour status is, however, limited only to the misleading impression and market distortion elements of market abuse: it does not extend to misuse of information. As regards any conduct outside safe harbours, compliance with the City Code will not of itself mean that behaviour does not amount to market abuse; equally, failure to comply with the City Code will not of itself mean that behaviour does amount to market abuse. However, these will be factors to be taken into account by the FSA in considering whether there has been market abuse. The FSA has also stated that it will attach considerable weight to the views of the Takeover Panel. A more detailed discussion of the Code of Market Conduct is contained at **1.8**.

8.15.3   Section 397

It should be remembered by all parties working on a takeover transaction that s. 397 FSMA makes it an offence to make any misleading statement (s. 397(1)) or carry on any conduct (s. 397(3)) which creates a false impression as regards any investment or induces a person to acquire or dispose of an investment.

8.16   Merger control

The term 'merger' refers to two businesses which have joined together under common ownership or control. This joining together can be by way of a hostile takeover bid, a recommended or agreed bid (for example to exploit perceived synergies between the undertakings or to eliminate a competitor from the market) or a joint venture.

Merger control provisions exist under both UK and European law, although the two regimes differ and are governed by different regulations. Two of the main overriding objectives of all merger control provisions are, firstly, to prevent the raising of barriers to entry into a particular market for potential competitors and secondly, to prevent the merger resulting in a reduction of competition in a particular market, often characterised by higher product prices, less choice for the consumer, a reduction of innovation and/or a reduction of the quality of the product.

8.16.1   United Kingdom

8.16.1.1   Reference by the Office of Fair Trading

The merger control regime of the UK is set out in Part 3 of the Enterprise Act 2002 ('the Enterprise Act') which came into force on 20 June 2003 and replaced the provisions of Part V of the Fair Trading Act 1973.

One of the main changes introduced by the Enterprise Act to the merger control regime includes the establishment of the Office of Fair Trading ('OFT') as an independent statutory body with a much expanded role in policing and enforcing mergers in the UK. There is a corresponding reduction of the powers of the Secretary of State in referring mergers to the Competition Commission—under the new regime the majority of mergers will be referred to the Competition Commission by the OFT. The Secretary of State does however retain the power to intervene before a reference has been made where he believes that a 'public interest consideration' is relevant.

Other changes from the old regime include a new turnover test, which has replaced the old current assets test, and the introduction of a new 'substantial lessening of competition' test, which replaces the wider 'public interest' test used in the old regime (although this test continues in relation to the Secretary of State's powers, as mentioned above).

The OFT has a duty, under s. 22 of the Enterprise Act, to refer a merger to the Competition Commission if the following criteria have been fulfilled:

(a) a 'relevant merger situation' has been created; and

(b) the creation of that situation either has resulted in, or may be expected to result in, a substantial lessening of competition within any market for goods or services within the UK.

The definition of a 'relevant merger situation' is set out in s. 23 of the Enterprise Act, which states that a relevant merger situation is created if:

(a) two or more enterprises have ceased to be distinct and either;

(b) the value of the turnover in the UK of the enterprise being taken over exceeds £70 million; or

(c) the merger results in at least one quarter of all of the goods or services of any description being supplied in the UK by one and the same person.

If a relevant merger situation has been created, the OFT must obtain evidence to support its reasonably held belief that there is at least a significant prospect that the merger may be expected to lessen competition substantially in any market for goods or services supplied in the UK. Guidance on the general principles that the OFT will apply in deciding whether or not a substantial lessening of competition has resulted or is likely to result from a relevant merger situation is published by the OFT, but its consideration is outside the scope of this book.

The OFT also has a duty under s. 33 of the Enterprise Act to refer 'anticipated' mergers to the Competition Commission if the arrangements made in preparation for a merger will result in the creation of a 'relevant merger situation' and the creation of that situation may be expected to result in a substantial lessening of competition within any market for goods or services within the UK. Similar rules to those applying to completed mergers apply to anticipated mergers.

For the purposes of the Enterprise Act, the definition of 'enterprise' is 'the activities, or part of the activities, of a business' (s. 129) and enterprises 'cease to be distinct' when two or more enterprises are brought under common ownership or control (s. 26).

In certain circumstances, the OFT has a discretion not to refer a merger which satisfies the s. 22 criteria (see above). These circumstances will be fulfilled if the OFT believes either that the market(s) concerned is/are not of sufficient importance to justify the making of a reference to the Competition Commission or that any relevant customer benefits relating to the merger outweigh the substantial lessening of competition concerned (s. 22(2)). Customer benefits include lower prices, higher quality, greater choice or greater innovation in relation to goods or services in the UK and such customer benefits must accrue as a result either of the creation of the relevant merger situation or of the substantial lessening of competition.

The Enterprise Act will not apply to a merger when the UK government has requested the European Commission to deal with a merger under the European merger control regime. In these circumstances, the OFT is barred from referring the merger to the Competition Commission as it will be dealt with by the European Commission (s. 22(3)). The Enterprise Act will also not apply in relation to newspaper, water or sewerage mergers, as these mergers are governed by the Communications Act 2003 (newspapers) and the Water Industry Act 1991 (water and sewerage entities). These alternative regimes are stricter than that of the Enterprise Act.

If a merger falls or is likely to fall within the merger control regime of the Enterprise Act, there is a system of voluntary pre-notification for the parties involved (ss. 96–100) which can only be used in relation to anticipated mergers which have already been made public. The Enterprise Act provides that the OFT must consider the notification within a period of 20 working days of receipt, with a maximum extension to this period of 10 working days. If no reference has been made during this period, the merger will be automatically cleared (subject to certain specified exceptions which include where false or misleading information has been given in relation to any material aspect of the merger (s. 100(l)(g)). A fee is payable to the OFT pursuant to the voluntary pre-notification system.

If the voluntary pre-notification system is not used, the parties to an anticipated or completed merger are able to make informal submissions to the OFT in order to advise the OFT of a merger. The OFT attempts to respond to informal submissions within 40 working days and a fee is payable to the OFT following the publishing of either a reference decision or any decision not to make a reference.

It is also possible to obtain either 'confidential guidance', 'informal advice' or to hold 'pre-notification discussions' with the OFT before a merger takes place to determine the likelihood of the merger being referred to the Competition Commission following its completion. The obtaining of confidential guidance or informal advice from, or the holding of pre-notification discussions with, the OFT prior to the merger is to enable the parties to evaluate the risk of a reference being made in relation to the merger and, if a reference were to be made, the risk of the merged businesses ultimately having to be separated if the Competition Commission were to decide that the merger had resulted or would result in a substantial lessening of competition.

If a merger is not notified, either formally or informally, the OFT may investigate the completed (or anticipated) merger regardless and refer it if it considers the s. 22 criteria to be fulfilled. Clearly this is a highly undesirable result for the bidder or buyer in a takeover situation, hence it is normal to advise the OFT in advance of a merger, generally by way of an informal submission. It is also typical to include as a condition to the bid or acquisition that no referral is subsequently made (see **8.16.3**).

8.16.1.2   Report by the Competition Commission

In practice, comparatively few mergers are referred to the Competition Commission. However, once a reference has been made, no person carrying on any enterprise to which the reference relates can complete any outstanding matters, make any further arrangements relating to the merger, transfer the ownership or control of any enterprises to which the reference relates or (in relation to anticipated mergers) acquire an interest in shares in a company to which the reference relates, without first obtaining the consent of the Competition Commission (ss. 77 and 78 of the Enterprise Act).

Following a reference, the Competition Commission has a period of 24 weeks within which to prepare and publish a report on (a) whether it considers that a relevant merger situation has been created and (b) if so, whether it believes that the creation of that situation has resulted in, or may be expected to result in, a substantial lessening of competition within any market(s) in the UK for goods or services (s. 35). If the Competition Commission decides that the above two criteria have been fulfilled by the merger then it must decide what, if any, action should be taken in relation to the merger (or anticipated merger).

Following the publication of its report, the Competition Commission has the power to accept undertakings or to impose orders on the enterprises concerned for the purpose of remedying, mitigating or preventing the substantial lessening of competition concerned and any adverse effects which have resulted in, or may be expected to result from, the merger (ss. 41, 82 and 84). See **8.16.1.3** for examples of the content of orders and undertakings.

8.16.1.3   Enforcement powers of the OFT and Competition Commission

The enforcement powers of the OFT and the Competition Commission are contained within Chapter 4 of Part 3 of the Enterprise Act.

Whilst the OFT is considering whether to make a reference to the Competition Commission, it has the power to request that the enterprises concerned provide it with undertakings. The OFT can also make orders in relation to the enterprises concerned for the purpose of preventing any pre-emptive action being taken by them which could either prejudice a reference or impede the taking of any enforcement action which may be required following the Competition Commission's decision on a reference.

The OFT may decide to accept undertakings from the enterprises concerned in lieu of making a reference, provided that the undertakings are for the purpose of remedying, mitigating or preventing the substantial lessening of competition which would otherwise result from the merger (s. 73). However, if the OFT has accepted undertakings in lieu of making a reference, but it later transpires that material facts about the transaction were not disclosed to the OFT, the OFT will then be able to make a reference in respect of that merger situation. The OFT can also make orders in relation to undertakings which are not being fulfilled or which were based on false or misleading information. Any orders which are made terminate the undertaking they replace and the prohibition on the OFT making a reference to the Competition Commission is also terminated by the making of the order.

Undertakings and orders may prohibit a completed or proposed merger, require the parties to dispose of shareholdings or interests in shares, provide for the break-up of a company or group by the sale of assets or a subsidiary or control the conduct of the merged company (for example by regulating the company's prices or charges) (Sch. 8 to the Enterprise Act).

The Competition Commission also has the power to accept undertakings and to make orders and, as with the OFT, its orders and/or undertakings must be made for the purpose of remedying, mitigating or preventing the substantial lessening of competition concerned and any adverse effects which have resulted in, or may be expected to result from, the merger.

Non-compliance with undertakings or orders may result in either the OFT, Competition Commission or Secretary of State (as appropriate) seeking an injunction against the enterprises concerned and may also result in civil proceedings being brought against the enterprises by any person who may be affected by a contravention of the undertaking (s. 94).

8.16.1.4 Chapters I and II of the Competition Act

Mergers are specifically excluded from the provisions of the Competition Act 1998 ('the Competition Act') in its Sch. 1, which means that agreements or conduct giving rise to a merger situation will not be regulated by both the Enterprise Act and the Competition Act, although in certain limited circumstances this exclusion can be withdrawn and the Chapter II prohibition of the Competition Act can be applied to specified agreements.

The Chapter I prohibition of the Competition Act applies to agreements which prevent, restrict or distort competition and which may affect trade within the UK. The Chapter II prohibition applies to conduct which amounts to abusive behavior by a dominant undertaking ('undertaking' includes any business entity). Both prohibitions are potentially applicable to UK mergers, but the exclusion in the Competition Act 1998 provides that the Enterprise Act will, in the majority of cases, be the regime under which they will be regulated.

8.16.2 European Union

8.16.2.1 Merger Control Regulation

The Merger Control Regulation (Council Regulation (EC) No. 139/2004) ('the Merger Control Regulation') came into force on 1 May 2004 and replaced the previous Merger Control Regulation 4064/89 together with its amending regulation 1310/97 in relation to concentrations following that date. However the old regulations will continue to apply in relation to concentrations to which they applied prior to 1 May 2004.

The Merger Control Regulation applies to all 'concentrations' with a 'Community dimension'. A 'concentration' is defined as a merger of two or more previously independent undertakings, or the acquisition by one or more persons (who already control at least one undertaking) of the whole, or parts, of one or more other undertakings (Art. 3). Takeover offers leading to a merger will therefore almost always give rise to a concentration. A joint venture may also be a concentration if it is performing on a lasting basis the functions of an autonomous economic entity (Art. 3(4)).

A concentration is defined as having a 'Community dimension' where:

(a) the combined aggregate worldwide turnover of all the undertakings concerned is more than € 5,000 million; and

(b) the aggregate Community-wide turnover of each of at least two of the undertakings concerned is more than € 250 million,

unless each of the undertakings concerned achieves more than two-thirds of its aggregate Community-wide turnover within one and the same Member State (Art. 1(2)).

Even if a concentration does not fit within the above criteria, if it may still be deemed to have a 'Community dimension' if it fulfils all of the following alternative criteria:

(a) the combined aggregate worldwide turnover of all the undertakings concerned is more than € 2,500 million;

(b) in each of at least three Member States, the combined aggregate turnover of all the undertakings concerned is more than € 100 million;

(c) in each of at least three Member States included for the purpose of (b) above, the aggregate turnover of each of at least two of the undertakings concerned is more than € 25 million; and

(d) the aggregate Community-wide turnover of each of at least two of the undertakings concerned is more than € 100 million,

unless each of the undertakings concerned achieves more than two-thirds of its aggregate Community-wide turnover within one and the same Member State (Art. 1(3)).

The residence or nationality of the parties is not relevant to the determination of a Community dimension, so in practice the Merger Control Regulation has previously caught mergers between Japanese and US corporations which had large EU interests. However, if each member of the merged entity (bidder and target in a takeover) has two-thirds of its turnover in the same Member State, the concentration will not have a Community dimension. It will instead be dealt with by the local regulator (the OFT in the UK).

A concentration with a Community dimension must be notified to the European Commission during the period prior to its implementation and following either the finalisation of the agreement, the announcement of the public bid or the acquisition of a controlling interest (see Art. 4(1) of the Merger Control Regulation). Within 25 working days of receiving the notification retired to above, the European Commission will decide whether to investigate the merger and, if an investigation is commenced, it will take up to 90 working days (with extensions possible in certain circumstances) to make a decision as to whether the concentration is compatible or incompatible with the common market. A concentration will be deemed to be incompatible with the common market if it creates or strengthens a dominant position and as a result competition is restricted.

Alternatively, in the event that a Member State informs the European Commission that either (a) the merger threatens to significantly affect competition in a distinct market within that Member State or (b) that the merger affects competition in a distinct market within that Member State and that market does not constitute a substantial part of the common market, the European Commission may decide to refer the merger back to that Member State to be dealt with under the national law of that Member State (Art. 9 Merger Control Regulation). In practice, consultation with the European Commission takes place before the bid to determine which of the European Commission or the OFT is likely to be dealing with the merger.

8.16.2.2 Articles 81 and 82 of the Treaty of Rome

Article 81 of the Treaty of Rome prohibits agreements made between undertakings which have an anti-competitive effect or intention and Art. 82 prohibits the abuse of a dominant position in a particular market. Both Articles are potentially applicable to arrangements leading up to a merger situation and/or to a merger itself.

Article 81 regulates agreements between undertakings (this includes all business entities) '. . . which may affect trade between Member States and which have as their object or effect the prevention, restriction or distortion of competition within the common market...'. Technically, arrangements in connection with a takeover offer could fall within Art. 81—for example, if the takeover would merge two competitors based in different Member States of the EU, leaving very few other competitors in the relevant market.

Article 82 prohibits 'Any abuse by one or more undertakings of a dominant position within the common market or a substantial part of it...in so far as it shall affect trade between Member States...'. A merger might result in the creation of a dominant position in the common market and if that dominant position is abused, then Art. 82 would appear to be relevant.

However, Art. 21 of the Merger Control Regulation provides that Council Regulation (EC) No. 1/2003 (on the implementation and enforcement of Arts 81 and 82) shall not apply to concentrations with a Community dimension. According to a Notice published by the European Commission simultaneously with the Merger Control Regulation, this means that, to the extent that restrictions of competition which arise from a merger are directly related and necessary to the implementation of the merger, Arts 81 and 82 will not be enforced against the entities concerned. In relation to any restrictions *not* regarded as directly related to the implementation of the merger therefore, Arts 81 and 82 remain potentially applicable.

Articles 81 and 82 should also be considered in connection with acquisitions and other transactions covered in this book, particularly joint ventures (see Chapter 6). Whenever Arts 81 and 82 are considered in relation to a transaction you should be aware that the provisions of Chapters I and II of the Competition Act could also be relevant.

8.16.3 Conditions

Due to the delays which would be involved if a merger were to be either referred to the Competition Commission in the UK or investigated by the European Commission in the EU, conditions to takeover offers always include a condition that the offer is subject to the merger not being either referred to the Competition Commission or investigated by the European Commission. Should any reference or investigation subsequently take place, the takeover offer would then lapse.

In the unlikely event that the OFT takes an excessive period of time in making its decision whether or not to refer a merger to the Competition Commission, the Takeover Panel may agree to freeze the bid timetable to await its decision. The OFT does however have a duty to decide whether to make a reference to the Competition Commission '...as soon as reasonably practicable' (s. 103(1) Enterprise Act).

8.16.4 Submissions to the OFT or European Commission

The preparation of any submissions (formal or informal) to either the OFT or to the European Commission (as appropriate) in relation to a merger can take on a key role in the success or failure of a takeover. If the regulator can be persuaded by the bidder that the takeover would not result in any restriction of competition in the relevant market or, alternatively, if the target company is successful in highlighting possible competition concerns, the outcome of the takeover could be affected.

Care taken in the preparation of a submission to the relevant regulator is therefore of prime importance to the outcome of the takeover. Submissions should be clear and complete, setting out the terms and proposed timing of the merger and outlining any competition issues that can be foreseen. The submission should also include detailed information to enable the regulator to analyse the relevant market, which will normally require the services of an economist in addition to legal specialists on merger control issues.

8.17 Common law

There are a number of areas of common law which will be relevant.

8.17.1 Contract

Clearly the law of contract affects the takeover offer. The principal concern, apart from ensuring that the offer document deals with everything necessary to bring a contract into effect (such as consideration and method of acceptance), is to spell out the conditions to the offer, and avoid any possible misrepresentations in the offer document. These may give rise to a right of action under the Misrepresentation Act 1967 (see **4.2.5.7**). Any failure by the bidder to perform its promises under the offer may also lead to actions for breach of contract.

8.17.2 Company law

The duties of the directors at common law, both to company and shareholders, are of course always present in addition to the regulatory requirements imposed by the City Code and the LSE.

8.17.3 Tort of negligence

Any misstatements in the course of an offer may be actionable if the maker of the statement owes a duty of care to the person relying on it. This has been covered in detail in the context of statements made in the course of an equity offering (see **4.2.5.7**). It is something which directors, the companies concerned and advisers need to be particularly cautious of.

8.17.4 Tort of defamation

This is often a particular concern in takeovers. A takeover will depend for its success on the quality of the case made by the bidder and target respectively in convincing target share-holders either to accept or decline the offer. The bidder will rely on commercial arguments about the strengths it can bring to the target's operation. The target will try to show that it is making a good fist of the task entrusted to it by investors. The arguments may go further than this and seek to stress the negative about the other side. A bidder may wish to show that the target has performed badly because of failures of management. The target may attempt to warn shareholders of the weaknesses of the bidder in some of its ventures, and perhaps the lack of relevant ability to manage the target.

The risk is that in putting the negative forward, both sides may wrongfully blacken the reputation of each other and so be liable in defamation. Any imputation about the man-agement or conduct of the affairs of either target or bidder runs this risk. Defamation proceedings are always best avoided as they are costly, cause significant embarrassment and are notoriously unpredictable in outcome.

If defamation becomes an issue, bear in mind the likely available defences:

(a) Justification, namely, that the defamatory statement is true.

(b) Fair comment, namely, that it is an honest expression of opinion on a matter of public interest.

(c) Qualified privilege, namely, that there was a duty or interest in publishing the state-ment and an interest in the recipient receiving it. This will generally not apply to statements released to the press nor to the offer document, but it will probably extend to the target's own document to its shareholders, as there is a pre-existing relationship based on a common interest (namely, the affairs of the company).

(d) Innocent dissemination, namely, where the defendant is a mere conduit (such as a distributor or seller) and did not know and had no reason to believe that it was contributing to any defamation.

Privilege will be overridden if the publisher acted with malice, or the statement is republished and republication was either intended or the natural and probable result of the original publication. This suggests that great care should be exercised when releasing any information to journalists.

Injunctive relief for defamatory statements is available but only where the case is clear-cut. If the document appears privileged or there is a defence of justification, an injunction is improbable. Summary relief is available by virtue of the Defamation Act 1996.

It is wise, if the statements being made appear defamatory, to research them thoroughly so that your defences are already prepared, but, better still, find some way of modifying them to avoid the need for legal action.

8.18 Takeover checklist

This is a checklist in the form of a timetable of a hostile bid made by one LSE listed company incorporated and based in the UK for another, where the consideration is the bidder's own securities. The intention of the timetable is to alert you to the principal activities of bidder and target at the various stages of the transaction, so that you have a better understanding of what the parties are doing, and what you will therefore need to consider as their legal adviser. It is not comprehensive and should be read in conjunction with the timetable in **8.5.1** which sets out the key moments of the transaction defined in the City Code. The earlier sections of this chapter also expand on many of the activities referred to below.

	BIDDER		TARGET	
Time	Activity	Document	Activity	Document
Before announcing offer	Buying shares in target—see **8.5.3.2**		Defence planning, track share purchases, keep up investor relations, prepare defence strategy (e.g., OFT submissions, likely defence circular)	Defence Manual
	Planning structure and finance for the bid			
	Due diligence on target		If offer is imminent, watch general principle 7 and r. 21—see **8.6.7**	
On and after announcing	Announce	Release press announcement	Communicate terms of bid to target shareholders	Preliminary circular

(Continued)

Time	BIDDER		TARGET	
	Activity	Document	Activity	Document
	Prepare offer	Offer document and listing particulars	Develop defence, influence investors	
	Continue share purchases			
	Begin lobbying regulators	OFT and EC submissions	Begin lobbying regulators	OFT and EC submissions
Posting offer and after	Offer document posted (by 28 days after announcing)	Offer document	Prepare first defence document (by day 0 + 14)	Defence circular
	Continue strategy from earlier			
First closing date (0+21)	Announce offer has closed or level of acceptances and next closing date	Press announcement		
After first closing date	Continue market purchases		Prepare any new information for shareholders	Day 39 circular
	Telephone campaign		Persuade shareholders to revoke acceptances (after 0 + 42)	
	Final offer (with increase— by 0 + 46)	Final offer document		
Final closing date (by 0 + 60)	Declare offer unconditional as to acceptances or announce failure	Press announcement		
0 + 81	Last date to satisfy all conditions			
0 + 95 and beyond	Settle consideration		Recommend remaining shareholders to accept	
	Exercise compulsory acquisition rights (s. 428)	Offer notice		
	Apply for de-listing of target	De-listing application		

8.19 Schemes of arrangement in practice

8.19.1 Examples

Here are some examples of where schemes have been used in practice in high profile mergers:

(a) *Granada and Carlton*

Early in 2004 Granada plc and Carlton Communications Plc merged to create ITV plc. The merger was based on two inter-conditional schemes of arrangement. Using reduction schemes, the ordinary share capitals of each of Granada and Carlton were cancelled and an equivalent number of new shares were issued by both companies to the newly formed ITV plc. ITV plc then issued new ordinary shares to the former shareholders of Granada and new ordinary and convertible shares to the former shareholders of Carlton.

(b) *Glaxo Wellcome and SmithKline Beecham*

At the end of 2000 these two companies joined forces to create GlaxoSmithKline. Again as a merger of equals, schemes of arrangements involving reductions of capital were used to merge the two companies under a new holding company.

8.19.2 Procedures and requirements

The detailed statutory requirements for a scheme are set out in CA ss.425 and 426.

(a) *Members' meeting*

Where a scheme of arrangement is proposed, the company must apply to the court for an order convening a meeting of the relevant class(es) of members (CA s. 425(1)). At the court convened meeting the majority in number (i.e. over 50 per cent) representing three-fourths in value (i.e. over 75 per cent) of the members present and voting (whether in person or by proxy) must approve the scheme (s. 425(2)). The statutory reference to 'majority in number' and 'three-fourths in value') makes this a two-legged test. Also due to the requirement to consider the value of the shareholders' holdings, the resolution is determined by way of poll. Any shares in the target held by the bidder are excluded from the vote.

(b) *Court approval*

Following the members' approval of the scheme. it needs to be sanctioned by the court at which point it is binding on the members (s. 425(2)). The court order must be filed with the Registrar of Companies and a copy of it annexed to every copy of the company's memorandum and articles of association (s. 425(3)). In determining whether to sanction the scheme the court has a number of duties (*Re Anglo Continental Supply Co Ltd* [1922] 2 Ch 723). It needs to satisfy itself that the statutory requirements have been complied with (for example, correct notice of meeting, resolution passed by requisite number and value). that each class was fairly represented by those attending the meeting, that the statutory majority acted bona fide and have not coerced the minority and that the arrangement is such that 'a man of business would reasonably approve' it. In determining reasonableness, the court will not judge the commercial merits of the proposals but will consider whether the scheme is fair and equitable. In effect, it looks at whether a shareholder could reasonably have approved the scheme, not whether the scheme is reasonable.

(c) *Explanatory statement*

The notice summoning the court convened meeting to approve the scheme must be accompanied by a statement explaining the effect of the scheme and setting out the material interests of the directors of the target and the effect of the scheme on those interests in so far as that differs from the effect of the scheme on similar interests of other shareholders (s. 426(2)). At the hearing to sanction the scheme the court will consider whether the explanatory statement is fair and whether, so far as possible, it gives all information reasonably necessary to enable the recipient to determine how to vote. In practice this statement will form part of the scheme document.

Further detailed requirements (set out in CA s. 427A and Sch. 15B) may apply where the target is a PLC but discussion of these is beyond the scope of this book.

It may appear that one of the advantages of using a scheme rather than a general offer is that it takes the bidder outside the City Code's jurisdiction. However, a scheme is a transaction which falls within the ambit of its review. Therefore, for example, the scheme document must contain all the information specified in rr. 24 and 25 of the City Code. Under r. 30.1 of the City Code the scheme document should be despatched within 28 days of the announcement of the bid but, in practice, the Panel will allow an extension to take account of the court's involvement. Therefore the timetable laid down by the City Code is subject to the timetable which the court determines for the scheme to be approved. That said, the Panel's approval of the overall timetable is required.

An important requirement which it is easy to overlook and can cause difficulties in practice is the determination of the relevant classes of members needed to approve the scheme. If the target fails to obtain the correct class approval of the scheme, then it will not be sanctioned by the court. The reference to 'classes' here does not necessarily equate to classes of shareholders in the usual sense (i.e. different classes of shareholders having different rights attaching to their shares). In the context of a scheme, there may be, say, two groups of shareholders within one class of ordinary shareholders whose rights are dissimilar enough for it to be necessary for them to have separate court approved meetings to consider the scheme. A class here is those persons whose rights are not so dissimilar as to make it impossible for them to consult together with a view to their common interest (*Sovereign Life Assurance Company* v. *Dodd* [1892] 2 QB 573). This issue has been complicated further by the decision in *Re Hawk Insurance Company Limited* [2001] BCLC 480. Discussion of that case is beyond the scope of this book but suffice to say that following the *Hawk* decision the Chancery Division of the High Court issued a practice statement which allows concerns regarding the composition of relevant classes to be determined early in the proceedings to avoid wasted time and costs. Another relevant issue here is the giving of irrevocable undertakings to vote in favour of the takeover by target shareholders which is common in the takeover context. It is not necessarily the case that the giving of such an undertaking prohibits the shareholder from voting in its class meeting to approve the scheme. However, it has been suggested that where the shareholder has special interests as the result of giving the undertaking then the court may not be bound by the vote at the court convened meeting and may use its discretion not to sanction the scheme.

8.19.3   Advantages of a scheme over an offer

The main advantages of a scheme are as follows.

(a) *Certainty of 100 per cent acceptance*

As stated above, under CA s. 425(2) a majority in number representing three fourths in value of those shareholders present and voting at the court convened meeting must approve the scheme, and once it is sanctioned by the court it becomes effective and binding on all members, whether they voted in favour or not. Under an offer the bidder is unlikely to get 100 per cent acceptance and must reach 90 per cent in order to put the compulsory acquisition procedures provided by the Companies Act 1985 in motion in order to sweep up the outstanding minority.

(b) *Shareholder profile*

With a general offer only 50 per cent of the voting rights is required for the bidder to obtain control. It needs to reach the 90 per cent level to be sure of getting 100 per cent ownership. As explained in (a), for a scheme to be approved the level of shareholder support can be lower. Therefore in a takeover situation, the parties must consider the likely course of action any large shareholder may take (if it may not accept the offer, reaching the nine-tenths threshold could be difficult). Equally, with a scheme only those shareholders who vote are taken into account, so shareholder apathy can be helpful for the bidder; if there are large numbers of small holdings unlikely to take action, then a scheme may be the preferred option. Conversely, if an organised minority is opposed to the bid, they have more opportunity to have their say with a scheme (they can put their case to the judge in court).

(c) *Period to acquire 100 per cent of the target*

This is shorter under a scheme because of the timetable involved in an offer's compulsory acquisition procedures (which can take up to five months).

(d) *No stamp duty*

As explained above, with a reduction scheme no stamp duty is payable as there are no transfers of shares to the bidder.

8.19.4   Disadvantages of a scheme over an offer

Certain issues may mean that a scheme is not a viable option.

(a) *Reliance on target directors*

The bidder has to rely on the target board as it has control over the timing and implementation of the scheme and could, for example, withdraw the scheme at any time until the court has made its order sanctioning it. This could happen if, say, the target receives a higher competing bid.

(b) *Timetable*

The court timetable is inflexible and so it may be quicker for the bidder to obtain *effective* control (i.e. 50 per cent acceptances) under an offer, although, as stated above, the period for obtaining 100 per cent control under a scheme can be quicker. Also, a scheme allows a competing bidder more time to intervene. It is possible to revise a scheme in light of a competing bid but it is not as easy as posting a revised offer document under an offer.

(c) *Market purchases*

Under a general offer, the bidder can purchase target shares on the market in order to achieve the relevant 50 per cent (effective control) and, once the offer document has been posted, 90 per cent (compulsory acquisition) thresholds. A scheme will not be affected by market purchases as such thresholds are not relevant; the scheme only becomes effective once it has been sanctioned by the court. Also, even if the bidder holds target shares, it will not form part of the class of shareholders approving the scheme.

(d) *Costs*

These can be greater with a scheme due to the involvement of the court and the use of counsel.

9

Corporate creativity

The art of remaining competitive in the commercial world is principally about the readiness to change, to move with new markets, essentially to be a dynamic rather than a static entity. Corporate finance advisers are faced with clients needing new products for new times, and new corporate structures for new situations. This chapter is devoted to reflecting on the principal ways in which these demands manifest themselves in the work coming to lawyers.

Looking first at corporate reconstruction, a company develops over time a structural framework for its operations in the form of holding companies, subsidiaries, groups of associated companies and businesses, and **9.1** looks at some of the considerations relevant when establishing that structure.

But the structure can become rigid and unresponsive to change and market forces. Pressures sometimes emerge for a reorganisation of the status quo, for a variety of reasons (the most important of which are considered later in **9.4**).

9.1 Forming a corporate structure

Most large corporate enterprises are structured today around groups of companies. These groups invariably consist of a parent or holding company at the top of a pyramid, and underneath it a myriad of subsidiary companies which it directly or indirectly (through other subsidiaries) controls. Why do these groups exist? Why not instead construct one single entity to encompass all the different subsidiaries?

9.1.1 Commercial factors

Groups are the usual product of expansion. As businesses develop, they spawn new businesses which operate *de facto* within the existing corporate stucture as separate units until eventually a business decision is taken that they should be represented as individual and legally independent entities. They will have their own management, employees and possibly premises—but of course they will remain linked to the original enterprise. Hence the subsidiary company is born.

Sometimes the same conclusion results from acquisitions or mergers. There may be benefits (particularly the preservation of goodwill) in keeping the name and notional existence of an acquired entity alive in the form of a wholly owned subsidiary rather than subsuming it within a lesser known acquirer.

An amorphous business unit can present problems of management and supervision. A group structure permits flexibility and the use of chains of command to improve efficiency in operational control and reporting.

9.1.2 Legal factors

A separate subsidiary company is a different legal entity from the parent company which owns it. Following *Salomon* v. *A. Salomon & Co. Ltd* [1897] AC 22, this means that the holding company owners have no legal responsibility for the liabilities accruing in the subsidiary. There are exceptions to this but that is the basic principle. As such, it provides a powerful rationale for enterprises to develop new (and possibly risky) business ideas through the medium of legally unrelated subsidiaries, where liabilities can be left to lie where they fall if the ideas fail.

9.1.3 Tax factors

The tax legislation has developed to offer certain benefits to groups of companies so they can be treated as one entity. But what constitutes a group for tax purposes varies for the different taxes—so you should take care to check whether your group will qualify for the particular benefit sought. These are the most prominent examples of available benefits:

(a) A disposal of an asset between members of the same group does not give rise to a charge for capital gains tax purposes—though if the acquiring company were subsequently to leave the group, there might be a CGT charge on the value of the asset. The basic rule, though, allows assets to be moved around within a tax group with relative freedom. Stamp duty relief is also available for transfers of assets within groups.

(b) Trading losses, certain expenses and capital allowances can be surrendered between members of a group. Companies are often set up in group structures as 'sink companies' into which losses are poured, to be set off against taxable profits or acquired gains so as to minimise the resulting group tax bill.

(c) VAT is not charged on the supplies of goods or services between members of the same group.

These tax factors do not necessarily improve the treatment of a group over that of a single entity, but they at least help to equalise the treatment of groups so that there is no appreciable tax cost in setting up or running a group.

Assuming, then, the advantages of using a group structure, what factors are relevant when setting a group up?

9.2 What is a subsidiary?

Since the Companies Act 1989 amended the Companies Act 1985, there has been a distinction between a subsidiary and a subsidiary undertaking.

A subsidiary is defined in s. 736 Companies Act 1985. This definition holds good for the use of the term 'subsidiary' throughout the Companies Act 1985 (for example, s. 151 of the Act, which makes it unlawful for a company *or its subsidiary* to provide financial assistance for the acquisition of the company's shares).

A subsidiary undertaking is defined in s. 258 Companies Act 1985, and although these two definitions are similar, they differ in some respects.

The subsidiary undertaking is the accounting version of the subsidiary. Where a company has subsidiary undertakings, s. 227 Companies Act 1985 requires the preparation of group accounts, that is, consolidated accounts which deal with the state of affairs, and the profit and loss, of the parent and its *subsidiary undertakings* through a consolidated balance sheet and profit and loss account.

Looking first at s. 736, four conditions will make company X a subsidiary of company Z:

(a) If Z holds a majority of the voting rights in X (s. 736(1)(a)).

(b) If Z is a member of X and controls a majority of the voting rights on its board (s. 736(1)(b)).

(c) If Z is a member of X and controls a majority of its voting rights through a shareholders' agreement (s. 736(1)(c)).

(d) If X is a subsidiary of another company (W) and W is itself a subsidiary of Z (s. 736(1)).

As for s. 258, any of five conditions will make entity X a subsidiary undertaking of parent undertaking Z (see s. 258 (2)). The first three of these conditions are identical to (a), (b) and (c) above. The other two are:

(a) If Z is entitled to exercise a dominant influence over X either through a contract or by X's constitution (see s. 258 (2)(c)). A dominant influence is exercised where X must act in accordance with Z's instructions (see Sch. 10A, para. 4 (1)).

(b) If Z has a participating interest in X and either actually exercises a dominant influence over it (see s. 258(4)(a)) or Z and X are managed on a unified basis (see s. 258(4)(b)). Dominant influence is not the same as for (a): there is in fact no clear definition for it in this context (see Sch. 10A, para. 4 (3)). A participating interest is presumed if Z holds 20 per cent or more of the shares in X (see s. 260(2))—otherwise it depends on whether Z is holding its shares in X on a long-term basis with the purpose of exercising control or influence through its interest (see s. 260(1)).

Two things in conclusion. The first is that the definition of subsidiary undertaking does not just apply to companies. A parent company may have an entity (such as an interest in a joint venture) which is not incorporated which falls within the term 'subsidiary undertaking' (see s. 259(1)). The second is the general point that essentially you should be guided not by majority ownership as your test of whether something is a subsidiary or subsidiary undertaking, but by majority control or influence (see Sch. 10A, para. 2(1) and 2(2)).

9.3   Why does it matter whether a company is a subsidiary or subsidiary undertaking?

We have already seen why it matters whether or not something is a subsidiary—it then gets caught within the net of various Companies Act 1985 provisions. It may, for instance, be a helpful escape from a s. 151 problem if the intended financial assistance is given not by the company or a subsidiary but by a vehicle which does not fall within the definition of subsidiary. This will involve some creative engineering to manufacture a structure falling outside the s. 736 definition.

The definition of subsidiary undertaking is vital in establishing whether an entity needs to be included in the group's consolidated accounts. Consolidated accounts present financial information about the group's various members as if they were a single unit rather than as separate entities. The detailed requirements are in Sch. 4A to the Companies Act 1985.

Before the Companies Act 1989, it was a good deal easier to create vehicles over which a parent company had effective control but which did not technically qualify as a subsidiary because the holding company's ownership rights were limited. The benefits of this to the parent were that these vehicles could be used to borrow money for the group when the group was already close to the borrowing limits in its articles of association. The vehicle, not a subsidiary, and therefore not a member of the group, would not be caught by the limits. This would also not aggravate the group's gearing ratio (its proportion of debt to equity).

Alternatively, a loss-making venture could be passed into such a vehicle so that its losses could not be seen to dent the group's consolidated profit figure.

Essentially, then, it was this process of so-called 'off balance sheet financing' (or 'window dressing', 'massaging the figures' or 'creative accounting', depending on how you looked at it) which the Companies Act 1989 was attempting to control with the introduction of the concept of the subsidiary undertaking.

There is still much creative energy exercised in finding a loophole in the legislation to achieve precisely the same objectives as before 1989, but of course these days it is somewhat harder. There are, though, a number of exemptions under which it is perfectly legitimate to exclude a subsidiary undertaking from consolidation in group accounts (see s. 229 Companies Act 1985).

A company's structure may of course start to present significant difficulties of cost and control—difficulties which the creation of further subsidiaries may not resolve. At this point a reorganisation, if you like, a root-and-branch reform, of the corporate tree may be needed.

9.4 Why restructure?

There are a host of reasons for reorganising a company's structure. Very often they are quite individual to the specific needs of the relevant company. There are, though, some general themes that we can point to.

9.4.1 Value for shareholders

This is the prime mover behind any demand for change in the corporate structure, namely, that shareholders are not getting value for money from their shares, given the way the company is currently structured.

9.4.2 Takeover defence

We saw in **Chapter 8** some of the characteristic defence strategies which companies vulnerable to a takeover bid adopt. A change in structure by a company is another such method, particularly if it can anticipate the arguments of a would-be bidder.

9.4.3 Rationalisation

A company may need to slim down its operations because of toughening competition, expensive overheads, difficult national economic conditions and so on. This is likely to lead to a disposal programme (see **Chapter 5**), which will generate much needed cash-flow, and accompanying this there will often need to be a reorganisation of the company's remaining operations to ensure they can be run more efficiently.

9.4.4 Survival

If the company mentioned in **9.4.3** is in particularly acute trouble, a reconstruction may effectively be forced on it as the only way of surviving in some shape or form—in other words, the only viable alternative to extinction as a going concern is to indulge in a wholesale reorganisation in the hope that something can be salvaged.

9.4.5 Break-up

To some extent this is related to value for shareholders (**9.4.1**). The 1980s saw companies expanding through acquisition, often accumulating disparate businesses under one roof. The 1990s have seen some of these companies responding to leaner times by returning to their 'core' businesses, and so selling peripheral activities. Often this is also because the stock market tends to place a lower value on a group of companies which bear little relation to each other than on those companies as separate entities. An alternative to a disposal programme in these circumstances is a reorganisation in the form of a break-up of the group into individual enterprises. The 'core' businesses can be prised away from the rest so the company is free to concentrate on these, and the reorganisation carries the added benefit of improving the value of shareholders' investments.

9.4.6 Financial engineering

Occasionally companies are in the position that they have accumulated significant reserves of capital which they cannot employ in financing continued growth or expansion through acquisitions. They may consider returning that capital to shareholders through various mechanisms, including a reduction of capital (see **9.7**) or a purchase by the company of its own shares (see **9.8**).

A company may be motivated to begin a process of reconstruction by a number of these factors at the same time. An example in point is the demerger by BAT of two of the businesses under its parental control, Wiggins Teape and Argos. At the time (this was a process which began in 1989), BAT was a large conglomerate with interests in industries as diverse as tobacco, life assurance, insurance, paper and packaging and retailing. BAT was the target of a takeover bid from Hoylake, which eventually failed. One of the key factors behind the bid was the argument that BAT would be worth more to its shareholders in separate entities than as a single unit (see **9.4.5**). In response to that bid (see **9.4.2**), and the investor and market pressure which Hoylake's arguments over shareholder value generated, BAT initiated its demerger programme. In a sense, this was a necessary step to prevent the prospect of another bidder emerging, as well as to satisfy the shareholders' best interests.

Given these pressures exerting themselves on a company, what options exist to carry out a reconstruction? Some of the transactions we have already looked at may achieve some of the things mentioned above—for example, it may be better for a company's break-up plans for it to sell some of its businesses or subsidiaries (see **Chapter 5**). Alternatively, the creative mind may prefer to toy with some of the ideas discussed below.

9.5 Demerger

As its name suggests, a demerger is a separation of two or more businesses currently operating under the same corporate roof: it is the opposite of a merger. The important point to note is that it is not simply a case of moving assets or businesses from one part of a company structure to another: it involves actual separation of the ownership of two or more parts of what is currently the same business empire.

The factors discussed in **9.4.1** to **9.4.5** tend to account for the majority of demergers. The commercial demands need to be strong to merit serious consideration being given to a demerger. The reason is cost. A demerger will inevitably eat quite heavily into the available time of hard-pressed managers, and most demergers will carry some sort of tax penalty: they are therefore not the sort of transaction to be undertaken lightly.

Demergers come in a variety of classic forms, which we will look at individually. Before we embark on that, though, we need to consider one common element of all these transactions, which is the preliminary preparation.

9.5.1 Preparing for a demerger

A demerger will involve separating a unified group of businesses or companies. This will require some shifting around of assets and businesses between a company's empire to ensure that, prior to the demerger scheme being announced, whatever is to be demerged has already been carved out of the existing corporate structure. The typical problem is that the business to be demerged is currently carried on, to a greater or lesser extent, by a number of subsidiaries, so that it needs to be brought together in one subsidiary and other aspects of that subsidiary's business taken elsewhere in the group.

In the ensuing examples, the subsidiary to be demerged is D, and its parent company (which wholly owns it) is P.

9.5.2 Dividend in kind (otherwise known as a dividend in specie)

This is the simplest route (**figure 9.1**). Currently, shareholders in P (S) have no direct shareholding interest in D. Under the dividend in kind method, shareholders in P receive shares in D by way of a dividend from P. The result is that shareholders in P now also have a direct shareholding stake in D, and D is no longer a wholly owned subsidiary of P at all. To achieve this:

(a) there needs to be power in P's articles to pay a dividend in kind to its shareholders, and

(b) P needs to have enough distributable reserves in its accounts to cover the value of D.

There is a major disadvantage. The dividend is a disposal by P for tax purposes and so will be subject to a capital gains tax charge. Furthermore, the dividend will be treated as taxable income in the hands of the shareholders (though they will qualify for a tax credit). The method is therefore expensive unless the gain is likely to be minimal.

9.5.3 Three-cornered demerger by way of dividend in kind

See **figure 9.2**. This is another dividend in kind route, but the differences avoid the tax disadvantages.

P sets up a new company (in this example referred to as Newco), to which it transfers the shares it holds in D. P meanwhile declares a dividend to its shareholders to be satisfied by Newco (currently its subsidiary) issuing shares in itself to P's shareholders. The result is that P's shareholders (S) now hold shares in P and Newco, and Newco is no longer a subsidiary of P.

The benefit of this is that the Inland Revenue treat this dividend in kind as an exempt distribution, provided various other conditions are satisfied, so that P is not liable to CGT on the disposal of D to Newco and the new shares received by P's shareholders in Newco are not treated as taxable income. P still has to have power in its articles to pay a dividend

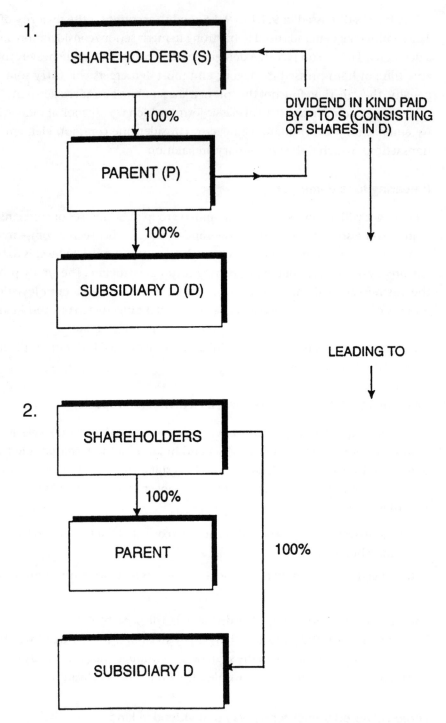

Figure 9.1   Demerger—dividend in kind.

in kind to its shareholders, and have enough distributable reserves in its accounts to cover the value of D, but at least the tax problems of the first method are overcome.

9.5.4   Scheme of reconstruction

See **figure 9.3**. This is a method available under s. 110 Insolvency Act 1986.

P is liquidated. Its assets are transferred to two or more newly formed companies (Newco 1 and Newco 2 for these purposes). Newco 1 and Newco 2 then issue shares in themselves to P's shareholders, which satisfies their rights in the liquidation. P's shareholders therefore end up with shares in both Newco 1 and Newco 2 and lose their interest in P altogether.

1.

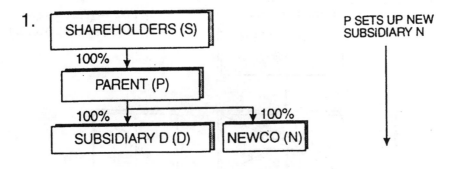

P SETS UP NEW
SUBSIDIARY N

2.

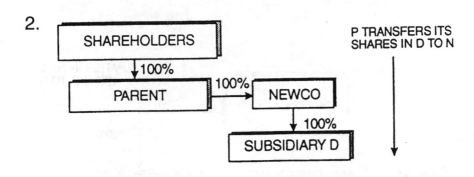

P TRANSFERS ITS
SHARES IN D TO N

3.

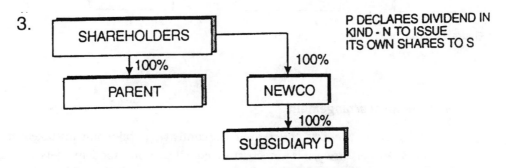

P DECLARES DIVIDEND IN
KIND - N TO ISSUE
ITS OWN SHARES TO S

Figure 9.2   Demerger—three-cornered.

This requires a special resolution of the shareholders in P to liquidate the company and authorise the transfer of P's business and assets to Newco 1 and Newco 2. (see s. 110 (3) Insolvency Act 1986).

The principal benefit under the scheme is that, because it is not being effected by way of dividend, it is not necessary to have sufficient distributable profits available in P's old accounts to cover the stated value of the two new companies.

The main difficulty with this route is that dissenting shareholders can insist on a cash payment under s. 111 Insolvency Act 1986 in lieu of receiving shares in Newco 1 and Newco 2. In addition, the directors have to make a statutory declaration of solvency (see s. 8.9 (1) Insolvency Act 1986), which may give rise to personal liability on their behalf if it turns out to be untrue.

The tax implications are minimised as there is no capital gains tax charge on the disposal of the business and assets to the Newcos, and distribution of the Newco shares is not treated as taxable income in the hands of the shareholders.

1.

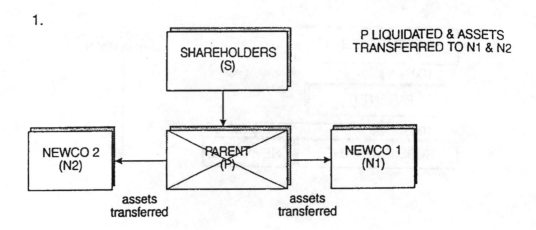

P LIQUIDATED & ASSETS
TRANSFERRED TO N1 & N2

assets
transferred   assets
                           transferred

2.

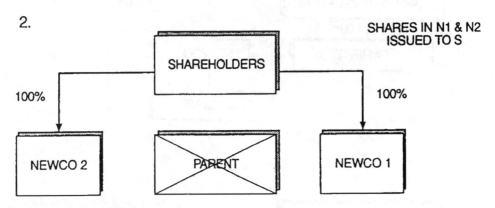

SHARES IN N1 & N2
ISSUED TO S

Figure 9.3 Demerger—scheme of reconstruction.

9.5.5 Scheme of arrangement

We have already encountered this in the context of public company takeovers (see **8.6.2.2** and **8.19**): perversely, it is a mechanism equally at home for demergers as well as mergers. It is a route governed by CA s. 425. What is needed is a scheme—and the benefit of this method is that it offers great flexibility in the nature of the precise scheme. Usually, in the context of a demerger, the scheme will be along the lines of a scheme of reconstruction, namely forming two new companies out of one old one and issuing shares in the new companies to the shareholders in exchange for the cancellation of their existing shares in the old company. (see s. 427).

The disadvantages are that shareholders need to approve the scheme by a majority in number voting at a general meeting and representing 75 per cent of the voting rights (see s. 425(2)), the scheme needs to be accepted by the court (see s. 425(1) and s. 427(2)), which can take time and is not something which can be guaranteed, and there may be tax liabilities otherwise avoided under the three-cornered demerger or the scheme of reconstruction—for instance, the issue of new shares to the shareholders may be treated as taxable income in their hands.

The scheme can be combined with some of the other methods (particularly the scheme of reconstruction under s. 110 Insolvency Act 1986) and in this way attract the tax benefits it will otherwise not qualify for.

9.5.6   Pervasive considerations

In all these transactions, consider the following issues carefully in addition to the specific requirements of the particular scheme:

(a) The transaction may not be a disposal for CGT purposes (for example, if it is an exempt distribution under a three-cornered demerger) but it may nevertheless be regarded as a transaction under the Listing Rules (see **5.6.4**). This would require (depending on the relative scale of the new company to be established) a possible circular to shareholders or their approval if the company is listed on the Stock Exchange or quoted on the AIM.

(b) If the parent company's share price is publicly quoted on either the Stock Exchange or the AIM and the dividend *in specie* route is used, the transfer of assets to the new company will cause the parent's share price to drop, as its value decreases. For the shareholders to feel as though they have received anything of value out of the demerger, the new company's shares will also need to be quoted on the same exchange so that the loss of value on their old shares is compensated by a marketable interest in the new company. Hence a demerger may also be accompanied by an application for admission to listing on the London Stock Exchange, or for a quotation on the AIM, of the new company's shares, and the consequent production of listing particulars or a prospectus (see **4.2** and **4.3**).

9.5.7   Conclusion

The dividend *in specie* routes are appropriate where the intention is to keep the existing parent company and create a new company alongside it in which the parent's shareholders also hold shares. The three-cornered demerger is the obvious procedure to select where the tax disadvantages of the simpler dividend in kind method are too great.

The scheme of reconstruction or scheme of arrangement are ideal where the intention is to create two or more new companies out of the existing parent and then remove the parent altogether. The reconstruction route is more tax-efficient and speedier but could be problematic where there are strong dissenting minorities or the company's future solvency is questionable.

It really is a question of 'horses for courses': it depends on your particular circumstances which route you would prefer to go.

9.6   Schemes of arrangement under section 425 Companies Act 1985

We have now looked at these in the context of mergers and demergers (see **8.6.2.2** and **9.5.5**). They are inherently flexible creatures available for use for any reorganisation, whether or not amounting to a demerger. An illustration would be changes to a company's capital structure including the alteration of special rights to shares, amendment of the terms of any loan or debt instruments or conversion of a class of shares from, for instance, ordinary irredeemable shares to redeemable preference shares. It is important to bear in mind, in this context, that s. 425 requires a 75 per cent majority in number of shareholders or holders of the appropriate class representing 75 per cent of the relevant voting rights to approve the scheme and make it binding on all.

A scheme can also be used for debt–equity swaps, where creditors substitute their secured debt holdings in a company for ordinary shares. This may be proposed as a way of relieving the debt burden on a company where this threatens to plunge it into insolvent liquidation: it will of course depend on agreement in this case of 75 per cent in value of the company's affected creditors and a majority in number voting at a general meeting.

9.7   Reductions of capital

Reductions of capital by companies are permitted by CA s. 135 provided there is authority in the articles, confirmation from the court in its role as protector of creditors, and approval from the shareholders by special resolution (see s. 135(1)).

Why might a company contemplate such a method of reconstruction?

9.7.1   Excess of wants

This means that the company is financially quite healthy but has more capital than it knows what to do with, for example, where the company has available cash reserves which are sitting idle (see s. 135(2)(c)). They can then be applied to repay shareholders their capital contributions and reduce the share capital account accordingly (see also **9.8** on purchases of shares).

9.7.2   Cancelling lost capital

A reduction of capital may be necessary where the company's financial position is unhealthy and its share capital no longer represents available assets but paints a misleading picture to shareholders of what is actually present to support their investment in the company. An example is a company with net assets significantly lower than the value of the share capital account (see s. 135(2)(b)). The share capital is then reduced to the level of the assets valuation. The court will usually be unwilling to confirm the reduction of capital in these circumstances unless it can be proved that the assets have declined to the stated value, so evidence of this will be needed. The court will also generally require an undertaking from the company that if any assets sold realise more than this stated value, the consequential profit shall be treated as capital for the benefit of the creditors.

9.7.3   Elimination of goodwill arising on an acquisition

We have seen in **Chapter 8** that goodwill arising on an acquisition must be written off against reserves immediately or through the profit and loss account over a number of years (see **8.6.3.6**). If the decision is taken to write off the goodwill straight away, available share capital may be reduced by the same amount as represents the goodwill, taken to a reserve and then written off against the stated goodwill. They cancel each other out and both items are eliminated from the balance sheet. It is not just the share capital account which can be used for this: we saw in **8.6.3.7** that a merger reserve created as a result of the availability of merger relief under CA s. 131 could also be used.

9.7.4   Shares at a discount

Section 100 Companies Act 1985 prevents the issue of shares at a discount to their nominal value. If the market value of a company's shares is lower than their nominal value, a further issue of shares is impossible: you cannot realistically expect investors to subscribe new shares at a price higher than the investors can currently buy them in the market. One solution is to reduce share capital by reducing the nominal value of the shares to below market value—then a new issue can be made at a discount to market value but not nominal value.

9.7.5 Redenomination of share capital into another currency

If a company is changing the currency in which its capital is denominated, the existing share capital account must be extinguished, and a reserve established with the capital. This is converted to the new currency at the appropriate exchange rate and then used to pay up shares in the new currency to the existing shareholders. The share capital account is then restored, now denominated in the new currency. Consequently no capital is actually lost.

9.7.6 What is the role of the court in these situations?

The court's principal function in a reduction is to ensure that the interests of creditors are protected. If the reduction involves repaying capital to shareholders, creditors are entitled to object (CA s. 136(3)). A court will only confirm the reduction if it is satisfied that creditors are safeguarded. This will usually require some sort of a third-party guarantee (such as a bank guarantee) to pay the debts the company does not discharge, or evidence that the company's assets are still sufficient to meet the combined effect of its liabilities, the repayment to shareholders and its outstanding share capital. The lawyer's role in this kind of transaction, apart from ensuring the requirements of s. 135 are satisfied, will therefore be to make out a satisfactory case to the court that the company's creditors will not be left high and dry by the reduction.

9.8 Redemptions and purchases of shares

You are aware of the right conferred upon companies by statute to redeem and purchase their own shares (CA ss. 159–181). We will look briefly at the rationale for such transactions as one technique for reorganising a company, and examine also some of the legal and practical issues which arise.

9.8.1 What are they?

What do redemptions and purchases actually involve? Simply put, the company is buying back from its own shareholders the shares it has issued to them. The principal difference between a redemption and a purchase is that a redemption refers to a buy-back of shares which were issued as redeemable, and a purchase refers to the acquisition of any shares.

Purchase or redemption will generally be at a price which is at or close to market value. The company will therefore generally be paying a premium to nominal value to the shareholders to buy back the shares: hence it is not simply a question of finding the amount to cover the value of the shares as stated in the share capital account.

When the shares have been bought back, the shares will be cancelled and the share capital reduced by the amount of the nominal value of the shares acquired.

9.8.2 Why do them?

Private companies are generally motivated by considerations such as the desire to buy out a dissenting or minority shareholder, or to develop a 'market' for their shares (which can otherwise not be traded publicly): if the company is prepared to buy back shares, it enables shareholders to realise their investment and encourages new shareholders to invest.

Public companies' reasons tend to flow from the performance of their share price in the market (whether traded on the LSE or the AIM):

(a) A buy-back of shares restricts the supply of shares in the market relative to demand, and so tends to increase the price of those shares remaining: this enhanced value may be particularly useful if the company uses or intends to use its own securities to finance an acquisition (it has to issue fewer of the securities to obtain the same value).

(b) Because a buy-back reduces the number of shares in existence, it will lead to an increase in earnings per share, which is much beloved by market analysts as a benchmark against which to measure the comparative performance of companies.

(c) When companies find that their shares trade at a discount to net asset value, a buy-back of shares enhances the asset value per share of the shares left.

(d) A buy-back concentrates more voting control in known hands: provided these are safe, it will therefore help as a long-term defence strategy against unwelcome takeover bids.

Hence, both private and public companies can find buy-backs helpful in certain contexts. Sometimes, companies do not have a choice about whether or not to launch a buy-back. Some redeemable shares, under their terms, must be redeemed on a certain date. Some convertible securities are converted by being redeemed and cancelled first, before the appropriate number of ordinary shares are then issued to the holders of the original securities.

9.8.3   How do you go about a buy-back?

The Companies Act 1985 (ss. 159 and 162) requires redemptions and purchases by private and public companies to be authorised in the articles (ss. 159(1) and 162(1)), the shares to be fully paid up (ss. 159(3) and 162(2)), and the cost of buying the shares to be paid out of distributable profits or the proceeds of an issue of new shares (ss. 160(1)(a) and 162(2)). Additionally, purchases under s. 162 must be approved by resolution of the shareholders. If the purchase is to be through the stock market (public companies only), a majority of shareholders in general meeting must approve (s. 166(1)); if the purchase is private (for example, a contractual deal with a particular shareholder), 75 per cent of shareholders in general meeting must approve (ss. 164(2) and 165(2)).

A private company may also purchase shares out of capital (CA s. 171). This involves an actual reduction of share capital—unlike buy-backs under ss. 159 and 162. Accordingly, the safeguards are more stringent, including the need for a special resolution (s. 173(2)), a statutory declaration of solvency from the directors (s. 173(3)) and a report from the auditors confirming the purchase (s. 173(5)). Creditors additionally can object to the court to prohibit the payment (s. 176(1)).

The one further requirement is to set up a capital redemption reserve. An amount equal to the nominal value of the shares bought back must be attributed to this account (s. 170(1)), which is a capital reserve not available for distribution (s. 170(4)) and so provides some financial security for creditors that the company is still properly capitalised. Money comes out of distributable profits and in reality is given to shareholders to buy the shares back. In accounting terms, that part of the money attributable to the excess over the shares' nominal value is a premium lost to the company, but the nominal value is treated as being transferred from share capital account (when the shares are cancelled) into the capital redemption reserve. Essentially an element of distributable profits is therefore being capitalised.

The accountants will advise the company on the accounting aspects described here: your role as the lawyer will be preparation of the appropriate resolutions, purchase contracts (if it is a private deal), and, of course, to check compliance with the articles and the Companies Act 1985.

9.8.4   UKLA requirements for listed company buy-backs

These are set out in ch. 15 of the Listing Rules. Of course they apply only to companies with securities listed on the Official List. In summary, the most important obligations are:

(a) to notify a Regulatory Information Service of any purchase of listed equity securities as soon as possible after the buy-back (see LR para. 15.9 for the precise timing required);

(b) not to make a purchase at times when a director of the company would be unable to deal under the Model Code (LR para. 15.1);

(c) where the purchase is of more than 15 per cent of the share capital of the company, to send shareholders a circular containing the information required by LR paras 15.4 to 15.5; where more than 15 per cent is bought back in a year, the purchase has to be by way of a tender or partial offer made to all shareholders so they all have the right to participate, LR para. 15.7 (see **8.6.2.4**).

9.8.5   Tax on buy-backs

If shareholders receive more than the nominal value of the shares in the buy-back, the excess over the nominal value (the premium) is treated as a distribution.

We have looked so far in this chapter at some of the more common forms of corporate reconstruction or reorganisation which may help a company respond to changing times and new demands. It is important always to bear in mind that all the transactions we look at in this book are forms of corporate reconstruction, whether it be a disposal, a merger, an acquisition, a management buy-out, a refinancing, a flotation, or taking the company private. There may be a number of different solutions to your client's longer term needs, so do not assume that only the methods of reconstruction described in this chapter are appropriate.

Some of the methods of reconstruction dealt with here may be particularly appropriate when a company is running into trouble: as we have seen, demergers and schemes of arrangement may be a way of keeping the company alive. We will look later at some of the other methods and techniques open to companies to help them survive—and what happens if they do not succeed.

First, though, one other aspect of corporate creativity: an alternative form of dividend.

9.9   Scrip dividends

You will encounter these quite commonly with publicly traded companies. The traditional dividend is of course a cash payment. A scrip dividend offers shareholders a dividend by way of new shares in the company rather than cash. They choose which to take.

The company benefits from a scrip dividend as it holds on to its cash reserves (and so reduces the level of borrowings necessary). The shareholders increase their shareholding in the company at a cheaper cost than buying shares in the market (there are no broker's fees or stamp duty to pay), and this may increase their loyalty.

The main disadvantage is that a scrip dividend carries a relatively high administration cost: all shareholders need to be told about it, but generally only a small percentage of them take up the offer.

What do you need to think about if a company is interested in introducing this option for its shareholders?

(a) If the company is listed on the Official List, the UKLA requires that the company must explain the scrip dividend scheme to shareholders in the form of a circular (usually sent with the annual report and accounts). The shareholder must positively elect for a scrip dividend. Other contents requirements for the circular are contained in LR para. 14.12.

(b) Do not forget that the company must have sufficient authorised share capital to meet the scrip dividend requirements, and directors' authority to allot the shares under CA s. 80. The articles must also permit the scheme.

So, here you have a number of ideas in various contexts which may prove useful for companies dealing with changing markets and different demands. Your clients operate in a creative environment. They will expect similar standards from their corporate finance advisers.

Company rescues and failures

This chapter will briefly consider some of the legal and practical issues that arise when a business fails, or is on the brink of failure. You have considered company insolvency as part of the compulsory LPC Business Law & Practice course, and you are advised to refer back to the detail covered at that point in your studies.

10.1 Circumstances of financial failure

A good starting point is s. 123 Insolvency Act 1986, which defines when a company is technically 'insolvent'. A company is insolvent when it is 'unable to pay its debts', which will occur if the company either:

(a) is unable to pay its debts as they fall due ('cash-flow' insolvency); or

(b) has liabilities that exceed the value of its assets ('balance sheet' insolvency).

The most frequent cause of corporate failure and insolvency is cash flow problems: the company simply does not have the cash to pay pressing debts. If a company is 'insolvent' (or is 'likely' to become insolvent), then a number of adverse legal consequences and formal insolvency procedures may follow (see below for some examples).

If a company has a cash-flow crisis, things will be coming to a head. Something must be done. The company may have reached the limit of its agreed overdraft with the bank; the bank may be refusing to extend the limit and threatening to 'call in' the overdraft; the company may have missed its interest payments and/or capital repayments to the bank; the landlord may be threatening to forfeit the lease of the factory or office premises because of unpaid rent; trade suppliers may be threatening debt recovery proceedings and/or refusing to supply further materials; there may not be enough cash to pay the employees (without whose support the company will collapse), or all of the above.

10.2 Where do you begin?

Clearly, directors of an ailing company will be trying hard to turn around the fortunes of the company. However, actual insolvency, or foreseen 'likely' insolvency, is an important legal milestone in the decline of a company, and directors must ensure positive action is taken. Such action may involve a formal or informal 'rescue' plan.

With an impending cash-flow crisis, the directors may seek your advice about what to do next (to try to save the company and to protect their own personal positions). There may be many options open to the directors. However, before any informed decisions can be made, you and the directors need hard and accurate information about just how dire the financial situation is. (What is the extent of the cash-flow crisis? What are the attitudes of key creditors?) The directors will have much of this information, but it is also extremely important to have an objective view on the financial position and, if the directors have not already instigated it, you should advise that the accountants be instructed to prepare a financial report. The information that is gathered may quickly and obviously eliminate some of what would otherwise be potential rescue plans. In reality, there may be only a few options available, and perhaps one will stand out as the best way forward.

Before going any further, do not forget your own professional responsibilities. Be clear on *your* position. Is your client the company? Is your client one of the directors seeking advice personally? Remember, the company is a separate legal entity, and you cannot act for two or more parties (e.g. the company and one or more directors) if there is a conflict or a significant risk of a conflict between the interests of the different parties. Particularly when advising at an early stage (when it is in everyone's interest to try to achieve the survival of the company as a going concern), there may not be any conflict (or significant risk of conflict) but, even then, there could be. Consider very carefully who you can and cannot act for, and make sure that everyone involved is clear on who it is you *are* acting for.

10.3 Possible rescue plans

The following is not an exhaustive list, but rather is indicative of options that may be viable in any given circumstances.

10.3.1 Negotiation with key creditors

Whether or not the company is likely to end up within a formal insolvency procedure (liquidation, administration, a company voluntary arrangement or receivership), it will be vital to recruit the support of key creditors. Without that support, an ailing company is probably doomed. It is vital to assess the attitude of those creditors who have the legal rights, and commercial muscle, to make or break the company. For instance, if the bank holds fixed and floating charges over all the assets of the company to secure an overdraft (which is repayable on demand), the bank holds many of the trump cards, and the directors will have to convince the bank to continue its support (otherwise the directors will have to find alternative sources of finance). Commercial landlords and major suppliers of stock and materials (particularly if there are no other viable alternative sources of supply) may also be vital to have 'on board'.

The critical objective for the company (via the directors) in any negotiations with creditors is to be able to offer something (whether with or without a formal insolvency procedure in place) that is a better commercial and financial alternative to the creditors than the directors simply calling it a day and calling an EGM of members to pass a resolution to go into voluntary liquidation. Of course, the directors may not wish to threaten creditors with winding up (it may not be in the company's best interests to imply that things have got that bad!), but creditors will know that that, ultimately, is the alternative. In any event, it may be the creditors who are threatening the directors with winding up the company! However, most creditors are businessmen (and women) at heart. If they can see that it is in their interest for the company to survive, they are likely to support a 'rescue plan'. It might be that the proposed plan is the best way of ensuring the creditors maximise the payments they receive from the company for current debts. It might be that the creditors see that by facilitating the survival of the company, they can continue to make money from the company (by continuing to lend money to the company; or to lease the premises to the company without having to find new tenants, or to supply further materials to the company—albeit perhaps on cash-only terms!).

The company may have a number of things to offer creditors, including (amongst others):

(a) completion of an on-going project which will result in significant cash being received by the company (e.g. a building company needing financial support to complete a new development, where failure to complete would be a breach of the building contract and would result in no (or reduced) payments being received by the company);

(b) the orderly and managed sale of viable parts of the company's assets (perhaps profitable subsidiaries of the faltering parent company);

(c) the orderly and managed sale of assets, the disposal of which will not prevent the company from being able to continue trading (e.g. the sale of freehold factory or office premises, with the 'lease back' of the premises from the new owners, resulting in an injection of the sale proceeds to the company);

(d) making arrangements for a further injection of share capital (equity) into the company (from existing shareholders and/or from new investors). Note that there will be special considerations where the company is listed on the LSE or on the AIM; or

(e) a change in the management of the company which will 'steady the ship' and restore confidence in the company (e.g. the replacement of the CEO, or the recruitment of a new managing director).

10.3.2 Informal arrangements with creditors

If the directors are able to negotiate with key creditors, and convince them to continue to support the company, it may be possible for the directors to keep the company going and to 'trade out' of the crisis. It may be that the ordinary trade suppliers and customers will not be aware of the crisis; that the goodwill of the company will not have been damaged, and that the company can recover and go from strength to strength. Informal arrangements might include one or more of the following (as well as a whole range of other possible deals that could be negotiated):

(a) the bank rescheduling the dates for capital repayments and interest payments;

(b) the bank extending the overdraft limit (perhaps in return for a (further) personal guarantee from a director, or further security on the company's assets); or

(c) landlords giving a rent 'holiday' or deferring the rent payments (again, perhaps against a personal guarantee, or a revised formula for rent increases in the future which will enable the landlord to take a share of possible future profits).

One of the main problems with informal arrangements with individual creditors is that they are with *individual* creditors. (Here, 'informal' refers to being outside the scope of formal insolvency procedures: not that they are not formally (legally) binding on the company and the creditors concerned.) Even if the directors can secure the support of some creditors, it may not be enough. Particularly with larger companies (Plcs, perhaps quoted Plcs), there may be many banks involved, each with different security and loan agreements with the company. There is no point in the directors doing a deal with nine of the company's ten banks, if the tenth will not 'play ball' and will 'pull the plug' on the company. Likewise, even relatively small, unsecured, trade creditors can thwart the rescue plan by petitioning for a compulsory winding up of the company. It is possible that even with the support of the key creditors, the only effective way of moving forward is for the directors to make the company subject to formal insolvency procedures (in order to prevent individual creditors unravelling a proposed 'rescue plan'). Indeed, even if the key creditors indicate their support for a proposed rescue plan, it is possible that they will only agree to it if the company is protected by formal insolvency procedures.

10.4   Formal insolvency procedures

These procedures were considered during the LPC Business Law & Practice course. What follows is a brief reminder and summary of the key aspects of these procedures (to highlight their differences and some of their relative strengths and weaknesses).

10.4.1   Administration

Administration was introduced by the Insolvency Act 1986 as an alternative to liquidation. The Enterprise Act 2002 introduced important changes to the rules on administrations (and administrative receivership—see below), with the expressed aim of ensuring that administration is the first and primary insolvency procedure for most companies in financial difficulties. The essential elements of administration are:

(a) It is primarily a collective procedure aimed at saving the business if possible and, if not, maximising the amount that all creditors will receive (rather than being a debt recovery procedure for a single creditor, as is the case with administrative receivership).

(b) The initiation of the procedure creates a 'moratorium' during which (most) creditors are prevented from enforcing their pre-existing individual legal rights (e.g. to recover property under retention of title clauses, to bring debt actions, or to petition the court for the compulsory liquidation of the company). The idea is that the assets of the company are preserved for the benefit of the creditors generally.

Following the changes introduced by the Enterprise Act 2002, administration can come about in one of two situations:

(a) by an application to the court (e.g. by the company, the directors or a creditor) for the making of an Administration Order (with the court appointing an Administrator); or

(b) by a Qualifying Floating Charge Holder (QFCH), a secured creditor with security, including a floating charge, over the whole or substantially the whole of the company's assets, appointing an Administrator.

The Administrator has a duty to act in the best interest of the creditors generally. He is an officer of the court and, as such, owes duties to the court. The Administrator must seek to achieve one of the following outcomes (in the following order):

(a) the rescue of the company as a going concern; or

(b) a better result for the company's creditors than would be likely on a winding up; or

(c) the disposal of assets to make a distribution to one or more secured creditors (e.g. the QFCH who appointed the Administrator) or preferential creditors.

10.4.2 Receivership (including administrative receivership)

For many years, secured creditors have been able to appoint a 'receiver and manager' in respect of assets subject to the security (under powers in the security documents and under statute). For example, if a bank has a fixed charge over the freehold of an office block owned by the company, and the company defaults under the loan agreement, the bank can appoint a 'receiver and manager' who can 'manage' the office block and 'receive' the rents from the tenants (passing the rent to the bank, rather than to the landlord company). The right to appoint fixed charge receivers has not been restricted by the Enterprise Act 2002.

The Insolvency Act 1986 introduced a special type of receiver, the Administrative Receiver (AR), and gave an AR additional statutory powers. Any creditor with security (including a floating charge) over the whole, or substantially the whole, of the company's assets (the same definition as a QFCH) could appoint an AR. An AR has a duty to the secured creditor to maximise the recovery by the secured creditor, even if that is not in the best interest of other creditors. Post-1986 experience showed that these rights gave secured creditors (particularly banks) too much commercial power, to the detriment of other creditors and enterprise generally. Consequently, the Enterprise Act 2002 significantly restricted those creditors who can appoint an AR. It is now only possible to appoint an AR in respect of the following security:

(a) if the charge was entered into before 15 September 2003 and was a charge which entitled the charge-holder to appoint an AR (under the IA 1986); or

(b) if the charge was made on or after 15 September 2003; where the charge-holder is a QFCH; the indebtedness secured by the charge exceeds £50 million, and relates to certain capital market or public/private project transactions.

10.4.3 Company voluntary arrangements ('CVA')

The CVA was also introduced by the Insolvency Act 1986 (now refined and improved by the Insolvency Act 2000), as an alternative to winding up. A CVA is essentially a special type of contract between the company and its creditors. It is a special type of contract as it is subject to rules set out in the Insolvency Act 1986 and the Insolvency Rules 1986. In particular, provided that 75 per cent of creditors (in value of the unsecured debts) approve the company's proposals, the arrangement is binding on all creditors who were entitled to attend and vote at the creditors meeting called to consider the proposals. A CVA cannot bind a secured creditor, which is free to enforce its security, unless the creditor agrees to be bound by the CVA. If approved by the required majority of creditors, the terms of the CVA proposals replace the pre-existing contractual and legal rights of individual creditors (provided the company complies with the CVA proposals). An insolvency practitioner (the 'supervisor') is appointed to monitor the implementation of the CVA proposals.

10.4.4 Liquidation (winding up)

There are two broad types of liquidation. With both types, a liquidator is appointed. The liquidator will be an insolvency practitioner, and will have two primary functions:

(a) *Collect in and sell the assets of the company*
This can include recovering assets of the company that were improperly disposed of before the commencement of the liquidation (i.e. 'antecedent transactions' such as 'transactions at an undervalue' (s. 238 IA 1986); 'preferences' (s. 239 IA 1986), and 'transactions defrauding creditors' (s. 423 IA 1986)). It can also include collecting

additional funds from third parties (e.g. directors in respect of 'misfeasance' proceedings (s. 212 IA 1986); 'fraudulent trading' (s. 213 IA 1986), and 'wrongful trading' (s. 214 IA 1986)—see below).

(b) *Distribute the funds collected in the statutory order of priority*.

Once the liquidator has completed his functions, he files a report at Companies House and three months later the company is dissolved (i.e. it ceases to exist). The two types of liquidation are:

(a) *Compulsory liquidation*—resulting from a petition being presented to the court (by an applicant identified in s. 122(1) IA 1986), and the court making a winding up order.

(b) *Voluntary liquidation*—resulting from the members passing a resolution to wind up the company (see s.84 IA 1986). There are two categories of voluntary liquidation:

    (i) *Members' voluntary liquidation*: the directors make a statutory declaration of solvency (a solvent liquidation) and the members appoint the liquidator.

    (ii) *Creditors' voluntary liquidation*: the directors do not make a declaration of solvency (an insolvent liquidation) and the creditors appoint the liquidator.

10.5   Reorganisations and schemes of arrangements

These can be either informal or under formal statutory procedures.

10.5.1   Informal arrangements

Individual creditors may agree to reorganise the company's liabilities to the creditor(s). For example, if creditors are faced with receiving nothing (or only a small percentage of the amounts owed to them) on a winding up, they may agree to convert all or part of the debt into shares. This may not be very attractive to creditors as it means that, as shareholders, they would be below all others in the statutory order of priority on a winding up (even unsecured creditors are further up the list than shareholders). However, if creditors think they will get nothing or very little on a winding up anyway, but believe that the company could survive and prosper given the chance (thereby eventually bringing value to the shares), they may agree to change their status from creditors to shareholders.

10.5.2   Scheme of arrangement—section 110 Insolvency Act 1986

Where a company is in (or proposes to go into) members' voluntary liquidation (a solvent liquidation: see above), the liquidator will normally sell the assets, pay the debts and distribute the surplus to members. A s. 110 scheme is where, with the approval of 75 per cent of members, the liquidator sells the assets and business of the company as a going concern to a new company (or to two or more new companies) in consideration of the purchasing company issuing shares in itself to the members of the original company. The procedure is also available where the company is in (or proposes to go into) creditors' voluntary liquidation (an insolvent liquidation), subject to the approval of the court and the creditors of the company. For some further details, see **9.5.4**.

10.5.3   Compromise or arrangement—section 425 Companies Act 1985

This is a procedure by which a binding compromise or arrangement between a company and its creditors or members (or class of creditors or members) can be imposed by the court. The company (acting by its directors, liquidator or administrator) can apply to the court for an order that there be a meeting of the relevant creditors or members to consider the proposed compromise or arrangement. The compromise or arrangement will be binding on the company and the relevant creditors or members if it is both approved by 75 per cent (in value) of the relevant creditors or members, and subsequently sanctioned by the court. For some further details, see **8.6.2.2**, **9.5.5**, **9.6** and **11.1.3.2**.

10.6   Advising the directors

You must ensure that there is no conflict of interest in advising a director, or more than one director (see **10.1**). In addition to seeking advice on how to deal with the company's financial difficulties, the directors may seek advice about their personal position (in particular, whether they may have any personal liability for the debts of the company or whether they may face any criminal action as a result of their conduct in respect of the company's failure). In addition, directors may have given personal guarantees to specific creditors (e.g. a bank or landlord). Such guarantee liabilities may have been secured by fixed charges on assets owned by the directors (e.g. a second mortgage on their home).

10.6.1   Possible civil liability of directors for debts of the company

Civil liability can arise on a number of bases, including (but not exhaustively), the following.

10.6.1.1   Misfeasance proceedings—section 212 Insolvency Act 1986

Section 212 does not create a new cause of action. Instead, it is intended as a quicker procedure by which actions can be brought (on behalf of the company) against directors to enforce pre-existing rights of action that the company has against the director.

Misfeasance proceedings can be brought by the Official Receiver, a liquidator, a creditor, or a 'contributory' (in essence, a shareholder). The grounds for misfeasance proceedings are if the respondent has either misapplied, retained or become accountable for any money (or other assets) of the company, or acted in breach of any fiduciary (or other) duty. If the proceedings are successful, the court can order the respondent to either restore or account to the company for any money or other assets, or pay compensation to the company.

10.6.1.2   Fraudulent trading—section 213 Insolvency Act 1986

To succeed in such a claim, the liquidator must show that:

(a) the business of the company was carried on with the intent of defrauding creditors or for some other fraudulent purpose; and

(b) the respondent was knowingly a party to the carrying on of the business in that way.

The requirements have been interpreted narrowly by the courts (the liquidator must show 'actual dishonesty' or 'real moral blame'). Consequently, relatively few claims have succeeded. If a claim does succeed, the court can order the respondent to make such contribution to the assets (i.e. to meet the liabilities) of the company as the court thinks fit.

10.6.1.3   Wrongful trading—section 214 Insolvency Act 1986

To succeed in such a claim, the liquidator must show that:

(a) the company has gone into insolvent liquidation;

(b) the respondent was a director (or a 'shadow director'); and

(c) at a date (before the liquidation) identified by the liquidator, the director knew or ought reasonably to have known that there was no reasonable prospect of the company avoiding going into insolvent liquidation.

If these conditions are established, the only possible defence is if the director can show that he took 'every step' to minimise the loss to creditors.

Section 214 has proved much more useful to liquidators (and, therefore, much more worrying for directors!), partly as a result of how the courts assess what the director knew "or ought to have known". Section 214(4) sets the test, being both (i.e. the higher of):

(a) the general knowledge, skill and experience that may be reasonably expected of a person carrying out the same functions as the director (i.e. objective standard); and

(b) the general knowledge, skill and experience that the particular director has (i.e. a subjective standard).

If a claim succeeds under s. 214, the court can order the director to make such contribution to the assets (i.e. to meet the liabilities) of the company as the court thinks fit.

10.6.2   Possible criminal liability of directors

Criminal liability can arise on a number of bases, including (but not exhaustively), the following.

10.6.2.1   Fraudulent trading—section 458 Companies Act 1985

Section 458 of the Companies Act 1985 is framed in the same terms as s. 213 Insolvency Act 1986, but makes fraudulent trading a criminal offence.

10.6.2.2   Disqualification from being a director—Company Director Disqualification Act 1986

For all companies that go into liquidation, the liquidator is obliged to file a report with the Secretary of State relating to all who were directors within the five years before liquidation, as to whether there is evidence which suggests whether disqualification proceedings should be brought against such a person. A Disqualification Order ('DO') can be made against a person who is shown to be 'unfit' to be a director of a company and/or who has:

(a) been convicted of an indictable offence in relation to the company; or

(b) persistently failed to comply with the companies legislation in respect of filing of documents to the Registrar of Companies (e.g. annual accounts); or

(c) participated in fraudulent or wrongful trading.

A DO can be made disqualifying the person from being a director of any company (or otherwise being involved with the management of a company) for up to 15 years. It is a criminal offence not to comply with a DO.

10.6.2.3   Directors of public and quoted companies

There are specific issues that directors of public companies (in particular, those quoted on the Stock Exchange or listed on the AIM) must be aware of when the company gets into financial difficulty. These may include (amongst others):

(1) 'Serious loss of capital'—section 142 Companies Act 1985

Where the net assets (assets less liabilities) of the company are no more than half of the company's called up share capital, the directors must (within 28 days of a director becoming aware of the fact), convene an EGM to consider whether any and, if so, what steps should be taken to deal with the situation. A director who is in default ('knowingly and willfully') commits a criminal offence and is liable to a fine.

(2) LSE and AIM Plcs: 'false market' in shares—section 397 FSMA 2000

As you will have identified elsewhere in this manual, the success of the LSE and the AIM as mechanisms for raising equity capital to finance business activity and economic growth, depends very largely on the transparent integrity of the markets. It is crucial that current and prospective investors can make informed decisions about whether to buy or sell shares. Whether or not a company is in financial difficulty is, of course, an important factor in the decision-making process. Section 397 creates various criminal offences, with the objective of trying to ensure the integrity of the markets.

Section 397(1) creates the offences of making 'misleading statements' to the market or engaging in 'misleading practices'. It is not just positive statements and actions that can constitute a criminal offence. For example, s. 397(l)(b) (read with s. 397(2)) makes it a criminal offence to 'dishonestly conceal any material facts whether in connection with a statement, promise or forecast made by him or otherwise' for the purpose of inducing (or recklessly as to whether it may induce) another person to buy or sell (or to not buy of sell) shares on the markets. Consequently, if a listed company is in financial difficulty, the directors will commit an offence if they fail to tell the markets of the position if the failure is for the purpose of inducing (or recklessly as to whether it may induce) an existing member to sell (or not sell) his shares.

Section 397(3) sets out the offence of creating a 'false market'. The offence is committed by any person who does an act or engages in conduct which creates a false or misleading impression as to the market in (or the price or value of) shares, if done for the purpose of creating that impression and of inducing someone to buy or sell (or to not buy or sell) listed shares. Again, directors of an ailing listed company must be careful to avoid falling foul of these provisions.

Case study

In this chapter, we look at two example transactions which illustrate some of the themes pursued in this book. These case studies do not look at the tax implications of these transactions, and you will need to consider these carefully when advising.

11.1 Acton plc

Acton plc has its ordinary shares listed and traded on the LSE. Your firm acts for Acton plc. Three of its eight directors, Messrs Garden, Crescent and Lane, who hold 10 per cent of the company's ordinary shares, want to buy the rest of it, de-list the company and take it back into their own private hands. They say they have talked to Avenue Bank, which is prepared to provide the financial backing. They need your advice on how to proceed.

(a) Is this a preposterous idea which cannot be done? Why might they want to do it?

(b) Can you act?

(c) How would such a transaction be structured? What choices are there?

(d) What problems do you foresee? How can they be overcome?

(e) What documents would you expect to be necessary?

(f) What should the three directors do next?

Let us look in brief at how you might deal with the questions posed.

11.1.1 Is this a preposterous idea which cannot be done? Why might they want to do it?

This process of taking a company into private hands is the reverse of offering shares in a company to the public. A few individuals end up owning the shares previously held by the public. The de-listing this involves simply means the company is no longer officially listed or dealt in on the AIM (depending on which it is).

Why might this prove attractive? There are a number of factors:

(a) The benefits of public ownership and trading of a company's securities bring with them the disadvantage of onerous disclosure obligations and restricted freedom of movement under the Listing Rules. There are also the costs (both financial and in terms of management time) of maintaining a listing, and keeping institutional investors, analysts and brokers regularly informed of the company's financial and trading progress and future.

(b) Some companies find the stock market undervalues their traded securities relative to the net worth of their assets. This may be because the company operates in a number of different sectors of the market and is valued on the basis that the whole is worth less than the sum of the parts. Alternatively the market may not find the future trading prospects of the company as attractive as the company feels they are. This may also be costly for the company if it plans to use its securities as consideration in acquisitions. Private ownership means that the value placed by the market on the securities is irrelevant.

(c) The market tends to place a premium on short-term qualities of a company's performance, such as dividend pay-outs, and has less regard for its longer term investment strategy. The company itself may then find it is subject to criticism for reinvesting substantial amounts of its profits rather than distributing them to shareholders. If it is determined to stick by its strategy, and the market continues to dislike this, the only long-term solution may be a parting of the ways.

Whatever the reason, there have been a number of such transactions in recent years.

11.1.2 Can you act?

Those who lead a bid to take the company private tend to be the company's directors (as here), sometimes in conjunction with its executive managers. Of course, their interests may not be the same as the company's. The company embraces not just the directors but the existing shareholders, employees and creditors. Solicitors who act for the company may therefore face a possible conflict of interests if they are asked to represent the directors here. The directors may therefore have to be told to seek their own independent legal advice.

The directors need always to be careful in such situations. Their duty of course is to the company (including all those parties mentioned above), and so any proposal on their part to take the company into their own hands must be based on their reasonable estimate not simply of their own best interests but also those of the company. Further, should they stand to profit from the transaction, they should be even more careful as any profits resulting from directors putting their own interests before their duty to the company belong to the company.

If the company and directors are to seek separate advice, who is then left to 'steer the ship' for the company? The independent and usually non-executive directors play a vital role here in representing the company's interests and consulting advisers. The Cadbury Code requires there to be a procedure under which such directors can obtain advice at the company's expense in such circumstances (see **2.2.3.1**).

11.1.3 How would such a transaction be structured? What choices are there?

Those wanting to take the company private are essentially proposing to buy a public company from its existing shareholders. As we saw in **Chapter 8**, this will have to be done by way of a takeover offer. As discussed in **8.6.2**, there are a number of ways of doing this:

11.1.3.1 By general offer under the City Code on takeovers and mergers

This of course brings with it the City Code Rules (see **8.8**). In this case, the offer can be made by the directors acting as a consortium or by a company which they form (X Ltd) and in which they hold all the shares. In both cases, the objective will be to offer cash so that the existing shareholders are all bought out. Once all the target shares are acquired (assuming the offer is a success), the public company will be re-registered as a private company.

One benefit of the general offer is that, if the target shareholders acquiesce in it, it is likely to be concluded by the first closing date, which is 21 days after the offer document is posted. This is likely to be a much quicker timetable than that for the scheme of arrangement described below. The only fly in this particular ointment is that any outstanding minority will have to be compulsorily acquired first (see **8.13**) before the target public company can be converted to a private company, and this will extend the time it will take to complete the transaction.

Its major disadvantage is that it requires a 90 per cent acceptance level from shareholders, as contrasted with the 75 per cent acceptance needed for a scheme of arrangement.

There will also be a stamp duty cost of $\frac{1}{2}$ per cent of the consideration offered for the securities in a general offer.

11.1.3.2   By a scheme of arrangement under section 425 Companies Act 1985 (see 8.6.2.2)

This will usually involve setting up a new private company (as with the general offer) and proposing a scheme whereby the target company shareholders agree either to transfer the securities they hold to the private company or to have them cancelled (which saves on stamp duty) in return for a cash payment. It will require approval from a majority in number of the shareholders representing 75 per cent in value of the shares, together with the sanction of the court. Court approval is sometimes a drawn-out process but once approval has been granted, the entirety of the target public company is bought out immediately (enabling speedy conversion to private company status), which means that there is no danger of the timetable dragging out.

Do not forget that the City Code applies equally to the scheme of arrangement as to a general offer.

11.1.4   What problems do you foresee? How can they be overcome?

There are two particular problems which will arise, other than those already indicated (depending on whether the general offer or scheme of arrangement is preferred).

(a) The new privately owned vehicle (X Ltd) will need cash to buy the target shareholders out. The directors and managers will not have sufficient personal resources available. They will need to borrow the sums they need. An institutional lender such as a bank will require some form of security. The only form of security which exists is the value of the assets of the target company to be acquired.

The difficulty with this is s. 151 CA, which prohibits a company from giving financial assistance for the acquisition of its own shares either before or after that acquisition (see **8.12**). If the target company gives the banks security after it has been acquired and is owned by the directors' private company, that will be caught as financial assistance.

The only escape from this in turn is if the target company is converted to a private company and the so-called 'whitewash' procedure is taken advantage of (see **8.12**). This is why it may be of particular significance to the directors to complete the transaction as soon as possible, so that the company's re-registration can be effected rapidly.

(b) Acton plc has its ordinary shares listed and traded on the LSE. As the company is to be bought by some of its own directors, will this be a related-party transaction under LR ch. 11 (see **5.6.4**)? The UKLA may take the view that it is in fact a transaction between the directors and other shareholders of the company, not between the directors and the company. If so, no issue under ch. 11 would arise. It is advisable to consult the UKLA on this issue. If the view is that ch. 11 does apply, the shareholders should be sent a circular and their consent to the transaction sought in general meeting.

If Acton plc were not listed (and even though it is), s. 320 CA also requires the approval of shareholders in general meeting to what is a substantial property transaction in which the company's shares are being sold to some of its own directors.

11.1.5 What documents would you expect to be necessary?

Let us assume the directors choose to make a general offer to acquire the target company. These are the most important of the documents necessary:

(a) Offer document (this will also double as a circular to shareholders complying with the related-party transaction requirements) and any other documents required in connection with the offer, such as press announcements.

(b) Notice of extraordinary general meeting of target and resolutions for it (if necessary for approval of the related-party transaction).

(c) Loan agreement with bank(s) and charge.

(d) Special resolution, directors' declaration and auditors' report for s. 155 'whitewash' exemption (see **8.12**).

(e) Brokers' letters to the UKLA and LSE to de-list the target on acquisition.

11.1.6 What should the directors do next?

After approaching different legal advisers, the directors should ensure the financing arrangements for their bid are secure and agreed with their lender. Thereafter, they need to determine how their bid is to be structured and put it into effect. Appointing financial advisers (accountants and investment banks) is therefore a priority, particularly to obtain necessary tax advice. With these advisers, they will need to decide the timetable for the transaction and how the bid dovetails with any shareholder approvals (usually the bid is simply conditional on obtaining the consent of the target shareholders at a general meeting).

The directors will need to be satisfied they are discharging their duty to the company when making the bid. In support of that, as a matter of urgency, they will need to declare their interest in making a possible bid for the company at a board meeting of the directors (s. 317 CA).

11.2 Brentford plc

One of the difficulties with companies that are taken private as with Acton plc (now Limited), is that they take on a very high level of debt. This has a number of effects. It makes it harder for the company to raise extra capital (particularly now it has withdrawn from the equity market) and it will have a pressing cash-flow requirement to satisfy the interest burden of the debt.

In this case study, the assumption is that Acton Limited has found the interest payment obligation too exacting, and the director-shareholders (Garden, Crescent and Lane) have decided they must sell. Their urgent need is for cash to pay off the banks.

The assumption here is that the three selling shareholders hold the shares in Acton through the private company (X Ltd) which made the acquisition described above in the first place. This may be tax disadvantageous in that the first sale (of the shares held in Acton) may attract a capital gains tax charge, and then a sale by Garden, Crescent and Lane of their shares in X Ltd may attract another charge. Tax advice will be needed on how to mitigate any such potential problems.

Brentford plc would like to buy Acton. Brentford is listed on the Official List. It can offer only its own securities as it has no ready reserves of cash. It will have to issue half as much share capital again as it already has in issue to pay for Acton.

(a) How can the mismatch in the needs of the parties be met and what considerations need to be taken into account in resolving this mismatch?

(b) What statutory and regulatory controls and restrictions will impinge on the transaction?

(c) What documents will need to be produced for the transaction?

11.2.1 How can the mismatch in the needs of the parties be met and what considerations need to be taken into account in resolving this mismatch?

Clearly the most appropriate method for resolving the parties' respective demands is through a vendor placing (see **3.6.5**). Brentford allots its securities to X Ltd as the shareholder of Acton. X Ltd sells the securities to a merchant bank, which has been appointed by Brentford to place those securities on behalf of X Ltd in the market. The cash provided by the placees passes into the hands of X Ltd, and, on receipt of the cash, Acton Ltd becomes Brentford's property.

There are a number of factors to consider with a vendor placing:

(a) Brentford will probably need to offer the securities to its own shareholders under the Listing Rules requirements. This would mean a clawback arrangement, and of the structures available a rights offer is the likeliest option (see **3.6.5.2**).

(b) The new securities will need to be listed alongside its existing securities. A prospectus or listing particulars will be required (see **4.2**).

(c) The point at which Acton will be transferred to Brentford will need to be interdependent with admission of the securities to listing. In other words, the sale of Acton will be conditional on admission to the Official List and the LSE of Brentford's shares, and the issue of shares will be conditional on the sale of Acton being completed.

11.2.2 What statutory and regulatory controls and restrictions will impinge on the transaction?

You will need to think about the impact of the following on the transaction:

(a) Companies Act 1985, s. 121 (does Brentford have sufficient authorised share capital in view of the size of the proposed transaction?), s. 80 (do its directors have the authority to allot?) and s. 89 (the need to issue the securities on a pre-emptive basis).

(b) Under FSMA and the Listing Rules, Brentford will need to issue a prospectus or listing particulars (see **4.2**).

(c) Under FSMA, you also need to think about the possibility that any document being issued is a financial promotion (s. 21) and the prospect of any exemptions which may apply to it under the Financial Services and Markets Act 2000 (Financial Promotion) Order 2001. You also need to be conscious of the criminal sanctions resulting from misleading statements or conduct in relation to the issue of shares as investments (s. 397 and see **1.5.1.3**).

(d) The Listing Rules will treat this as a Class 1 transaction for Brentford under LR ch. 10. Where that company is issuing equity as consideration for an acquisition, and that consideration is more than 25 per cent of its current market capitalisation, that acquisition will need to be notified to shareholders in the form of a circular and will be subject to their approval in a general meeting. If none of the other comparisons are above 25 per cent then The Listing Rules may allow you to treat this simply as a Class 2 transaction requiring only notification to a Regulatory Information Service and a press announcement.

You can ignore the City Code on Takeovers and Mergers, as Acton Ltd is a private company and the Code only applies to the acquisition of public companies in the UK.

11.2.3 What documents will need to be produced for the transaction?

Some of the items in the list below have already been mentioned:

(a) Prospectus or listing particulars, incorporating the circular to shareholders required by the UKLA.

(b) Vendor placing agreement, under which Brentford will appoint an investment bank to arrange the issue and placing of its shares.

(c) Sale agreement, under which X Ltd, as the seller of Acton, agrees with Brentford's merchant bank to sell the shares in Brentford it is allotted to the bank for placing in the market.

(d) Share purchase agreement between Brentford on the one side and X Ltd on the other. This will govern the sale of the shares in Acton to Brentford. This agreement will need to be inter-conditional with the vendor placing agreement. It will contain various warranties from X Ltd to Brentford regarding X Ltd's title to the shares in Acton, any changes in the financial position of Acton since the last audited accounts, any deterioration in asset values and the like (see **5.5.1.6**). The shareholders of X Ltd may feel it is difficult, particularly if they have only owned Acton for a very short period, to give extensive warranties, but given their former relationship as directors of Acton, Brentford is unlikely to be sympathetic.

(e) Various notices and resolutions required for a Brentford EGM.

(f) Share transfers for the shares in Acton to be sold to Brentford.

(g) Documents required for any UKLA and LSE listing of securities (see **4.2.6.5**).

(h) Documents required to discharge any security taken by X Ltd's banks over Acton's assets. The banks will be repaid out of the proceeds realised by the placing.

As ever, there will be a host of other supporting documents prepared for the transaction, including verification notes, board resolutions and the like. This list covers only the most significant documents you will need to consider.

INDEX